GW00870908

# Boston, 1086–1225
# A medieval boom town

*For my parents, Ron and Maisie*

# Boston, 1086–1225
# A Medieval Boom Town

Stephen H. Rigby

THE SOCIETY FOR LINCOLNSHIRE HISTORY AND ARCHAEOLOGY
2017

SOCIETY FOR
LINCOLNSHIRE
HISTORY &
ARCHAEOLOGY

First published by the Society for Lincolnshire History and Archaeology 2017

© Society for Lincolnshire History and Archaeology

ISBN 978 0 903582 56 8

British Library Cataloguing in Public Data
A CIP catalogue record of this book is available from the British Library.

All rights reserved

No part of this publication may be reproduced or transmitted in any form or by any means, electronic or mechanical, including photocoying, recording, or by any information storage or retrieval system, without permission in writing from the publisher.

Designed by Ros Beevers

Printed in the United Kingdom by T J International, Padstow

*Cover illustration: Lion's head knocker on the south door of the tower of St Botolph's. The knocker is the only remnant, above ground, of the church which preceded the fourteenth- and fifteenth-century building that now stands on the site.*

# Contents

# *Preface and acknowledgements*

This study of the early growth of Boston has been written with two rather different audiences in mind. The first is made up of those readers who have an interest in the local history of Boston or of Lincolnshire but who may be less familiar with wider debates in medieval urban history. In writing for this audience, I have tried to make the subject-matter as accessible as possible. For instance, technical terms are either explained in the text when they first occur or are defined in the glossary at the end of the book. The richness of Pishey Thompson's nineteenth-century studies of Boston has meant that his work has cast a long shadow over modern accounts of the town's history. One of my aims here has been to show how a return to the primary sources, in manuscript and in print, allows us to see the history of the town afresh and to dispel some of the myths about it which have inevitably accumulated over the years. Although the book focuses on the period before 1225, I have also provided detailed bibliographical references to studies of Boston in the later Middle Ages to guide those who are interested in reading further about the history of the town. My second intended audience is comprised of academics and students with an interest in medieval economic history. In addressing them, I have attempted to demonstrate how the rise of Boston in the twelfth century related to wider trends in the English economy. The survival of sources means that most histories of medieval English towns tend to focus on the period after 1200 and particularly on the years after the mid-fourteenth century. Here I have sought to show what the sources can reveal to us about Boston in the twelfth and early thirteenth centuries whilst also acknowledging that many conclusions about the town must remain provisional and that important aspects of its history remain almost entirely hidden in the surviving archival and archaeological evidence.

Medieval Boston was originally suggested to me as a research topic in 1976 by Caroline Barron, who patiently supervised my doctoral thesis on 'Boston and Grimsby in the Middle Ages' (University of London, 1983) and who has been a source of academic guidance ever since. Both my thesis and my subsequent publications on Boston focused on the history of the town in the thirteenth, fourteenth and fifteenth centuries. I am glad here to be able to turn my attention to the growth of Boston in the years before *c.*1225, a period which was hardly touched on in my previous work. This study is thus the product of new research based not only on the printed sources but also on manuscripts held at The National Archives, the British Library, Lincolnshire Archives, the John Rylands Library, Manchester, and at St Bartholomew's Hospital, London. I am grateful to the staff of all of these institutions for their patience and help. Particular thanks are owed to Neil Wright, who guided me around Boston and willingly responded to my many requests for advice on the topography of the town.

viii

I am also extremely grateful to Mark Bailey, not only for commenting on drafts of my text and for suggesting a number of ways of approaching the early history of Boston but also for providing me with accommodation in London which allowed me to carry out much of the research for this volume. Both the structure and the content of this work were also greatly enhanced by the perceptive comments of Rosalind Brown-Grant, Wendy Childs and Richard Goddard. Maryanne Kowaleski read two draft versions of the book and offered many ideas which clarified both its detail and its overall argument. Keith Lilley was equally generous with his time and came up with a number of helpful suggestions about how to analyse Boston's town-plan. As always, Robert Nash's close reading of my text resulted in innumerable improvements to its logic and to its prose style. I have also benefited greatly from the encouragement of Pamela Cawthorne and from the advice of Sally Badham, Mike Baillie, David Crouch, Cathy Delaney, Caitlin Green, Richard Holt, Stephen Mossman, Carole Rawcliffe, Max Satchell, Mustapha Sheikh and Jenny Young.

I owe my colleague Nick Higham a particular debt of gratitude for preparing Maps 1, 2, 5 and 6, below, for publication. Thanks are also owed to Spalding Gentlemen's Society for providing me with photographic copies of the sources in their possession, which are cited below, and for permission to reproduce a folio from the Wrest Park cartulary (Figure 27). I am also grateful to the British Library for permission to reproduce Saxton's map of Lincolnshire (Figure 7), to Historic England for permission to reproduce Figures 4, 13, 15, 16, 26 and 32, to Richard Kay Publications for permission to reproduce Hall's map of Boston (Figure 10) from F. H. Molyneux and N. Wright, *An atlas of Boston* (1974), which is an indispensable work for any student of the history of Boston, and to Katie Carmichael and John Minnis who supplied the photographs used for Figures 1, 2, 18, 21, 24 and 34. The other photographs used in the figures below are by the author. Particular thanks are also owed to Ken Redmore and Ros Beevers for their help in preparing this volume for publication and to Ken for providing Map 4 and to Ros for providing Figure 22.

I am glad here to have been able to correct some of my own earlier errors of fact and interpretation about medieval Boston but the inevitable mistakes in the text below remain my own responsibility. Finally, this study is dedicated to my parents, Ron and Maisie Rigby, whose support and encouragement allowed me the privilege of becoming a medieval historian.

ix

# Illustrations

# Maps

# Abbreviations used in the notes and bibliography

**BL** British Library (London)

**CChR** *Calendar of the charter rolls preserved in the Public Record Office* (six volumes; London, 1903-1927).

**CCR** *Calendar of the close rolls preserved in the Public Record Office, 1227-1509* (sixty volumes; London, 1902-1963).

**Chartulary of Fountains** *Abstracts of the charters and other documents contained in the chartulary of the Cistercian abbey of Fountains in the West Riding of the county of York*, ed. W. T. Lancaster (two volumes; Leeds, 1915).

**CIM** *Calendar of inquisitions miscellaneous (Chancery) preserved in the Public Record Office* (eight volumes; London, 1916-2003).

**CIPM** *Calendar of inquisitions post mortem and other analogous documents preserved in the Public Record Office* (twenty-three volumes; London 1904-2004).

**CLR** *Calendar of the liberate rolls preserved in the Public Record Office* (six volumes; London, 1916-1964).

**The complete peerage** *The complete peerage*, by G. E. C[okayne], enlarged by V. Gibbs *et al*, 13 volumes (new edition; London, 1910-1959).

**CPR** *Calendar of the patent rolls preserved in the Public Record Office, 1216-1509* (fifty-three volumes; London 1901-1916)

**CRR** *Curia Regis Rolls* (twenty volumes; London 1922-2006).

**EcHR** *Economic History Review*

**EHR** *English Historical Review*

**JRLM** John Rylands Library, Manchester

**KAO** Kent Archives Office (Maidstone)

**LAO** Lincolnshire Archives (Lincoln)

**LHER** Lincolnshire Historic Environment Record

**LRS** Lincoln Record Society

**n.s.** new series

**Pipe Roll** *The great roll of the pipe, 31 Henry I-7 Henry III* (Publications of the Pipe Roll Society, 1884-2012).

**SBHAO** St Bartholomew's Hospital Archives Office (London)

**TNA** The National Archives (London).

**TRHS** *Transactions of the Royal Historical Society*

# Part 1

# The early history of Boston

Although the twelfth and early thirteenth centuries were a decisive period in the formation of the urban hierarchy of medieval England, the dearth of written evidence for these years means that they still retain 'an air of mystery' about them when compared to the much better documented years from the mid-thirteenth century onwards.[1] This lack of sources is particularly evident for the town of Boston, which is situated near the mouth of the River Witham in the Holland division of Lincolnshire (see Map 1). By the start of the thirteenth century, Boston was perhaps second only to London amongst the ports of England in the scale of its overseas trade, yet the town's origins and its early development are now very obscure. While late medieval Boston, particularly the decline of its overseas trade[2] and the role of Hanseatic merchants in its commerce,[3] has attracted much attention from historians, the town's development in the period before c.1225 has been little studied. This concentration on the later Middle Ages has continued in the most recent studies of medieval Boston, which have mainly focused on St Botolph's parish church, its monuments, and the piety of its parishioners and guild members in the pre-Reformation period.[4] As a result, the early history of Boston has often become the stuff of local myth and legend.

All modern studies of Boston remain in the shadow of Pishey Thompson's *The History and Antiquities of Boston*, an excellent antiquarian account of Boston that was published in 1856 and which, to this day, remains an invaluable source of information about the history of the town.[5] As a result of the high quality of Thompson's work, modern studies of the town have often rehearsed his claims uncritically. Yet, as a pioneering essay by Dorothy Owen showed, much new information remains to be discovered about the development of Boston in the century or so following its emergence as a new town.[6] This study develops Owen's work by drawing on a variety of manuscript and printed sources, as well as on the findings of archaeologists, to trace the rise of Boston in the period between Domesday Book and c.1225, after which date the sources available for the history of the town become much richer. Here, we begin by locating the origins and early growth of Boston (part 1) before exploring the topography of early Boston and tracing the history of the lordships that made up the town (part 2). We then examine the town's trade and communications (part 3), set out the history of its fair (part 4) and assess the role of borough privileges in the growth of the town (part 5), before concluding with an assessment of Boston's role in the wider changes in the English economy in this period (part 6).

## 1.1.  BOSTON IN AN AGE OF URBANISATION

The twelfth and thirteenth centuries were a period when the English economy, like that of Western Europe as a whole, was becoming increasingly commercialised as local, regional and international trade expanded and markets and fairs proliferated.[7] As a result, England's population became increasingly urbanised. Thus, whilst national population at least doubled, and may have almost trebled, in this period, rising from around 1.7 to 2.5 million in 1086 to about 4.7 to 6.0 million in 1315,[8] the number of people living in England's towns grew even faster, probably rising from around 10 per cent of the country's inhabitants in 1086 to perhaps 15 per cent or more by the early fourteenth century.[9] This growth in urbanisation was achieved not only by the expansion of England's long-established urban centres, such as York and Lincoln, but also by the foundation of hundreds of new towns. Among these new creations, Boston was one of the most successful.[10]

Boston emerged as an urban settlement in the late eleventh and early twelfth centuries. Like Lynn, across the Wash, which rose in the same period, it benefited from being established early on in the wave of urban growth: it was those towns that were created first in the process of urbanisation that tended to be the most successful.[11] The success of the 'boom town' of Boston was certainly evident by the start of the thirteenth century.[12] At this date, the account for the royal duty of a 'fifteenth' levied on trade, which was included in the Exchequer pipe roll drawn up in the Michaelmas term of 1204, shows that Boston was already one of the busiest ports in the country: its payment of £780 15s. 3d. meant that it ranked second only to London (£837) amongst the ports of the south and east coasts.[13] If we add Lincoln's payment (£667) to that of Boston, as in Maryanne Kowaleski's ranking of England's ports, the trade of these two Witham ports at this date was even greater than that of London, although some of Lincoln's trade must actually have passed along the Foss Dyke and the Trent, rather than via the Witham and Boston.[14]

Unfortunately, the earliest surviving source that allows us to estimate Boston's medieval population comes from as late as 1377, at which time England's population was only around a half of the total it had reached before the famines and plague outbreaks of earlier in the fourteenth century.[15] In theory, the 2,871 Boston townspeople who contributed to the first poll tax in this year included all its male and female lay inhabitants aged fourteen and over, apart from beggars. They may have represented a total population of about 5,500, which meant that Boston was then the tenth largest urban community in the country.[16] In the absence of direct evidence, it is difficult to estimate Boston's population before the arrival of the plague. In particular, as the town seems to have been flourishing in the second half of the fourteenth century, we cannot simply assume that its population had declined at the same rate as national population in the years between 1348 and 1377.[17] Nevertheless, some indication of its significance in the pre-plague period is given by its valuation of £1,100 for the lay subsidy (or taxation) of 1334, which was the fifth highest of any town in the country.[18] Another sign of Boston's prominent position in England's urban hierarchy at this time is the fact that it was one of only just over a dozen towns in England in which the houses of four different orders of friars were located[19]. When did Boston's growth begin and what were the factors that promoted the success of this new town?

## 1.2. THE ORIGINS OF BOSTON

There had been some Roman occupation in the area around Boston in the second to fourth centuries, and archaeological evidence suggests that renewed settlement took place in nearby villages, such as Skirbeck, Frampton and Fishtoft, from the seventh and eighth centuries onwards. Yet, despite speculation about the existence of a Roman site to protect the outfall of the River Witham, there is little evidence for a settlement at Boston itself during this early period, particularly in what was to become the medieval core of the town.[20] One problem here is that Roman and pre-Roman sites may have been covered by later marine deposits, particularly in the early Anglo-Saxon period when the fens were flooded. There have been finds of Roman origin in Boston, including pottery and coins, to the south of the Market Place and at the Hussey Tower (see Map 2, nos 9 and 29, and Fig. 1). There have also been some late Anglo-Saxon finds, including coins from the reign of Athelwulf (639-58) and Cnut (1016-35), as well as pottery, in West Street, on the west side of the River Witham (see Map 2, no. 15). However, apart from these scattered discoveries, very little is known of the history of Boston as a settlement before Domesday Book.[21]

Boston's medieval name of 'St Botolph's' ('Sanctus Botulphus/Botulfus') or 'the town of Saint Botolph' ('villa Sancti Botulphi/Botulfi'), along with its Latin and English variants such as 'Sanctus Botulfistan', 'Botolfston', 'Botulfston', 'Botulvestan', and 'Bothelstane', was derived from the dedication of the town's parish church (see Map 2, no. 5 and Figs 3 and 5).[22] Its modern form of 'Boston' was in use by 1366.[23] According to the *Anglo-Saxon Chronicle* (and hence to later medieval chroniclers), St Botolph had founded a 'minster' at 'Icanhoh' in 654 A.D. (or in 653 A.D. according to the E Text of the chronicle).[24] As a result, Boston has sometimes been identified as the site of Icanhoh, an identification that remains popular to the present day. Thus the latest edition of the guide to St Botolph's church claims that 'Christians have worshipped on this site since the seventh century when St Botolph, an Anglo-Saxon missionary, is believed to have preached here'.[25] Yet this identification of Icanhoh with Boston is very speculative. After all, over sixty other English medieval churches were also dedicated to St Botolph. Many alternative sites have been suggested for Botolph's foundation, which was destroyed by the Danes in 870, with Iken (Suffolk) now seeming to be the most likely.[26]

Boston does not appear by name in Domesday Book and its site must have been subsumed into the survey's entries for the 'hundred' of Skirbeck, which took its name from the village whose parish church lay a mile downstream from Boston on the River Witham (Fig. 2). A 'hundred' in the Lincolnshire Domesday refers not, as it does in most of England, to the subdivision of the shire whose equivalent in Lincolnshire was the wapentake, but rather to a much smaller unit of twelve carucates of land, which was assessed for geld and which had some legal responsibilities.[27] The 'hundred' of Skirbeck was located in what the Lincolnshire Domesday refers to as the wapentake of 'Wolmersty' (that took its name from a now extinct village in the parish of Wrangle) which, in the late twelfth century, became known as the wapentake of Skirbeck.[28] Nearly all of Skirbeck hundred in 1086 belonged to Alan Rufus (Alan I), count of Brittany.[29] Alan had probably fought at the Battle of Hastings alongside William of Normandy, his second cousin, by whose favour he became one of the richest and most powerful magnates in England. He held over four hundred manors in eleven counties of England and his estates included the honour of Richmond, which was granted to him after the Revolt of the North in 1070, which was comprised of land in eight counties of England. Its many Lincolnshire manors included the part of Boston which lay on the east side of the River Witham.[30]

Since the compilers of Domesday Book were not attempting to list all the vills in England, the fact that Boston is not explicitly mentioned in the Domesday survey does not mean that a settlement had yet to be created there or that the town of Boston was founded after 1086 on an 'empty site'.[31] Rather, it seems likely that, just as one of the two churches in the Domesday entry for the nearby village of Butterwick was probably that in the unnamed Benington, one of the two churches in the Domesday entry for Skirbeck hundred was actually St Botolph's and that it was served by one of the two priests who are mentioned in the entry for Count Alan's lands in the hundred.[32] The parish of St Botolph thus seems to have been carved out of the parish of Skirbeck, which was itself divided into two parts by the River Witham, with the portion later known as 'Skirbeck Quarter' (see Map 2, no. 32) lying to the west of the river.[33]

For most of the medieval period, St Botolph's church belonged to the Benedictine abbey of St Mary, York. The abbey had been founded c.1086 when Alan Rufus had persuaded a group of monks, who had previously left Whitby abbey to settle at Lastingham, to move to a site in York. His new foundation soon found support from William II, who enlarged the abbey's precinct as part of his continuation of his father's policy of encouraging monasticism in the north of England. With this royal backing, as well as the patronage of Count Alan, his successors and other northern lords, St Mary's grew to be one of the wealthiest and most powerful monasteries in the north (Fig. 4).[34] The supposed charter of William II to the abbey, which confirmed previous donations of land to the monks and granted them a range of liberties, has been described as 'either a forgery or grossly interpolated'.[35] Nevertheless, it does seem to record a genuine grant of the church of St Botolph's and its appurtenances to St Mary's, which was made by Count Alan some time prior to his death in 1093, perhaps as early as his initial foundation of the abbey.[36] In connection with this grant, the charter also mentions a carucate of land and the site of a mill and it is possible that these were also located in the settlement that was to become Boston. However, later confirmations of the grant refer to them as being in 'Skirbeck', which may refer specifically to the village of Skirbeck, where the abbey also held land, rather than to the larger 'hundred' of Skirbeck, within which Boston lay.[37] Alan Rufus was succeeded by younger brother Alan Niger (Alan II), who confirmed the grant of St Botolph's to St Mary's.[38] St Botolph's then remained in the possession of the abbey until Edward IV's reign, when it passed, via the hands of the king, to the Knights Hospitaller.[39] As a possession of the abbey, presentations to St Botolph's were made by the abbot and convent, as in 1227–8 when Johannes Romanus, the subdean of York Minster, was instituted as rector there.[40]

The present St Botolph's church is mainly a product of the fourteenth and fifteenth centuries; it is such a familiar sight that it is now difficult to imagine the building that stood in its place at the time of Domesday Book (Fig. 3). Of the church that was there in 1086, nothing now remains above ground. In the eighteenth century William Stukeley referred to the discovery of the remains of vast stone walls, along with a leaden cross, on the south side of the present church (Fig. 5). Restoration work at St Botolph's in the 1850s uncovered the foundations of what was identified as an Anglo-Norman church, consisting of nave, aisles, tower and chancel, which was approximately half the size of the current building.[41] However, it is possible that these foundations included work done to enlarge St Botolph's in the late twelfth or thirteenth century, by which time the earlier church may no longer have matched the town's rapidly-growing population and wealth.[42]

Nonetheless, if the presence of two churches in Skirbeck hundred at the time of the Domesday survey suggests that some form of settlement already existed at Boston at this date, there is no evidence to support the view that Boston was an 'important' market centre or landing place as early as the tenth century or to uphold the claim that Skirbeck 'hundred', including Boston, accounted for 'more than a quarter' of the population of the parts of Holland in 1086.[43] After all, only 19 sokemen and 13 villeins are noted in the Domesday entry for Count Alan's manor in Skirbeck hundred and only a further 8 villeins in the entry for the land in the hundred belonging to Eudo, son of Spirewic.[44] These 40 tenants, who actually made up less than 4% of the heads of households in Holland, represented a total population of perhaps only 170 to 240 people, many of whom must have lived in the village of Skirbeck rather than in Boston itself.[45] The Domesday entry for Skirbeck includes land which was a 'berewick' (i.e. a detached portion of a manor) of Drayton which, in 1066, had been held by Ralf the Staller, a leading courtier of Edward the Confessor. Drayton's valuation of £70, along with £20 tallage, may include revenues drawn from Boston, although many other local villages were also berewicks of this manor.[46]

It has been argued that, since the Domesday Book commissioners were given little guidance on how to gather information about England's towns, the Domesday survey leaves out many inhabitants of the towns it describes, that the urban characteristics of some of the settlements it lists are neglected, and that some towns, including the urban part of the manor of Coventry, were excluded from the survey altogether. Such omissions are certainly possible, although if they occurred on a significant scale, the oft-quoted figure of 10% for England's urban population in 1086 would have to be revised upwards, thereby reducing any estimate of the scale of urbanisation that took place between 1086 and 1300.[47] It is possible that Boston was already a town by 1086 but that it was omitted from the Domesday survey. However, in the absence of any other indication of the existence of an urban community within Skirbeck hundred at this date, it seems likely that the site of what was to become the town of Boston was then occupied by a small community of peasants, fishermen (as indicated by Domesday's mention of two fisheries in Skirbeck) and perhaps salt-makers, who were served by the church of St Botolph.[48]

### 1.3.  BOSTON'S EMERGENCE AS A TOWN

If Boston was not an urban community at the time of the Domesday survey, the settlement clustered around St Botolph's was soon to develop into one of England's major towns and busiest ports, and to become the site of one of the country's leading fairs. Few historians would now see the Norman Conquest as a decisive turning-point in the history of English towns and trade but, nevertheless, the country's new rulers did encourage settlement by French traders in existing towns and were keen, as at Boston, to found new towns and boroughs.[49] With its French and Breton overlords, who held the Richmond, Croun and Tattershall fees within the town (see below, sections 2.2. and 2.6.), it is likely that Boston was one of those towns that attracted migrants from across the Channel in its early years. It has even been suggested that such an early influx of migrants may explain the frequent occurrence of Breton personal names in the Boston area in the late twelfth century.[50] However, as the lords of the honour of Richmond, who held one of Boston's main manors, were first the counts, and later the dukes, of Brittany, the use of Breton names locally may actually have been a product of contacts with the duchy that continued through to the thirteenth century.[51] For instance, although Earl Conan (1146–71) became duke of Brittany in 1156 and was often in his duchy, he also spent much time in England where he issued charters at Boston at some point between 1156 and 1158.[52] Similarly, shortly before her death in 1201 Constance, countess of Richmond and duchess of Brittany, who was Conan's daughter and heiress, granted £10 a year from the honour of Richmond to the abbey of Villeneuve, which she had founded in the diocese of Nantes, to be paid at Boston fair. She also gave a tenth of various sources of income, including that which the honour drew from the fair, to the Breton abbey of Bégard, which had been founded by her great-grandfather Count Stephen, and which was her father's likely burial place.[53]

Perhaps the earliest indication that Boston was beginning to emerge as an urban community is the fact that it was important enough to be home to a coppersmith named Fergus, who, according to Ingulph's chronicle, presented the monks of Crowland abbey with two small bells for the new belfry that they built following the fire at the abbey in 1091.[54] Another sign of Boston's commercial growth is the appearance of its fair, which was eventually to become one of the busiest fairs in the whole country. It is possible, as Owen suggested, that the fair was created by Alan Rufus but there is no actual evidence for its existence during the lifetimes of Alan Rufus or of his brother Alan Niger (i.e. prior to 1098).[55] The first reference to the fair is often said to be that in the charter granted to St Mary's abbey by Alan Niger's successor and younger brother, Count Stephen of Brittany.[56] The identification of Conan, a witness to the charter, as archdeacon of Richmond means that this grant can be dated to the period after 1125, and probably after 1132. Its *terminus ad quem* is the death of Count Stephen but unfortunately the exact year of his death is uncertain. Clay dated the charter to 1125 to 1135 even though he himself noted that Count Stephen may have died in 1135 or 1136, and the same date as is given in the second edition of the *Complete Peerage*, as opposed to 1137 which had been cited in the first edition.[57] More recently, however, Stephen's death has also been dated to 1138.[58] In the charter, Count Stephen not only confirmed the grant of St Botolph's church, which stands on the east side of the river, to the abbey of St Mary's which had been made by his older brother, Alan Rufus, but also gave the monks the right to take their profits in the time of the fair, both in and out of the churchyard at Boston (Fig. 5).[59] However, the fair may have been in existence at an even earlier date since, if the first continuation of the *Croyland Chronicle* is to be believed, it was already being held within the Croun fee, on the west side of the river, around 1114, when Alan de Croun and his wife, Muriel, made a grant of the tithe of the monies received from the fair ('*denarium de feria nostra*') to Crowland abbey.[60]

These references to the fair are the first hint that Boston was beginning to be distinguished from the rural settlements around it. By the early 1150s Boston was significant enough to be mentioned in the account of Britain included in the Arabic geographical encyclopaedia, which was compiled by Muhammad al-Idrisi at the court of Roger II of Sicily.[61] What was the nature of the new urban and commercial community that was emerging at Boston and what were the reasons for its success?

# Part 2

# Lordship and topography

Unfortunately, no buildings now remain in Boston from the years of the town's early growth and, apart from archaeological findings, other material remains from this period are equally scarce. The town's earliest surviving building is the refectory of the Dominican friary, which was rebuilt after being destroyed by fire in 1288. The Guildhall and the town's other brick and timber-framed medieval buildings all date from after *c*.1390. The lion's head knocker, with a ring of two lizards, on the south door to the tower of St Botolph's church (Fig. 6) has been claimed as a relic of the Anglo-Norman church, although even this may actually date from the thirteenth century.[1] What does survive from this period is the town's street-plan, much of which is preserved in the modern centre of Boston, which was established in the early years of its history (Maps 2 and 3). A key influence on the town's plan was the sinuous course of the River Witham, which divided medieval Boston into two main parts, to the east and west of the town bridge (section 2.1.). On the east bank were the manors of the honour of Richmond and the soke of the abbey of St Mary's (section 2.2.) Much of this part of the town lay inside the Barditch and it was here that the town's main streets, which focused on St Botolph's parish church, the bridge over the River Witham, and the Market Place (sections 2.3.), were to be found. Claims for the existence of town walls, a castle and a priory at Boston are problematic (section 2.4.) while the history of the Hospital of St John, which stood just outside the Barditch, poses a number of problems of interpretation (section 2.5.). On the west bank of the river were the Croun and Tattershall fees (section 2.6.) where the merchants of Lincoln concentrated their activities (section 2.7.).

## 2.1. BOSTON AND THE RIVER WITHAM

Boston is situated where the River Witham, flowing southeastwards from Lincoln towards the North Sea, cuts through the 'townlands', a crescent of silt and clay, ranging from about one to five miles wide and standing 10 to 15 feet above sea level, which extends for many miles around the Wash. As is shown with particular clarity on Christopher Saxton's 1576 map of Lincolnshire, the townlands form a barrier between the Lincolnshire fenland to the west, parts of which are at or below sea level, and the saltwater marshlands to the east, and so gave rise to a string of settlements, including Benington, Butterwick, Freiston, Fishtoft and Wyberton (Map 1 and Fig. 7).[2] Boston thus stood advantageously on an island of slightly higher land in an area that was and, as was shown by the tidal surge that hit the town in December 2013, still is extremely prone to flooding (Fig. 8). For instance, in 1175 (or, perhaps 1176), a 'deluge' from the sea 'engulfed many men and herds in Holland' and in 1178 'an infinite multitude of men and animals' was said to have been cut off when Holland was submerged by the sea.[3] Ironically, despite the danger of flooding, Boston may have suffered from a lack of good drinking water. In 1568, the corporation discussed bringing fresh water to the town from as far away as Keal Hill and Hildike while attempts at boring for water were made in the mid-eighteenth century. At the start of the nineteenth century Marrat noted that water was carted to Boston from over sixteen miles away, with its inhabitants collecting rainwater in cisterns for domestic use; only in 1849, when water was piped to the town from Miningsby, was the problem solved.[4] That the inhabitants of medieval Boston faced similar difficulties is suggested by the fact that in 1327 the Boston Dominicans were licensed to build a conduit from Bolingbroke, twelve miles away, to bring water to their friary and to the town.[5]

The River Witham flows approximately north-west to south-east through Boston where, according to John Leland, who visited the town around 1544, it sometimes ran as fast as an arrow.[6] In the medieval period, the river was crossed by a single bridge situated along a stretch where the river narrows, spanning only 100 feet of water at high tide. When the town bridge was originally built is unclear. It has often been said that the first mention of the bridge comes in 1305 when John of Brittany, earl of Richmond, obtained a three-year grant of pontage at Boston.[7] In fact, a bridge was already in place as early as c.1210 when Cecily, the widow of Norman le Mercer, quitclaimed two shops in the mercery ('la mercerie') in Boston fair, 'next but two before the bridge', to St Bartholomew's Hospital, London (Map 2, no. 34).[8] 'Briggestrate' (or 'Briggestrath') is also named in a St Bartholomew's Hospital deed of the second quarter of the thirteenth century (Map 2, no. 33).[9] In all likelihood, the bridge was in existence from a very early date in the town's history and it may well have been used as the site of the sluice which was constructed in the river at Boston in 1142 and which, according to the jurors at an inquisition of 1315, improved the navigation of the Witham at Boston (see section 3.1., below).[10]

The bridge was rebuilt a number of times in the early modern and modern periods. The present Town Bridge was erected in 1913 on the site of John Rennie's cast-iron bridge of 1807. The latter had been located a few yards to the south of the previous bridge, which had been built in 1742 but which incorporated the massive pier that was part of the bridge and sluice that had been built under the direction of Matthew Hake in 1500 (Map 2, no. 6). The pier is mentioned by Leland and is marked on the earliest surviving map of Boston, which was made by Robert Hall in 1741. If the bridge of 1500 was built on the site of its predecessor then the medieval bridge would have lain a little upstream of the present crossing of the Witham, slightly closer to St Botolph's church (Fig. 9).[11] Another possibility is that the bridge was originally well to the south

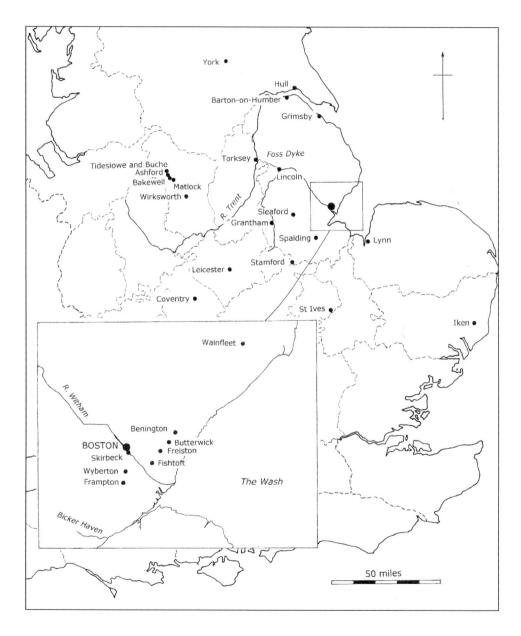

*Map 1. Boston in its national context, with places named in the text.*

of the present bridge and that the road leading to it on the west side of the river was a continuation of the line of what is now West Street (Map 2, no. 15). However, this seems much less likely as it would place the bridge well away from St Botolph's and from the Market Place.

## 2.2. THE LORDSHIPS ON THE EAST SIDE OF THE RIVER

Control of medieval Boston was divided between the jurisdictions of four different lords, two on the east side of the town bridge and two to the west. Some knowledge of the descent of these lordships is important for an understanding of the town's history. This is partly because, as we shall see, the town's overlords played an important role in encouraging its development but also because Boston is most likely to appear in the surviving sources from this period during those years when the honour of Richmond, whose fee made up much of the town, was in the king's hand. On the east bank lay the soke of the abbey of St Mary's, York which, in 1242-3, was said to comprise a twelfth of the eastern part of the town.[12] This soke, which in 1212 consisted of one bovate and a sixth part, was held in free alms, by gift of the count of Brittany, its origins lying in the grant of St Botolph's church to the abbey by Alan Rufus (see section 1.2, above).[13]

Also on the east bank was the Boston manor of the honour of Richmond, which was held in chief and comprised a large part of the medieval town.[14] As we have seen, at the time of the Domesday survey the honour was held by Alan Rufus, count of Brittany, who granted St Botolph's church to St Mary's abbey, York. After his death in 1093 Alan was succeeded by his younger brother, Alan Niger (Alan II), who died in 1098.[15] In turn Alan Niger was followed by his younger brother, Stephen, whose charter to St Mary's abbey contains, as we have noted (section 1.3., above), one of the earliest mentions of Boston fair. The year of Stephen's death is, as we have seen, uncertain, with dates from 1135 to 1138 being possible.[16] Stephen's son Alan III was the first lord of the honour to be referred to as the 'earl of Richmond', a title that he used in 1136.[17] On Alan's death in 1146, his son Conan inherited the earldom as a minor. In 1156 he took on the title of 'duke of Brittany', which he claimed through his mother, Bertha, who was daughter of Duke Conan III, and he referred to himself by this title in his own charters, although the English crown only allowed Conan and his heirs the style of 'count of Brittany'.[18] In 1166 Conan was forced to abdicate as duke but he retained the earldom until his death in 1171. He was succeeded by his daughter Constance who was a minor, which meant that the honour once more fell into the hands of the king. In 1181, Constance married Henry II's fourth son, Geoffrey, who used the titles of duke of Brittany and earl of Richmond until his death in 1186, although he only obtained effective possession of the earldom in 1183. Following Geoffrey's death, Constance was married to Ranulf, earl of Chester, perhaps in 1189, but she repudiated the marriage in 1199 and in the autumn of that year took Guy de Thouars, the brother of the vicomte de Thouars, as her third husband.[19]

Following the accession of King John in 1199, the history of the honour becomes extremely complicated. At this date, the twelve-year-old Arthur of Brittany, the son of Constance and Geoffrey, began to use the title of 'earl of Richmond'.[20] With the support of his mother and the backing of the French king, Philip Augustus, Arthur claimed the counties of Anjou, Maine and Touraine, a claim that brought him into conflict with his uncle, King John, by whom he was captured in 1202 and who was responsible for his death in the following year.[21] At Michaelmas 1200, the lands of the Countess Constance were in the hands of the king and the accounts for them in the royal pipe roll (which includes accounts for monies received at the royal exchequer) include the income that was received by the honour from the two previous Boston fairs.[22] However, the countess seems to have been seised of the honour at the time of her death in September 1201, at which point her husband, Guy de Thouars, was granted the right to lease out the lands of the honour. The honour was still in Guy's hands in April 1203 but, in September of that year, it was forfeited following Guy's transfer of allegiance to Philip Augustus.[23] The honour was then granted to Robert de Breteuil, earl of Leicester, but he died just over a year later, in October 1204, at which point it returned once more into the hands of the king.[24]

In 1205, Guy de Thouars, having briefly returned to King John's allegiance, used the title of earl of Richmond, whilst in 1208 Eleanor, the daughter of Constance and Geoffrey, who was a prisoner of King John, was referred to as countess of Richmond.[25] Eleanor's half-sister, Alice, the elder daughter of Constance and Guy de Thouars, also used the title of countess of Richmond (along with that of duchess of Brittany) perhaps as early as 1205 and definitely by 1214.[26] In 1213, Alice married Pierre de Dreux (or 'Mauclerc'), the second son of the count of Dreux and a member of a cadet branch of the Capetians, who then adopted the title of earl of Richmond although, like Guy, Eleanor and Alice, he had no actual dominion over the lands of the honour which remained in the king's hand. As early as 1215, King John had offered Pierre the honour of Richmond if he would come to England to provide him with military aid. However, as Pierre joined Prince Louis' invasion of England, the honour remained in the king's hand, although some of its lands were granted to Ranulf, earl of Chester in 1218, while 200 marks of the honour's income from Boston fair were assigned to the bishop of Winchester.[27] In 1219, the honour was divided, with thirty of its knights' fees being retained by the crown and the rest of its lands being awarded to Pierre, although William Longespée, earl of Salisbury, seems to have had possession of the honour's rights in Boston fair from 1220 until his death in 1226.[28] Pierre was deprived of the honour for a few months in 1223, for his failure to perform military service in Wales, again in 1224-5, for supporting a French attack on Poitu and Gascony, and once more in 1227–9 when he betrothed his daughter to the brother of Louis IX of France. Finally, in 1235, his English estates were permanently confiscated when he definitively transferred his allegiance to the French king.[29] The honour then remained in the king's hand until 1240, when its estates, although not the actual title of earl of Richmond, were granted to Peter of Savoy, the uncle of Henry III's queen, Eleanor of Provence. Peter surrendered some of the honour's lands to the Lord Edward (the future Edward I) in 1262, while in 1266 the honour was granted to John of Brittany, although Peter continued to claim the lordship until his death in 1268.[30]

## 2.3. THE BARDITCH AND THE TOWN ON THE EAST SIDE OF THE RIVER

One of the key elements determining the plan of the eastern part of Boston, where the soke of St Mary's and the Richmond manor lay, was the Barditch. This was a ditch and a bank about 1,300 yards long which, as can be seen on Robert Hall's 1741 map of the town, encompassed the north, east and south sides of the eastern part of Boston, with the River Witham on the fourth side (Map 2, no. 3 and Fig. 10).[31] The Barditch was covered over from the mid-eighteenth century but its line can still be traced on the basis of the modern street-plan and property divisions (Fig. 11).[32] The ditch was linked to the Witham at its north end at what, in the sixteenth century, was called 'Wormgate End' and at its south end at 'St John's Bridge' (Map 2, no. 20).[33] Beyond the Barditch at the north end was the pool called 'Deppol' (Map 2, no. 21) which in 1248 was mentioned as the site of two mills, which were presumably tidal, in a grant to the monks of Fountains abbey.[34] The existence of the Barditch suggests some form of co-ordinated town-planning, probably on the part of the Richmond honour, but when it was originally dug is uncertain. It was certainly in place by about 1160 when the 'Barredic' is mentioned in a grant of land to Bardney abbey made by Eudo, son of Sigar.[35] Owen tentatively suggested that the Barditch may have been designed for defensive purposes during the disturbances of Stephen's reign. However, given the discovery of eleventh-century pottery at an excavation on the site of the Barditch in the grounds of Fydell House in South Square (Map 2, no. 11 and Fig. 12), it is likely that, as Owen also speculated, the ditch dates from the very earliest years of the town.[36] Indeed, the Barditch may not necessarily have had a defensive function; given the liability of Boston to flooding, the ditch may have helped with the drainage of the area, and it could also have facilitated the collection of tolls by forcing horses and wagons to enter the town via its main roads.[37] The 'Barredich' was described as a 'common sewer' of the town in 1337 and was used as a rubbish tip by the townspeople.[38] In the sixteenth century all those who held properties with frontages along the 'Bardike' had the responsibility to 'scour and carry away' manure and filth from the ditch.[39]

Within the area defined by the Barditch, the eastern part of the town formed a long strip laid out along the course of the Witham.[40] It was here that St Botolph's parish church was located (Map 2, no. 5). Churches were the major public buildings of medieval towns and, as at Boston, where the churchyard was the site of part of the town's fair, they could be used for a variety of secular purposes.[41] While England's

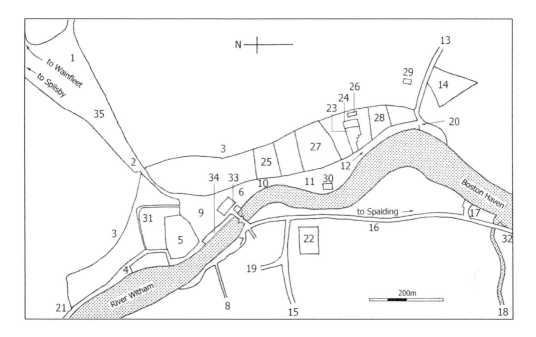

*Map 2. The town of Boston, with places named in the text.*

*Key to Map 2*

1. Wide Bargate
2. Bargate
3. Barditch
4. Wormgate
5. St Botolph's church
6. Bridge and sluice (1500)
7. Stanbow Lane
8. Lincoln Lane
9. Market Place
10. South Street
11. South Square
12. South End
13. Skirbeck Road
14. St John's churchyard
15. West Street (Forde End Lane)
16. High Street (Goat or Gowt Street)
17. St Anne's Lane
18. Hammondbeck
19. Rose Garth Street
20. St John's Bridge
21. Deppul
22. Carmelite friary
23. Mart Yard (sixteenth century)
24. Grammar School (1567)
25. Dominican friary
26. Possible site of Richmond manor house
27. Franciscan friary
28. Possible site of Austin friary
29. Hussey Tower
30. Gysors' Hall
31. Fountains Lane
32. Skirbeck Quarter
33. Possible site of 'Briggestrate'
34. Possible site of 'La Mercerie'
35. Horse Market

older towns were honeycombed with tiny parishes, with York, Lincoln, Norwich and Winchester each having over forty churches, later urban foundations, such as Boston, often had only one main parish church, although part of Boston on the west side of the bridge did lie within the parish of Skirbeck.[42] St Botolph's church (Figs 3 and 5), the Market Place (Map 2, no. 9 and Fig. 13) and the nearby bridge formed the central focus of Boston (Figs 9 and 14).

The town received a formal market charter at a very late date, in 1308, when, as part of a grant that included a number of fairs and markets, John of Brittany, earl of Richmond, was awarded a weekly Saturday market at Boston.[43] However, those places that had held a market before 1199 enjoyed the prescriptive right to do so, even if they did not possess a market charter.[44] This was certainly the case at Boston. Here the first mention of the market dates from the late twelfth century when the marketplace ('*forum*') in Boston is referred to in a grant of land in the town to the Gilbertine house of Alvingham by Reiner of Waxham.[45] Boston fair, which was in existence by 1138 and, perhaps as early as 1114, was held in the Market Place and in the churchyard, although it also extended over the town bridge to the Croun fee.[46] The market must have been in existence from the town's early days and it is likely that the lords of the honour of Richmond had taken the initiative in laying out the basic plan of the eastern part of the town, with its large marketplace and associated tenements, its main streets and the Barditch at the turn of the eleventh and twelfth centuries.[47] Few English new towns had the rectilinear grid-plans and regular chequers of the sort found in later urban foundations in Gascony and Wales but rather, like Boston, tended to be market-based. Markets were often sited adjacent to a parish church, as was the case at Boston, although here the full extent of the town's triangular marketplace is now obscured by market infill on the western side (Fig. 19).[48]

The main streets of Boston within the Barditch formed a Y-shape, with the church and the Market Place at the centre. From here, Wormgate led north-westwards along the river bank; Strait Bargate ran north-eastwards out of the Market Place and, after passing over a bridge over the Barditch (Fig. 11), became Wide Bargate; whilst South Street was the main street from the southern end of the Market Place.[49] It has been suggested that Wormgate (Map 2, no. 4) was originally named 'Dipple Gate' or 'Depul Gate', after 'Deppol', the pool, with its mills, to which it led, and only later became Withamgate and then Wormgate. Certainly an account of St Mary's guild for 1523 refers to a property in 'Depulgate or Wormgate'. Nonetheless, Wormgate (or 'Wrmegate') was in use as a street-name by the late twelfth century and archaeological excavations here have identified a timber building and evidence of lead-working from this period (Figs 15 and 31).[50] From the northeast corner of the Market Place, Strait Bargate and Wide Bargate (Map 2, nos 1 and 2, and Fig. 11) led to the roads towards Wainfleet and Spilsby. Here, beyond the town bar ('*extra barram*'), was found the horse market ('*forum equorum*') where, around 1200, Lincoln cathedral acquired properties (Map 2, no. 35).[51] It is likely that, as in other towns, the funnel shape of Wide Bargate was created to help herd livestock. Certainly, nineteenth-century maps and pictures of Boston indicate Wide Bargate as the site of sheep and cattle markets.[52] By contrast, references to the southern part of the town are lacking in the period before *c.*1225 and it is likely that this area was not yet intensively developed (Figs 16 and 17). The fact that the houses of the Franciscan,[53] Dominican,[54] and Austin friars,[55] were all established in this part of the town in the thirteenth and early fourteenth centuries certainly suggests that there was still ample room for development here during this period (Map 2, nos 25, 27 and 28 and Fig 18).[56] The excavation of the Haven Cinema site, in South Square (Map 2, no. 11), similarly indicated that this area was not densely occupied in the twelfth and early thirteenth centuries.[57]

As can still be seen on the Ordnance Survey map of Boston of 1905 (Map 3), Boston's main streets were lined with long, thin tenement plots, creating the layout that was characteristic of English medieval towns since it allowed access to these major thoroughfares to the maximum number of householders.[58] The pattern is particularly obvious in the Market Place, where the properties, which were each about 24-25 feet wide and 200 feet long, ran as far back as the Barditch. Here the plots were laid out as adjoining double tenements with a shared passageway down either side giving access to the rear, a pattern similar to that which developed on the Bergen harbour-front from the early twelfth century (Figs 19 and 20).[59] Whether these property divisions were in place before the fires which struck the town in 1279[60] and 1288,[61] with the latter being said to have burnt down the greater part of the fair as well as the Dominican friary, cannot be known for certain. However, a number of early grants of property in the town do refer to plot widths of 24 feet, although this was by no means always the case.[62] Plots could also be subdivided – and later reassembled – as can be seen in the case of the four plots of land which were granted, *c.*1190, to Roger, son of William Huntingfield by Roger, William and Eudo, the sons of Asloc, which had been part of their father's '*curia*'.[63]

## 2.4. TOWN-WALLS, A CASTLE AND A PRIORY?

The influence of Pishey Thompson's nineteenth-century work has led to claims that Boston in the Middle Ages was walled and that there was also a castle and a priory in the town. In reality, however, the existence of town-walls of a castle or of a monastery in medieval Boston is unlikely. Thompson's citation of a grant of murage (i.e. of a toll levied to pay for the building or maintenance of town walls) by Edward I in 1285 'to the bailiffs and burgesses, and other good men of the town' established the view that medieval Boston was walled. Later studies then speculated that the bank

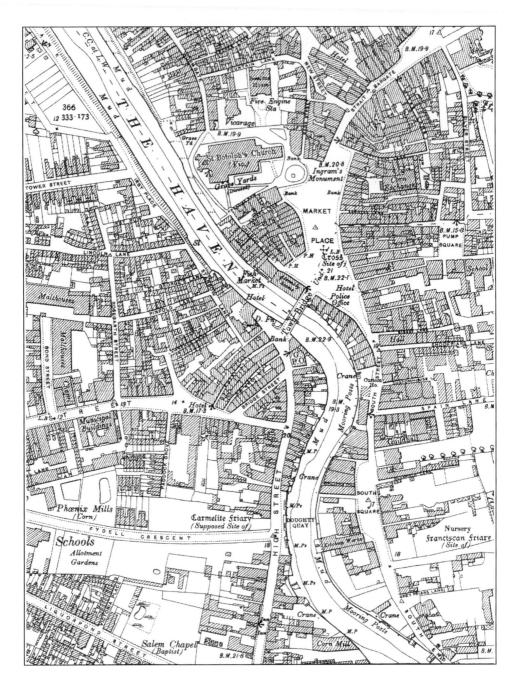

*Map 3.  Boston, Ordnance Survey map, 1:2500, second edition, 1905.*

of the Barditch marked the line on which the town walls were built and that their construction had perhaps begun in 1285, even though Thompson himself referred to the grant of this year as being for repairs to existing town walls.[64] In fact, although the marginal annotation for the 1285 grant in the patent roll does refer to it as being for 'murage' ('*De muragio ville Sancti Botulphi*'), the text of the grant itself states that it was for the levying of pavage, a toll levied to raise money for the paving of the town.[65] There is thus no secure documentary evidence that medieval Boston was ever walled.[66] In the early 1150s, al-Idrisi's geographical account of Britain, which was compiled in Sicily, perhaps from information provided by a source who was familiar with England's south and east coasts, or perhaps even on the basis of a visit to England by al-Idrisi himself, does refer to Boston as a 'fortress', but the town is not shown as walled on the fourteenth-century Gough Map.[67]

Nearly all English towns of a similar rank to Boston did acquire walls, although, as at Lynn, these were often built in the late thirteenth and fourteenth centuries rather than in the initial period of urban development.[68] Whether the substantial walls, including foundations six feet thick, perhaps dating from the early fourteenth century, which were identified by test-excavations in the garden of Fydell House, in South Square (Fig. 12), in 1957 and 1960, were actually part of a circuit of walls in Boston remains uncertain.[69] The walls may have been part of the Franciscan friary, which was located in this area of the town, but another possibility is that they were built to prevent the Barditch from overflowing.[70] Certainly, the Barditch was tidal. In 1561 Boston's council ordained that the 'Bardike' should be made to 'Rune, ebbe and fludde', while in 1569 it instructed that 'clowes' (i.e. sluice-gates) should be constructed at each end of the ditch to help scour and clean it, one having previously been ordered to be set up at St John's Bridge in 1567.[71]

Many towns that were founded in the late eleventh and early twelfth centuries were linked with Norman castles, as was the case at Richmond (Yorkshire) which, like Boston, belonged to the Breton lords of the honour of Richmond.[72] Yet, this does not seem to have been the case at Boston where, despite the existence of a plot of land known as 'Castle ground' in 1570, there is no evidence for a medieval castle.[73] Thompson claimed, on the supposed authority of John Stow, the sixteenth-century antiquarian, that a castle, or at least a 'manorial residence', had been constructed at Boston in 1220 by Ranulf, earl of Chester and of Richmond.[74] In fact, Ranulf was no longer earl of Richmond by 1220 and Stow's text actually refers to Beeston castle ('Beston' or 'Bestone') in Cheshire rather than to Boston.[75] Nevertheless, the honour of Richmond must have had its own manor house in Boston from an early date, perhaps the 'house of the Richmond steward in Holland', which was referred to in 1198, and it was probably here that the honorial court convened when it was held in Boston, as it was by Henry II's reign.[76] The Richmond manor of 'Hallgarth' was granted to the corporation of Boston in 1545 and Thompson identified the site of its manor house as being at the south end of the town (Map 2, no. 26), between the Barditch to the east, the Grammar School (which was built in 1567; Fig. 30) to the west, and the Franciscan friary to the north, but whether this was its original location cannot be known.[77]

Like castles, monastic houses frequently functioned as nuclei of medieval town-life, shaping town plans and encouraging urban development, but once more this was not the case at Boston.[78] It has often been claimed that, following its acquisition of St Botolph's parish church, St Mary's abbey, York, founded a small priory in Boston, perhaps in 1098.[79] Certainly, a house called 'The Priory' once stood on the north side of St Botolph's church until it was demolished to make way for the Sessions House (Fig. 21) which was built from 1841-3.[80] Yet, although St Mary's did establish dependent cells in Lincolnshire, there is no evidence that such a cell ever existed in Boston and, like 'The Priory' in the Cathedral Close at Lincoln, the name of the house in Boston may be a post-medieval invention.[81] Alternatively, 'The Priory' in Boston has been suggested as the site of a nunnery, but the existence of such a house of female religious in the town also lacks any basis in the documentary evidence.[82]

## 2.5. HOSPITALS

Although there is no clear evidence for monastic institutions in Boston prior to the arrival of the four orders of mendicants in the town in the thirteenth and early fourteenth centuries, there were a number of hospitals in the area.[83] Unfortunately, their complicated histories are rather difficult to disentangle and any conclusions about them must be very tentative. Following his visit to the town, John Leland asserted that the church of the Hospital of St John in Boston had once been the town's chief parish church and that St Botolph's had originally only been a chapel of it, although it is not clear why he thought that this was the case.[84] In fact, the earliest evidence we have of the existence of St John's dates only from the early thirteenth century, well over a century after the first reference to St Botolph's.[85] Perhaps, as the parish of St Botolph's seems to have been carved out of the parish of Skirbeck, Leland was confusing St John's, which was situated at the southern end of the town ('towards Skirbeck', as an early thirteenth-century grant to the hospital put it), with Skirbeck parish church, although the latter was actually dedicated to St Nicholas (Fig. 2).[86] The Boston hospital of St John, which was situated outside the Barditch, to the south of the town (Map 2, no. 14), certainly had its own chapel, most of which was demolished in 1584, leaving only the chancel, which was itself taken down in 1626.[87] Nonetheless, its churchyard, which was enlarged in 1715 and 1827, remained in use for burials until 1856. It was marked on Hall's 1741 map and the Ordnance Survey map of 1905 and can still be seen in Skirbeck Road (Map 4).[88] Like the parish church of St Botolph, the Hospital of St John originally belonged to St Mary's abbey, York, and, as at St Botolph's, the right of presenting priests to the hospital's chapel was possessed by the abbey. Only in 1480 did St John's pass into

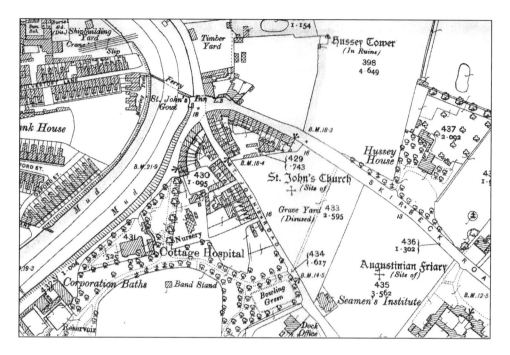

*Map 4. Ordnance Survey map of Boston, 1905, showing the site of St John's Hospital in Skirbeck Road.*

the hands of the Knights Hospitaller, who had recently acquired the advowson of St Botolph's.[89]

The date of the foundation of the Boston Hospital of St John is uncertain, although it is usually seen as being in existence by the early 1280s.[90] Rigby has claimed, on the basis of references in the bishop of Lincoln's rolls, that the hospital had been created by 1218.[91] However, these references to the Hospital of St John 'outside Boston' seem actually to relate to the Hospital of St John in the neighbouring village of Skirbeck, rather than to the Boston foundation: the dedication of hospitals to St John the Baptist was particularly popular at this time.[92] The Skirbeck Hospital of St John was founded when Sir Thomas Multon granted the existing Hospital of St Leonard, of which he was the patron, to the Knights Hospitaller, but the date of his gift is uncertain. Traditionally, the foundation of the Skirbeck Hospital of St John has been dated to around 1230 but a date of *c*.1220 has also been suggested and, as we have seen, it was probably in existence by 1218.[93] The Boston and Skirbeck hospitals of St John have been conflated in some accounts but, given that the Skirbeck house belonged to the Hospitallers long before 1480, when the Boston house passed to the order, they can definitely be identified as two separate institutions.[94] In 1776, Stukeley said that the church of the Skirbeck hospital was standing 'within memory of man' and Thompson located its site as being on what was, by then, the west side of the Maud Foster Drain (dug in 1568) where Norfolk Street meets Hospital Bridge, with Hospital Lane continuing on the eastern, Skirbeck, side of the bridge (Fig. 22). Thompson speculated that an old house called Jerusalem House, which was then standing on the site, had been constructed using materials taken from the hospital but that it had not formed part of the hospital's original buildings (Fig. 23).[95]

Nevertheless, even if the 1218 references to the Hospital of St John are to the hospital of that name in Skirbeck, the Boston Hospital of St John does also seem to have existed by the early thirteenth century, as is evident from a grant recorded in the cartulary of St Mary's abbey, York. The grant was made to the 'brothers and sisters' of the Hospital of St John the Baptist '*de novo loco in villa Sancti Bothulphi versus Skyrebeck*' by William de Huntingfield, who was dead by October 1225.[96] The early date of this grant is supported by the fact that it was witnessed by Alexander Gernun, who also witnessed a grant of a property in Boston to Lincoln cathedral around 1200, acted as a pledge in 1202, was named in the pipe roll of 1204 and appears in a list of essoins from 1212.[97] The early thirteenth century was a peak period in the creation of non-leper hospitals in England, with many foundations in this period being sited in towns. Sometimes, they were established by individuals or by groups of townspeople, and some would eventually pass into the control of the civic authorities. However, as was the case with St John's in Boston, which belonged to St Mary's abbey, they were often linked to a Benedictine monastery, even if they drew upon local townspeople for support.[98]

To complicate matters even further, while the Skirbeck hospital of St John was originally dedicated to St Leonard, Boston itself also had a hospital of St Leonard. The hospital was in existence by 1222, at which date Emma, the widow of Stephen the son of Reginald, brought a case concerning her dower rights to land in Boston against a number of men including the master of the Hospital of St Leonard in the town.[99] If, as was suggested above, the Hospital of St John in Skirbeck was no longer dedicated to St Leonard by 1218, then this 1222 reference to St Leonard's must be to a separate institution. St Leonard was a very popular dedication for leper-hospitals and this may also have been the case in Boston. When St Leonard's was founded is not known, although the main wave of leper-house foundations in England (if such St Leonard's was) occurred in the twelfth century, slightly earlier than the peak for the creation of non-leper houses.[100] Neither do we know the location of St Leonard's although, if it was a leper-house, it is likely that, for reasons either of public health or of theology, it would have been sited away from what was then the main built-up part of the town that clustered around either end of the town bridge.[101] Its location can be very speculatively identified as being indicated by the row of houses once called the 'Hospital Houses', which was situated on the west side of the Witham, between High Street and the river, immediately north of

St Anne's Lane, on the site where the building known as 'The Barracks' now stands (Map 2 no.17 and Fig 24).[102] Urban hospitals could be ephemeral institutions and we do not know how long St Leonard's was in existence or whether it had any connection with the 'house of lepers' at Boston that was mentioned in 1510 in the will of a man from Hogsthorpe (Calcewath wapentake, Lincolnshire).[103]

## 2.6. THE LORDSHIPS ON THE WEST SIDE OF THE RIVER

In addition to the Richmond manor and the soke of the abbey of St Mary's on the east bank of the River Witham, medieval Boston also comprised two other lordships that lay on the west side of the town bridge, those of Croun and Tattershall. The fee of the Croun (or Craon or Creon) family lay immediately to the west of the bridge. This part of the town may have been included in the Domesday survey within the eleven bovates of land in Wyberton belonging to Guy I (or Wido) de Craon, whose family originated in Anjou and who had arrived in England with William I. Wido was a considerable landowner who, at the time of Domesday, possessed 61 lordships, mainly in Lincolnshire itself.[104] It is difficult to disentangle the members of this family who bore the names Alan and Maurice. The Domesday Wido de Croun was succeeded by his son, Alan I, who was the founder of Freiston priory, three miles to the east of Boston, as a dependency of Crowland abbey (Fig. 25). The first continuator of the *Croyland Chronicle* extols his virtue and describes him as the beloved steward and trusted counsellor of Henry I. According to Thompson, this Alan died in 1114, although he cited no evidence for this claim.[105] Alan's eldest son was Maurice de Croun I, who was also a benefactor of Crowland.[106]

In 1315, it was said that an Alan de Croun had been responsible for the building of a sluice at Boston in 1142. If this was the case, he may have been the Alan de Croun (who would thus be Alan II) who, according to Marrat, died in 1150 (although he gave no source for this) and so was perhaps the son of Maurice I.[107] If so, the Maurice de Croun who, at some point between 1147 and 1156, having inherited from his father, confirmed the grant that the latter had made during Stephen's reign to William, son of Roger de Huntingfield, would be Maurice II.[108] In 1183, this Maurice gave lands in Boston to Roger de Huntingfield,[109] and this grant was confirmed by Maurice's son, Guy II (or Wido), who succeeded his father in 1187-8.[110] Guy II's only heir was his daughter Petronilla who, at some point during the reign of Richard I, married William de Longchamp (who died *c.* 1205), the nephew to William Longchamp, who was bishop of Ely and chancellor to King Richard.[111] Her second husband was Henry de la Mare, who died in 1211, and she finally married Sir Oliver de Vaux (or de Vallibus).[112] Their son John de Vaux was succeeded in 1287-88 by two daughters, the younger of whom, Maud or Matilda, who was married to William de Roos (or Ros) of Hamelake, received the lands her father had held in chief in Boston when his estates were divided between his two heiresses.[113] The manor then remained in the hands of the Roos family for the rest of the medieval period, apart from a period of attainder under the Yorkists.[114]

When John of Brittany petitioned for a grant of the toll of pontage in order to maintain the bridge at Boston in 1305, the bridge was said to connect his honour of Richmond with the land of William de Roos (i.e. with what was previously the Croun fee) and with that of the heirs of Robert de Tattershall.[115] The Tattershall fee was the fourth main administrative division of Boston and lay to the south of the Croun fee along High Street (Map 2, no. 16). At the time of Domesday Book, this land belonged to Eudo, son of Spirewic, an important Breton tenant-in-chief who held manors in Lincolnshire, Norfolk and Suffolk, and the survey lists eight villeins on Eudo's manor, which was said to be 'sokeland belonging to Tateshale'.[116] By 1118, Eudo had been succeeded by his son Hugh, who in 1139 founded Kirkstead abbey and who died c.1166.[117] Hugh was followed by his son Robert, who gave the monks of Kirkstead a new site. He was dead by 1185, when his estate was inherited by his son Philip, who had died by 1200.[118] The manor then passed through the hands of six Robert de Tattershalls, the first two of whom died in 1212 and 1249.[119] On the extinction of the male line, following the death of Robert de Tattershall VI in 1306, the manor passed to Joan de Driby, who was probably the daughter of Robert IV, and in 1367 came into the hands of Ralph Cromwell.[120]

## 2.7. THE TOWN ON THE WEST SIDE OF THE RIVER

After John Leland had visited Boston he declared that the 'greate and chifiest' part of the town lay on the east side of the Witham and described the western part of the town as consisting of 'one long street'. This was presumably a reference to what is now High Street, which runs parallel with the river, southwards from the bridge towards Skirbeck Quarter (Fig. 26).[121] On Hall's map it is labelled 'Goat Street or High Street' (Fig. 10) but it was originally known as 'Gowt Street' - a 'gowt' being a channel of water or a sluice.[122] It has been suggested that the Richmond fee was the original nucleus of the town of Boston and that the growth of the urban community on the Croun fee was a later development which may have resulted from the building of the town bridge at the time of the construction of the sluice in 1142.[123] Yet the date when the bridge was built is unknown and it is equally possible that a bridge was in existence before the sluice and was therefore chosen as the site for it. The new town of Boston and its fair may thus have clustered around both ends of the bridge well before the building of the sluice in 1142 and, as we have seen, the fair may have been held on the Croun fee, on the west side of the river, by as early as c.1114.

Moreover, despite the comments made by Leland in the mid-sixteenth century about the relative unimportance of the western side of Boston, it may be unwise to underestimate the development of this part of the town in the early years of its history. After all, while the honour of Richmond drew £8 0s. 5d. from rents of assize in Boston in 1199-1200, four years later the rents of assize of the Croun fee were worth as much as £11 17s. 4d.[124] That in 1142 it was Alan de Croun, rather than the earl of Richmond, who was responsible for the building of the sluice at Boston, also suggests that the lords of the Croun manor were taking an active interest in encouraging the development of the town in this early period.[125] It is possible that the manor-house of the Croun fee was situated near the modern Rose Garth Street, off West Street (Map 2, no. 19). As noted above, the fee was eventually acquired by the Roos family and it is likely that Rose Garth Street takes its name from the site of the Roos Hall manor-house, which was bought by the corporation of Boston in 1557 and was perhaps the successor to a manor-house of the Croun fee.[126]

From the west end of the bridge, the road which is now West Street, which was previously known as Forde End Lane, led out towards Sleaford and Lincoln.[127] The merchants of Lincoln seem to have concentrated their activities in this part of the town from an early date, perhaps as early as the twelfth century if complaints made by the citizens of Lincoln in 1265 are to be believed. At this date, the men of Lincoln alleged that they had been excessively charged for tronage in Boston even though they had previously paid only half a mark (6s. 8d.) to Wido de Croun (who died in the 1190s) and to his heiress, Petronilla, the wife of William de Longchamp, in lieu of all tronage.[128] Nine years later, the Lincoln Hundred Roll jurors complained that the mayors of the city had paid £10 a year to Peter of Savoy (who had died in 1268), the lord of the Richmond honour, in order to trade at Boston fair. An extent of the honour made in 1280 specified that this payment was made for permission to trade on the Tattershall and Croun fees (with the latter by then being in the hands of John de Vaux), on the west side of the river, even though, as we saw above, the fair had probably been held on the Croun fee from the early twelfth century.[129]

That Lincoln men were active in the western part of Boston from an early date is also shown by the grant made to the monks of Durham cathedral priory, around 1200, by Godwin the Rich, a citizen of Lincoln, of a house that he held of the Croun fee.[130] Lincoln Lane, leading westwards from the western bank of the Witham is shown on Hall's map of 1741 (Map 2, no. 8): this may be the 'Lincoln Row' which was amongst the properties listed on the 'west side of the water' in the 1489 extent of the Boston guild of Corpus Christi.[131] Another Lincoln connection in this part of town is Stanbow Lane, which is also marked on Hall's 1741 map (Map 2, no. 7). The name of the lane, which still exists, may be derived from that of the Stonebow, the main gate of the city of Lincoln. It was in use as a Boston street-name by 1577, whilst the mid-fourteenth-century cartulary of Crowland abbey includes a marginal annotation to the 'part of the town called Stonbow' (Fig. 27).[132] The Croun-Vaux-

Roos fee was also, from at least 1307 and probably earlier, the site of the Carmelite friary, the white friars being the only one of Boston's four orders of mendicants to have a house on the west side of the bridge (Map 2, no. 22).[133]

The part of Boston belonging to the Tattershall fee lay within the portion of the parish of Skirbeck that was on the west side of the River Witham and was eventually known as Skirbeck Quarter (Map 2, no. 32).[134] Thompson identified this area of the town as lying to the south of St Anne's Lane and of the stream known as the Hammondbeck (Map 2, no. 18).[135] It is likely that, as in the eastern part of the town, urban development on the west side of the river spread downstream from the bridge. Thus, by 1211-12, the Tattershall fee received £17 10s. 10½d. in income from Boston fair and, as was noted above, in the thirteenth century the city of Lincoln paid the lord of the honour of Richmond for permission to trade on the Tattershall and Croun fees during fair time.[136]

It has been suggested that Boston on the west side of the River Witham may have been walled.[137] However, this claim is even less plausible than those made for the existence of walls around the eastern part of the town. The supposed evidence for such walls is a royal writ of 1356, which appointed two men to organise repairs of bridges, houses, walls and buildings in Boston and elsewhere. In fact, this writ actually refers to work at Boston on the honour of Richmond's manor, on the east side of the river, as well as on a number of other Lincolnshire manors of the honour, and does not specify that these repairs were to town walls, as opposed to walls around manorial properties.[138]

As we have seen, Boston at the time of Domesday Book was only a minor settlement within the hundred of Skirbeck yet, by the start of the thirteenth century, it had emerged as one of the most successful new towns in the country. Unlike many other new towns, Boston's layout and growth were not explained by the presence of a castle or of a monastic community; instead, from its birth, Boston was a purely commercial plantation.[139] What, then, were the branches of trade that promoted the growth the town enjoyed during this period?

# Part 3

# Boston's early trade

The surviving sources for the history of Boston in the twelfth and early thirteenth centuries are, as we shall see, mainly concerned with its fair, which came to play a central role in England's wholesale trade. Yet, as is shown by the case of St Ives (Huntingdonshire), the fact that a settlement possessed a successful fair was not, in itself, sufficient to elevate it to the ranks of England's major towns.[1] After all, before 1218, Boston fair lasted for only eight days, from St Botolph's day to the feast of St John the Baptist ( i.e. from 17 to 24 June), at which date it was extended for another eight days.[2] What was crucial for the early growth of the town was not only that it was the site of one of England's busiest fairs but also, as is shown by the returns of the fifteenth on trade levied by King John, that it had developed into one of the country's leading ports.[3] The rise of Boston was part of a wider process whereby deep-water estuarine ports prospered at the expense of inland ports (section 3.1.). Boston was particularly well-placed to take advantage of links with Germany and Scandinavia (section 3.2.) and of the growing trade in wool, textiles, lead and wine (sections 3.3. to 3.6.), although we are far less well-informed about its trade in foodstuffs (section 3.7.). The emergence of Boston was connected not only with the growth of overseas trade but also with the drainage and colonisation of the Lincolnshire fens in this period (section 3.8.). Finally, whilst much of Boston's commerce is now hidden from us, the occupations of the artisans and retailers who must have made up the bulk of the town's population are even less likely to appear in the surviving sources (section 3.9.).

## 3.1. BOSTON AS A PORT

At a time when sending goods by road could be six or even ten times as expensive as using water transport, access to river and coastal trade dramatically increased the effective size of a town's hinterland.[4] Above all, it was international trade which promoted urban expansion and generated mercantile wealth.[5] In 1334, for instance, of the seven wealthiest towns in England, five were estuarine ports involved in overseas trade (London, Bristol, Newcastle, Boston and Yarmouth) and the other two (York and Norwich) were inland ports.[6] In particular, with its position at the mouth of the River Witham, Boston benefited from its role as the out-port for the city of Lincoln, over thirty miles upstream (Fig. 28). It also functioned as a trans-shipment point where commodities were transferred between larger sea-worthy vessels and river-going craft, although as is shown by the boat ('*batella*') that carried 78 quarters of grain from Lincoln to Boston in the early fourteenth century, the latter could be of a considerable size.[7]

Lincoln's growth had perhaps taken off as early as the middle of the ninth century and its southern commercial suburb of Wigford emerged from the early tenth century. The city underwent renewed expansion from the mid-eleventh century, despite the short-term destruction caused by the construction of the Norman castle. The evidence of minting, of the city's Domesday population, and of its tallage payments suggests that, in the late eleventh and twelfth centuries, Lincoln stood behind only London, York and Winchester in its size and wealth and it was, along with York, the major cloth-making centre in the country; it was still the ninth richest English town in 1334 and the sixth largest in 1377.[8] The earliest reference to Lincoln merchants trading in Boston comes in 1202 when they were fined for selling wine against the assize, which controlled its price and quality and, as we have seen, it is likely that they concentrated their business in Boston on the west side of the river.[9] Lincoln men, as noted above, owned property in Boston and these included Pictaululus, son of Yanasser the Jew, of Lincoln, who, in the late twelfth century, made a quitclaim to Malton priory of all the land in Boston which he had previously been granted by Walter Bars.[10] However, although Jewish credit played an important part in the commercialisation of the English economy in the twelfth century, Jewish communities tended to be found in royal towns, such as Lincoln and York, rather than in seigneurial boroughs such as Boston, where there is no evidence for Jewish settlement.[11]

The emergence of Boston as a port in the twelfth century also seems to have been linked with improvement in the navigation of the River Witham, with the development of Boston's harbour facilities, with changes in ship design, and with the expansion of its hinterland as a result of the port's enhanced access to a network of inland waterways. The early course of the River Witham has been the subject of some debate. Following a suggestion by Stukeley, Miller and Skertchly claimed that the river once flowed into the sea at Wainfleet, north of Boston, and that its present course was once a lesser outflow of the river, but this theory was subsequently refuted by Jukes-Browne.[12] An alternative view is that Bicker Haven, to the south of Boston, was once an outfall of the Witham although when the river changed its course is not clear.[13] Hallam, for instance, argued that the main course of the Witham once flowed to the sea via Bicker Haven and that Boston was originally a lesser outfall of the river. For Hallam, it was the construction of a sluice at Boston in 1142 (see below) that caused the main course of the river to shift to Boston, with this shift explaining the 'late, but meteoric ascent' of the port.[14] Yet, as we have seen (in section 1.2., above), Boston's commercial growth seems to have begun before 1142 with St Botolph's fair being in existence by 1138, and perhaps as early as 1114. The construction of the sluice may thus have been a response to the growth of the town's trade rather than the cause of it.

Indeed, it has also been suggested in a number of popular and academic works that the main outlet of the Witham did not shift from Bicker Haven in 1142, following the building of the sluice, but rather that the river altered its course as early as 1014, as a result of the great flood which hit England on 28 September of that year.[15] The flood is noted in the *Anglo-Saxon Chronicle* and is also reported in William of Malmesbury's *Gesta Regum Anglorum* where it is described as a 'tidal wave' of 'astonishing size' that submerged villages and drowned people many miles inland.[16] It is possible that this flood was a tsunami caused by the impact of comet debris landing in the North Atlantic. It seems to have affected a number of places around the English coast, from Cumbria to Cornwall, and may even have caused flooding in the Netherlands.[17] However, any claims for the impact of this flood on the course of the River Witham remain very speculative and it is possible that the present course of the river was actually in place by the ninth century or even earlier.[18] Moreover, even if the course of the Witham did alter in 1014, this did not immediately cause the rise of Boston as a port. Rather, as we shall see, the emergence of Boston was part of a more general trend for estuarine ports to grow, which was evident in late eleventh- and twelfth-century England as ships increased in size and new types of harbour facilities became available.

Nevertheless, if Boston Haven was already the main outlet for the Witham even before the construction of a sluice there in 1142, the new sluice may well have improved the condition of the port. Unfortunately, the only evidence for the building of the sluice is provided by the claims made by the jurors at an inquisition held in 1315 before three royal commissioners *de walliis et fossatis* (later known as the commissioners of sewers, i.e. of watercourses) who were responsible for overseeing the measures in place to ensure the drainage of low-lying land and its protection against flooding.[19] Very few records of these commissioners have survived for the period before 1427 and the original return of the Boston inquisition of 1315 no longer seems to exist.[20] The text of the 1315 inquisition is now known only from the copies and translations of it that were made in the early modern period and that can be traced back to an entry in the 'Black Book of Sewers' which was in the custody of the clerk of the commissioners of sewers in Holland.[21] Of course, this source cannot simply be taken at face-value. After all, in 1623, it was claimed at Sleaford that many people suspected that the old records upon which the decisions of the contemporary commissioners of sewers were being based were actually 'false counterfeit and forged' documents for which no authentic original could be found.[22] Nevertheless, the later versions of the text of the 1315 inquisition do seem to be based on a genuine original return since they state that the inquisition was held before Lambert de Trikyngham, Roger de Coppledyk and Robert de Mablethorp. These men were indeed three of the four commissioners *de wallis et fossatis* who had been appointed by the king on 4 August 1315 in response to complaints made by men dwelling along the Lincolnshire coast.[23] What is more problematic, however, is what sources were available to the jurors in 1315 in order for them to make claims about the building of a sluice in the mid-twelfth century. In the absence of other corroborative evidence, their account of the building of the sluice naturally has to be treated with caution. Nevertheless, just as the story concocted by a jury of Gloucester men at an inquisition of 1356 about the building of the town's Westgate Bridge in the twelfth century was inaccurate without being a 'complete work of fiction', so the return of the jurors in 1315 may preserve, even if in a muddled form, some of the details about the origins of sluice at Boston.[24]

The jurors returned that in the seventh year of King Stephen's reign (26 December 1141 to 25 December 1142), Alan de Croun, who was lord of the Croun fee on the west side of the River Witham, had, out of his piety and charity, caused a *'magna exclusa sive cateracta'* (i.e. 'a great sluice or conduit/floodgate') to be built in the middle of the river at Boston where the wapentakes of Skirbeck and Kirton met. The purpose of the sluice was to deepen the channel of the Haven by increasing the flow of the river, which was said to be blocked up by the abundance of sand and silt which were brought in each day by the tide, and to allow the waters from the marshes of Lindsey, Holland and Kesteven to descend more easily to the sea. The jurors of 1315 reported that the sluice was then 'ruinous and in great decay', with many posts missing and iron bonds, beams and planks being in need of replacement, and they returned that the cost of repairing the sluice and of maintaining the banks and dikes along the Witham should be borne by the entire district.[25] Similar complaints about the condition of the sluice and about the dangers of tidal flooding were made in Henry VI's reign and a new sluice was eventually built in 1500.[26] By holding back freshwater, which could then be released to scour out the Haven below Boston, the sluice, which was said to have been constructed in 1142, may have made it easier for sea-going vessels to gain access to the port. It perhaps also enhanced the navigation of the Witham above Boston, as well as helping to protect the fens from tidal flooding.[27] Certainly, in 1500, one of the advantages of the new sluice for Boston was said to be the 'deeper harbour that would be created', although complaints about the shifting mud-banks in the Haven, which were formed as the mud-laden Witham met the silt-laden tide, continued down to the modern period.[28]

The emergence of Boston as the out-port for Lincoln was part of a general trend in this period for new coastal and estuarine ports, such as Newcastle, Hull, Lynn and Yarmouth, to develop at the expense of England's inland ports. The growth of trade, particularly in bulky goods rather than in luxuries, encouraged the development of larger ships with deeper draughts and stern rudders. These included the cog, the flat-bottomed, keeled, high-volume cargo-carrier, which needed greater depths of water in order to moor and so was particularly suited to coastal and estuarine harbours.[29] In turn, the availability of larger ships, which by 1250 could each carry five times the cargo of those of 1000, itself promoted the growth of trade as their economies of scale reduced unit transport costs and so made it more viable to send goods over long distances. These larger ships could not simply be run up onto the foreshore, as had previously been the normal practice, but required improved waterfront facilities. For instance, at London, quays with timber revetments had been built by the late eleventh century whilst stone quays were introduced from the early thirteenth century. Loading and unloading via gangplanks onto quays was easy and cheap although the use of cranes is also known from the second half of the twelfth century.[30] The existence of such facilities in Boston is indicated by grant made around 1190 by William de Longchamp which mentions the place in Boston 'where ships tie up' ('*athachiamentis navium*'), whilst a mid-thirteenth century bond about a plot of land in Boston made by Roger the Goldsmith specified that he was to maintain the buildings and '*le kay*', which were attached to the plot (Fig. 29).[31] References to properties whose rights stretched from the middle of the plots 'to the middle of the river' may also indicate the existence of private staithes for mooring ships.[32]

The importance of Boston as a port was enhanced not only by its role as the out-port for Lincoln at the mouth of the River Witham but also by its position at the entrance to an important system of inland waterways - the Trent, Humber, and Ouse - by which goods could be sent to Nottingham, York and Hull. Access to this system was provided by the Foss Dyke, a canal which connected the Witham at Lincoln with the Trent at Torksey, eleven miles away. When the Foss Dyke was originally built is not clear. It may have been created by the Romans, although a late tenth- or early-eleventh-century date is also possible, either for its construction or at least for when it was re-dug. The canal seems to have become obstructed after the Norman Conquest but was re-opened in 1121.[33] This network of inland waterways meant that Boston was able to function as a port which served a much wider area than its immediate hinterland. This may have particularly been the case in the period before the last decades of the twelfth century, at which time the newly-created port of Hull began to compete for the trade of Yorkshire.[34] The reopening of the Foss Dyke in 1121, the building of the sluice at Boston in 1142, and the improvement of the port's harbour facilities all formed part of the expansion of the material infrastructure of the English economy in this period, an expansion also evident in the construction of bridges and the spread of water- and wind-mills.[35] Such innovations set in motion a process of positive feedback so that the reopening of the link between the Witham and the Trent or the improvement of the navigation of the Witham were not only a response to the expansion of trade but, in turn, facilitated commerce and generated further growth.

Nonetheless, while Boston benefited from the advantages of water transport provided by the Witham and the Foss Dyke, it would be wrong to see roads and rivers as competing, rather than as complementary, methods of distributing goods in this period.[36] This was, after all, a period when road transport was also being improved with the building of bridges, the extension of the road network, the increased use of horse haulage and improvements to cart design.[37] Certainly, when monastic houses acquired properties in Boston for use during fair time, they made sure that they came with guaranteed access for horses, wagons and carts.[38] As a bridging point, Boston benefited from being the meeting point of a number of roads. These included the road that follows the line of the sea-banks northwards to Wainfleet; that which leads southwards to Spalding, which King John took when he passed through the town in October 1216; those to Lincoln and to the ferry across the Humber at Barton to the north; those on the causeways linking Boston to the Wolds; that on the causeway between Holland and Kesteven, which linked Boston and Grantham; and the roads from the south end of the town to Freiston and Skirbeck.[39]

## 3.2.  SCANDINAVIAN AND GERMAN TRADE

Unfortunately, we lack detailed evidence about the trade which flowed along the road and water routes which led to Boston in the twelfth century; only from the thirteenth century onwards do the royal Chancery enrolments (including the close, patent, liberate and fine rolls) and the records of the royal customs service allow us to explore the town's commerce in any detail. We do know that Scandinavian links were important in Lincolnshire's early trade, with Henry II ordering all Norwegians coming to the county's ports to pay tolls on their goods to the city of Lincoln.[40] Stockfish imports from Bergen were central to this trade, which was expanding from the late eleventh and early twelfth centuries, while other Scandinavian imports included furs, hawks, timber, walrus ivory, and horses. In return, grain, ale, honey and cloth were shipped to Norway.[41] In the twelfth and early thirteenth centuries, English and Norwegian merchants dominated this branch of commerce, although it is possible that Lynn, rather than Boston, was its main focus in this period.[42] Boston's involvement in the trade is evident in the earliest references to royal purchases at Boston fair, which relate to hawks and girfalcons, probably from Norway, with £20 being paid by the king for birds bought there in 1175 and £8 in the following year.[43] Goshawks were bought at the fair for the king's use in 1207 and 1213, as were two girfalcons and one goshawk sent to Winchester in 1213-14.[44] These purchases were usually made by members of the Hauvill family, which, from the reigns of Henry II to Edward III, provided falconers for the crown.[45] In the thirteenth century, the Hauvills held the manor of Hacconby (Aveland wapentake, Lincolnshire) in serjeanty and had received a grant of the toll of lastage in Boston in return for receiving falcons for the king at Boston.[46]

German merchants were also present in Boston in this early period. At this date, merchants from Cologne virtually monopolised Anglo-German trade, exporting English wool and importing wine, cloth, metalwork and other goods.[47] Cologne merchants were active in Lincolnshire in the twelfth century and can be seen trading at Boston fair in the early thirteenth century. In 1213, for instance, Arnulf Ungfother, merchant of Cologne, was licensed to attend Boston fair to trade along with his cog ('*goga sua*'), while in 1224 Terricus de Stamford, a Cologne man who dealt in wool, cloth and wine, was exporting goods from Boston.[48] In the thirteenth century Hanseatic merchants from the Baltic ports took over an increasing share of Anglo-German and Anglo-Scandinavian commerce, and Hansards, particularly those from Lübeck, came to control the trade between England and Bergen, with Boston replacing Lynn as their main centre from the early fourteenth century onwards.[49] However, these 'Esterlings' only became a significant presence in England from around 1220, with their trade particularly taking off in the second half of the century when the direct sea route from the Baltic to the North Sea was established and goods no longer had to be taken by land across the Jutland peninsula.[50] The purchase of 'greywork', i.e. winter squirrel skins, for the king's use at Boston fair in 1222 may be an early sign of the arrival of the Esterlings in the trade of the port, whilst in 1226 the men of Gotland were also claiming exemption from paying lastage on their trade in Boston.[51]

### 3.3. THE WOOL TRADE

A key factor in the emergence of Boston in the century and a half after the Domesday survey was the role the port played in England's expanding wool trade with the Low Countries. In the thirteenth century, when raw wool overwhelmingly dominated England's export trade, the evidence of the advance contracts for wool sales and of the returns of the royal custom on wool exports (which survive from 1279) shows that Boston was the most important port in the country for the shipment of wool, a position it was to retain until the last decade of the century when it was overtaken by London.[52] Nevertheless, the wool trade had much earlier origins. It is possible that England was supplying wool to the growing Flemish cloth industry as early as the eleventh century, although the first direct evidence of English wool exports to the Low Countries dates only from the early twelfth century and the trade undoubtedly expanded from the middle of the century. There was a further spurt of growth in the late twelfth century as rising population meant that Flemish sheep runs were being converted to arable, which increased the dependence of the Flemish textile industry on imported raw materials. By the end of the century, England was the main supplier of high-quality wool in Europe, a fact which allowed Richard I and King John to use the trade as a diplomatic lever in their dealings with France and Flanders.[53] The collapse of fair income in Boston in 1173 and 1174 (see Table 1, below), at a time when Anglo-Flemish trade was disrupted, points to the significance of the wool trade at Boston at this time, although Flemish merchants not only dealt in wool but also imported wine, silk, cloth and woad.[54]

The prominence of Boston in the returns for the fifteenth on overseas trade levied by King John must, to a large degree, have been a reflection of the scale of its wool export trade at this early date.[55] Although London was the main port of England at this date, accounting for 17 percent of the total raised by the fifteenth from the ports of the south and east coasts, its primacy was rivalled by Boston's 16 per cent, as well as by the trade of other provincial ports such as Southampton, Lincoln and Lynn (on 14, 13 and 13 percent respectively). At this date, the capital no longer dominated England's overseas trade as it had perhaps done before the Norman Conquest and as it was certainly to do once more from the late thirteenth century.[56] Indeed, London merchants were themselves active in Boston from an early date, at least if we accept the date of 1189 for the assize which said that the capital's Husting court was only to be suspended during the time of Boston and Winchester fairs and at harvest-time.[57] Londoners were also acquiring property in Boston by the start of the thirteenth century.[58]

We have little evidence for the area from which Boston drew its shipments of wool in the twelfth century. Lincolnshire itself was a major supplier of the expensive wool that supplied the export trade and there may have been extensive flocks in the county, including in the Holland fens and the Lincolnshire Wolds, by the late tenth century, or even earlier.[59] By the thirteenth century, when Boston and Winchester were the leading fairs for wool, Boston exported the wool of a wide area including not only Lincolnshire itself but also many other northern and Midland counties, particularly Leicestershire, Derbyshire, Northamptonshire, Nottinghamshire, Rutland and Warwickshire, and even from as far west as Flintshire, Cheshire and Staffordshire.[60]

The nationalities of the merchants who dealt in wool in the twelfth and early thirteenth centuries are also obscure. In the years immediately before 1270, Flemish merchants seem to have dominated England's wool export trade, particularly that in high-quality Midland wools, and merchants from Ypres, Douai and other Flemish towns were very active in Boston's trade, both as exporters of wool and as importers of cloth.[61] It is likely that they enjoyed a similar primacy in the twelfth and early thirteenth centuries, although references which specify their involvement in the trade, such as the pipe roll entry for 1219, which refers to the wool of St Katherine's priory, Lincoln, which was said to have been arrested at the instance of merchants from Ghent, are very much the exception.[62] Royal policy meant that the wool trade was periodically disrupted. For instance, in 1195-6, Simon de Kyme, the sheriff of Lincolnshire, was fined the huge sum of a thousand marks for allowing foreign merchants to take their goods away from Boston fair by ship, an offence which may have arisen from the restrictions on wool exports and the levying of a tax of a tenth on foreign trade which were associated with the collection of Richard I's ransom.[63] In addition to the Flemings, other merchants from the Low Countries traded through Boston, including the men of Holland, whose goods were arrested at Boston fair in 1226, and merchants from Antwerp (Brabant), who brought wine to the fair in 1227.[64]

### 3.4. THE TEXTILE TRADE

In addition to exporting raw wool, Boston also profited from the trade in manufactured woollen cloth. In 1201 merchants at Boston fair were willing to bribe royal justices so as to be allowed to evade the requirements of the 1196 royal assize of cloth and so be able to sell cloth of whatever width they pleased.[65] Thompson saw this incident as evidence for extensive cloth production at Boston itself during this period but it is more likely to have involved cloth sold at the fair.[66] Certainly, Boston was not included among the many English cloth-making towns, including five in Lincolnshire (Lincoln, Grimsby, Stamford, Sleaford and Barton), which, in 1202, paid to be exempted from the assize.[67] Lincoln, in particular, was a centre of production for high-quality textiles from an early date and had a guild of weavers as early as 1130. We can see Lincoln merchants selling cloth to the king at Boston fair in the mid-thirteenth century.[68] Cloth from other English towns, including those belonging to merchants from Bristol, Beverley, Coventry, Thetford, Stamford, Worcester, Oxford and Leicester, was also seized at the fair for being against the assize in 1225 and 1226.[69]

The English cloth industry needed to import dyestuffs but we lack evidence for this trade in Boston, although we may speculate that the goods of the Abbeville man seized at Boston and Lynn fairs in 1218 would have included Picard woad.[70] Furthermore, since it is likely that the assize of 1196 originally applied to imported cloth as well as to those made in England, it is not certain that the merchants noted above who attempted to evade its restrictions in 1201 were actually English.[71] For instance, French textiles, including those belonging to Norman merchants, were arrested at Boston fair in 1227.[72] Flemish cloth, often made with English wool, was being imported into England on a large scale by 1220, by which time it was beginning to undermine the production of high-quality woollens in the towns of eastern England. It was a major commodity at Boston fair in the thirteenth century, alongside English cloth, and it is likely that cloth from Flanders had been sold at Boston fair during the previous century.[73]

### 3.5. THE LEAD TRADE

As is shown by the references to the hawks which were bought for the king in Boston, our evidence for the port's trade in the twelfth and early thirteenth centuries is disproportionately concerned with royal purchases. As a result, we know more about shipments of lead through Boston in this period than we do about the trade in wool and cloth. Lead-mining had been established in Derbyshire in Roman times and was flourishing once more from the late Anglo-Saxon period. At the time of Domesday Book, the industry was centred on the areas around Wirksworth, Matlock, Ashford and Bakewell. Then, as production took off from the 1170s, mining shifted northwards, into the High Peak area north of the River Lea, including Tideslowe and Buche (Map 1), although output contracted once more in the first half of the thirteenth century.[74] In 1179-80, the sheriff of Nottinghamshire and Derbyshire sent 40 cartloads of lead, which the king had given to the Cistercian order, from the Peak District to Boston. In the same year, he also arranged for 100 cartloads of lead to be taken to Boston and then shipped via London to Waltham abbey (Essex), the house of Augustinian canons which

Henry II had vowed to build as part of his penance for the death of Thomas Becket.[75] In 1184, Ranulf de Glanvill accounted for 31s. 3d. for the carriage of 20 cartloads of lead (worth £13 6s. 8d.) from 'Holland', which in this context almost certainly meant from Boston, to Rouen in Normandy for use on the king's works at Gisors, an important fortress on the border between Normandy and France. Lead was also shipped from Boston to Sandwich for the king's use in 1199-1200 and was sent to Winchester castle, via Southampton, in 1222 and 1224.[76]

### 3.6. THE WINE TRADE

Imported wine was one of the major commodities sold at Boston fair in the thirteenth century, but the trade had its origins in the previous century.[77] At some date between 1146 and 1171, Earl Conan had granted the right to all the empty wine casks at Boston fair to Richard Pinchard. In turn, by July 1188, Richard had transferred this right to the Cistercians of Sibton abbey (Suffolk), which had been founded in 1150, with his gift then being confirmed by Conan's daughter, Countess Constance, sometime between 1181 and 1201.[78] The monks of Sibton certainly enforced this privilege as men with properties in Boston were prepared to pay the abbey to obtain exemptions from its monopoly.[79] Our main source for the trade in wine in this period is, once more, the evidence of royal purchases. In 1183-84, for instance, ten tuns of white and red wine, which had cost £8 8s. 4d., were sent for the king from 'Holland' to Nottingham and Clipston (Nottinghamshire) at a cost of 41s. 5d., whilst in 1199-1200 the sheriff of Nottinghamshire and Derbyshire paid 25s. for the carriage of wine bought for the king at the fair.[80] Royal purchases of wine were also sent from Boston to York and Knaresborough in Yorkshire; to Hareston, Laxton, and Southwell in Nottinghamshire; to Northampton, Cliffe, Geddington, Silverstone, and Yarwell in Northamptonshire; to Melbourne in Derbyshire; to St Ives in Huntingdonshire; to Woodstock in Oxfordshire; as well as to Bedford and Chester (Map 5).[81] Of these destinations, Clipston, Silverstone, Geddington, Cliffe and Laxton were all royal hunting lodges within the bounds of the forest.[82] In 1202, nineteen traders were accused of having sold wine at Boston against the assize and these included men from London, Lincoln, Yarmouth, Bury St Edmunds, Lynn, Northampton and Limoges.[83]

The origins of the wine that arrived in Boston are less clear. By the early thirteenth century, substantial amounts of Gascon wine, shipped from Bordeaux, were being sent to England and this region was dominant in the wine trade after 1225. Wines from Gascony and Blanc-en-Berry were purchased for the king's use at Boston fair in 1224, including the £104 paid for 48 tuns of wine bought from Peter Buzun, a merchant of Bordeaux. However, prior to the fall of Normandy in 1204, imports of wine from the Ile de France, which were shipped to England via Rouen, had also been significant and, from c.1137 until the conquest of Poitu by the French king in 1224, wine from Anjou and Poitou was also sent to England via La Rochelle.[84] In 1200, for instance, 20

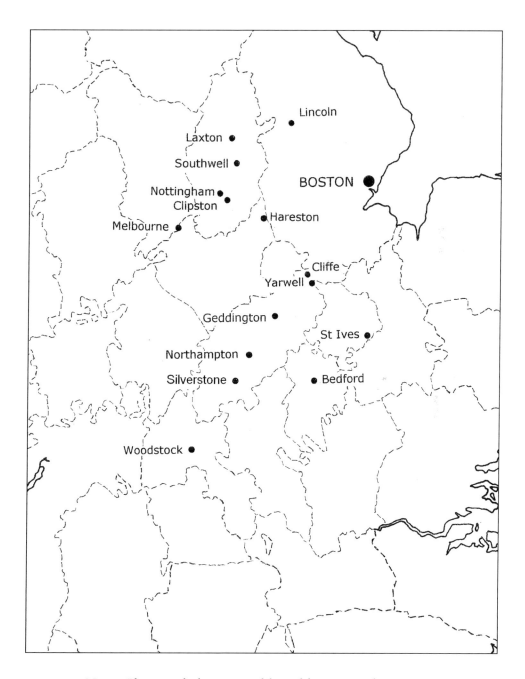

*Map 5.  Places to which wine was delivered from Boston fair, pre-1225.*

tuns of wine from Anjou and Auxerre were carried from Boston fair to Lincoln for the king's use.[85] In the thirteenth and early fourteenth centuries, Rhenish wines were also imported into Boston but there is no evidence for this trade in the twelfth century.[86] Henry II's injunction, of *c*.1174, that wine imported from Cologne should be sold at the same price as French wine, has been cited as an indication of the existence of the Rhenish trade at Boston in this early period. However, while Cologne men may well have shipped wine to Boston at this date, the king's order did not specifically refer to Boston but applied nationally.[87]

### 3.7. THE TRADE IN FOODSTUFFS

The rise of Boston in the twelfth century was bound up with the contemporary European 'commercial revolution', which not only involved a marked growth in the volume of international exchanges, but also meant that raw materials, foodstuffs and everyday consumer items, such as wool, grain, wine, cloth, timber and fish, rather than luxuries for a limited elite, came to make up an increasing proportion of commerce.[88] Unfortunately, much of this everyday trade is absent from our surviving sources. The emergence of Flanders as the most industrialised and urbanised area of northern Europe generated demand for food imports but what evidence we have for this period suggests that English grain was shipped through the ports of Norfolk and Suffolk, such as Lynn, Yarmouth, Dunwich and Ipswich, or via the Cinque Ports, rather than through Boston.[89] We have little information about this trade in Boston, although grain was sent from the port to Newcastle-upon-Tyne in 1212 and to Scarborough in 1225, while in 1227 Breton merchants were permitted to export grain from the port.[90]

Similarly, as salt does not feature among the royal purchases recorded in the pipe rolls, we can know nothing of Boston's role in the salt trade at this date. Yet, by the early fourteenth century, Boston was the pre-eminent port in England for the export of this vital commodity. It was able to draw upon the produce of the principal English salt-making areas of Norfolk and of Lincolnshire itself, where the Lindsey marshland and the Holland fens had been the site of a salt industry since the Iron Age, with 34 Lincolnshire villages being noted as possessing salt-pans in Domesday Book.[91]

### 3.8. THE OPENING-UP OF THE FENS

Despite the importance of overseas commerce within Boston's economy in the twelfth and early thirteenth centuries, the town's rise should not only be understood as part of the contemporary expansion of England's overseas trade but should also be seen in the context of the reclamation of the Holland fenlands, which took place during this period. As the thirteenth-century chronicler Matthew Paris said in his famous description of the fens: 'Concerning this marsh, a wonder has happened in our time', with places that were once 'accessible neither for man nor beast' being 'changed into delightful meadows and also arable ground' or being used to produce 'sedge, turf and other fuel'; the Croyland chronicler similarly referred to the fens as 'drying up' in this period.[92] If Domesday Book is to be believed, the fenland in 1086 was among the poorest and least populous areas of Lincolnshire, although the wapentake of Skirbeck, where Boston itself was located, was already one of the most prosperous and intensively occupied areas within the county's fens. Yet, by the early fourteenth century, what Darby referred to as a 'great revolution in economic geography' meant that the fens were now one of the wealthiest and most densely populated areas in the county and, indeed, in the whole of England. Between 1170 and 1240 alone, 100 square miles of land were reclaimed from the Holland fens, quite apart from land won back from the sea. In Skirbeck wapentake, as Hallam has shown, 'intakes from the fen were extensive', with much of this work having already been completed by 1150 and most of it by 1180.[93] The long history of reclamation means that although Boston now stands six miles inland, at the time of Domesday Book, the coastline would have been closer to the town.[94]

With the large and growing population of the town of Boston to be fed, it is not surprising that, by the thirteenth century, arable products dominated in the agriculture of the wapentake of Skirbeck, even though pasture was an important element of agriculture elsewhere in the newly-colonised fens. As with the improvement of the Witham and the Foss Dyke, the growth of Boston was both a cause and an effect of the transformation of the Fens. Once more, however, the essential local trade that supplied the townspeople of Boston with their food is invisible in our sources for the period before 1220.[95]

### 3.9. INDUSTRY

Given that occupational diversity is usually seen as one of the defining characteristics of an urban community, the limitations of our sources for Boston's history in this period are particularly highlighted by the lack of information they contain about the retail and craft occupations that must have provided a living for the vast majority of the town's inhabitants.[96] A rare exception is the use of craft by-names to identify three of the six Boston men who appear in a list of those who went on the Third Crusade: William the Tanner, Robert 'le Poter' and Robert the Fuller.[97] Otherwise, apart from other occasional uses of craft by-names, such as those of Geoffrey the Cobbler, Ordinerus the Cobbler, and John the Cook, the occupations – or even the names – of the artisans and retailers who provided their fellows with food, drink, clothing, housing and manufactured goods in this early period are virtually unknown to us.[98]

Even when archaeological excavation has found evidence of manufactured goods, as with the leather knife-sheath dating from the late twelfth-century, which was excavated from the Barditch, it is not possible to say whether these goods were produced in

Boston itself.[99] Equally invisible in our sources are the many crafts and trades, from carters, stable- and tavern-keepers to porters and shipwrights, which must have existed to service the fair and the port. The very partial survival of evidence for this period means that we now know more about occasional royal purchases of hawks, wine and lead than we do about the routine economic activities that sustained the bulk of the town's growing population. Similarly, as Boston's population was rising at a much faster rate than England's population as a whole, the town must have been reliant on immigration to maintain its growth but, while the evidence of place-name surnames allows us to trace the area from which Boston drew migrants in the early fourteenth century, we lack the sources to establish the origins of the people who helped to fuel the town's expansion in the twelfth century.[100] What the sources for this period do emphasise is the importance of Boston fair within England's trade and it is to this topic that we now turn.

# Part 4

# Boston Fair

Although hundreds of fairs were created in medieval England, it was, as was also the case for new towns, those fairs that were founded at an early date which tended to be the most successful.[1] This was certainly true of Boston where the fair, as we have seen, may have been in existence by 1114 and was certainly trading by 1138 (section 1.3., above). The fair of St Botolph rose to become a central part of the series of great fairs, alongside those of Lynn, Stamford, St Ives and Winchester, which dominated England's overseas and wholesale trade in the period from the twelfth to the early fourteenth century.[2] Indeed, Boston's fair, like that of Winchester, was used as a model for the liberties granted to fairs in other towns, including Portsmouth in 1200 and Marlborough in 1204.[3] As was noted above, Boston's fair originally lasted from the 17 to 24 June but in 1218 it was extended for another eight days.[4] Here we discuss where the fair was located within the town (section 4.1.), examine the administration of the fair (section 4.2.), assess the income which the lords of Boston drew from it (section 4.3.), establish the main commodities that were traded at the fair (section 4.4.), and look at the monastic houses that were attracted to Boston by the chance to sell wool and to buy imported goods at the fair (section 4.5.).

## 4.1. THE SITE OF THE FAIR

Owen distinguished 'Boston fair', which she believed was held in the Richmond fee on the east side of the Witham, from the 'fair of Holland', which she believed was held in the Croun fee on the west side of the river.[5] It is true that the fair was held on the Croun fee, perhaps, as we saw above, from its very early days. Nonetheless, as is made clear in the royal pipe rolls for the years before 1183, when the honour of Richmond was in the king's hand, the fair on the Richmond fee could also be called 'Holland fair'; it was Boston fair in general, rather than a specific part of it, which was referred to in this way.[6] This confusion may have arisen from a grant to St Bartholomew's Hospital, London, of a shop in the 'fair of Holland' which was located in 'Breggestrate', which Owen assumed was a reference to the modern Bridge Street, on the west side of the river, when what was actually meant was the narrow Bridge Street, between the river and the Market Place, on the east side of the bridge (Map 2, no. 33).[7]

Further uncertainty about the location of the fair has been caused by the existence of the 'Mart Yard' by the Grammar School, in the southern part of Boston (Map 2, no. 23 and Fig. 30). By the late sixteenth century, the Mart Yard was a privileged site for shops and for trading within the town and, as a result, it has sometimes been assumed that it was also the location of the medieval fair.[8] However, there is no evidence that this site was used before the sixteenth century and it seems more likely that the town's medieval fair had a more central position in the town, taking place near to St Botolph's church, in the Market Place, and around both ends of the bridge over the Witham (Figs 5, 13, 14, 19). Thus, *circa* 1210, when two shops in 'la mercerie' in Boston fair were quitclaimed to St Bartholomew's Hospital, London, they were said to be located 'next but two before the bridge' (Map 2, no. 34).[9] Count Stephen's charter to St Mary's abbey, which was granted at some point between 1125 and 1138, gave the monks the right to take their profits in the time of the fair, both in and out of the churchyard of St Botolph's (Fig. 5).[10] Similarly, in 1240, when a dispute at Boston fair between Nicholas Kipping, of Winchester, and Peter Balg, of Ypres, led to an attack on Flemish merchants by men from a number of English towns, including Winchester, Beverley, York, Nottingham, London, Oxford, Lincoln, Hertford and Boston, Kipping's 'hospice' (i.e. the house where he lodged) was said to be located in the churchyard and the Flemings' houses to be situated nearby.[11]

### 4.2. THE ADMINISTRATION OF THE FAIR

The administration of Boston fair was separate from that of the town and its structure was similar to that of other fairs. Overall responsibility for the smooth running of the fair lay with its 'keepers' (*'custodes'*) whose tasks included holding the fair court, collecting and accounting for the fair revenues, and arranging payment to those people and institutions, such as the abbey of Bégard, which had been assigned a share of the fair's profits. The keepers also had to co-operate with royal officials, such as those responsible for holding the assize of wine in the fair or who had been sent to buy wine. In addition, they themselves had to implement royal orders, as in 1220, when they were commanded to arrest the goods of Danish merchants in retaliation for the seizure in Denmark of the merchandise of Londoners, and in 1222 when they were ordered to take hawks on behalf of the king.[12] Unfortunately, we only know the identity of the keepers of the fair when the honour was in the king's hand and appointments were being made by the crown. Given the prominence of Boston's fair and the scale of the revenues it produced, the government thought it expedient to choose experienced royal officials as keepers during these periods. In 1218, for instance, one of the three keepers of the fair was Henry of Ponte Audomari, a royal officer who also served as keeper of the fairs at Lynn and Northampton and who received royal commissions in Hampshire, and Devon.[13] In 1226, the keepers were Thomas de Multon, a royal justice and prominent local landowner who founded the Skirbeck Hospital of St John, and William de Haverhull, an important royal clerk who later rose to be royal treasurer.[14]

The day-to-day running of English fairs was carried out by a group of officials who were often referred to as 'bailiffs'.[15] However, this title could also be used for the fair's keepers and it is likely that a number of the writs that were addressed to the 'bailiffs' of Boston fair were actually meant for its keepers.[16] At Boston, the officers below the keeper could also be described as 'serjeants' ('*servientes*'). For instance, in 1240, when Peter Balg of Ypres complained to the chief 'bailiff' of the fair that he had been assaulted by the servants of Nicholas Kipping, two '*servientes*' of the fair were sent to arrest Nicholas and his men and to obtain surety from him that he would pay the debt he owed to Peter.[17] It is likely that Boston fair would also have needed the constables or watchmen of the kind who maintained law and order and protected property at other English fairs, although our sources do not explicitly mention them.[18] The fair court would certainly have had its own clerk to help run the court and to produce its records but, once again, this official does not appear in our sources for this period.[19] Perhaps the earliest reference to the clerk of the fair at Boston for the Richmond honour comes in 1289, although even this is ambiguous, with a list of witnesses to a grant of two plots of land in Boston beginning with Roger de Sordehyll, steward of Boston fair, and Thomas de Beverlaco, bailiff of the fair, and their names then being followed by 'William le Clerk' of Boston.[20] Since the Croun and Tattershall fees also received income from the fair and had their own courts during fair time, they too would have needed their own stewards and bailiffs to administer the fair for them, although our sources do not reveal them to us in the period before 1225.[21]

## 4.3. FAIR INCOME

The importance of Boston fair meant that it was extremely profitable in terms of the revenues generated by stall rents, court fines and tolls. Inevitably, the income received from the fair fluctuated from year to year: as an inquisition of 1185 noted, Countess Margaret, the widow of Earl Conan, drew eight marks of rent in Boston fair 'when the fair is good' ('*quando nundine sunt bone*').[22] We are particularly well-informed about the profits of the fair received by the honour of Richmond in the period from 1172 to 1183, during the minority of Countess Constance, when Ranulf de Glanville, one of Henry II's chief ministers, who had been appointed as custodian of the honour, rendered account for its revenues at the royal exchequer (see Table 1).[23] In the first year, he accounted for £67 of the fair's issues but the fair's profitability was then hit by the rebellion of Henry II's sons in 1173, Flemish involvement in which led to seizures of the goods of Flemish merchants, and by the continuing disturbances of 1174, with the issues falling to £22 and then £10.[24] However, income from the fair soon recovered and even exceeded its previous levels, so that by 1182–3 it was worth almost £105.[25]

The fair's revenues continued to fluctuate after 1183. For instance, in 1190 and 1191, when the honour of Richmond was again in the hands of the crown, the issues of the fair, which then stood at £50 7s. 7d. and £61 respectively, were well below the £105

| | |
|---|---|
| 1172 | £67  1s  6d |
| 1173 | £22  2s  5d |
| 1174 | £10  6s  1d |
| 1175 | £61  7s  2d |
| 1176 | £70  2s.  9d |
| 1177 | £72  1s  2d |
| 1178 | £66  13s  2d |
| 1179 | £79  7s  8d |
| 1180 | £61  3s  9d |
| 1181 | £76  14s.  2d |
| 1182 | £91  15s  4d |
| 1183 | £104  19s  5d |
| 1190 | £50  7s  7d |
| 1191 | £61  0s  0d |
| 1199 | £54  7s  7d |
| 1200 | £71  0s  0d |
| 1209 | £106  6s  4d |
| 1210 | £97  5s  6d |
| 1211 | £90  3s  0d |
| 1212 | £87  10s  6d |

*Table 1.  Income of the honour of Richmond from Boston fair accounted for at the royal exchequer, 1172-1212.[26]*

which had been obtained in 1183. In 1199 and 1200, the honour's profits from the fair amounted to £54 5s. 5d. and £71, but they had again recovered to £97 5s. 6d., £90 3s., and £87 10s. 6d. in 1210, 1211 and 1212. These totals do not quite match those for the fairs of St Ives and Winchester during this period although they relate only to the honour of Richmond and so exclude any profits made from the fair by the Croun and Tattershall lordships within the town.[27] We have little information about these other fees, although the pipe roll for 1203-4 reveals that the Croun fee obtained £6 1s. 2½d. for the rents of stalls in Boston fair, quite apart from the income which it must have drawn from tolls and court fees.[28] Similarly, in 1212, the Tattershall fee received £17 10s. 10½d. from the fair, although this amount was dwarfed by the £87 10s. 6d. which the Richmond honour obtained from the fair in the same year.[29] It has been claimed that the income of £105 received by the exchequer from Boston fair in 1212 shows its growth by this date when compared with the early 1170s, when revenues were around £70.[30] However, the total for 1212 is inflated by the inclusion of the Tattershall revenues (although it does not include any income from the Croun fee), whereas the income recorded for the 1170s was drawn only from the Richmond fee.[31] In 1209, the Richmond honour did receive £106 6s. 4d. from the fair but even this total was only slightly greater than the income which it had received in 1183. Thus, while the income received by the honour from the fair was certainly higher in the years 1209-12 than it had been in the early 1170s, it was not significantly above the levels that it had attained in the early 1180s.

## 4.4. COMMODITIES

Although the royal pipe rolls reveal the profitability of Boston fair during the twelfth and early thirteenth centuries, they give us little indication of the nature of the commodities available at the fair and tell us little about the origin of the merchants who traded there. Rather than recording the normal course of trade, our evidence for this period disproportionately concerns ships and merchants going to and from the fair when they were the targets of crime, as when William Algar was murdered at King's Norton (Worcestershire) when returning from Boston fair, or when Walter le Fleming was said to have been killed at the fair by two Londoners in 1220.[32] Nevertheless, we do know that the fair attracted men from right across northern Europe, from Denmark in the east to Bayonne in the west, with ships from the latter importing cordwain (i.e. leather) in 1208.[33]

  As we have already seen in part 3, wool, wine, cloth and hawks were sold at the fair in the twelfth and early thirteenth centuries, but our sources for this period do not allow us to see the huge range of commodities that we know to have been available there later in the thirteenth century, including furs, wax, textiles, manufactured goods such as chests and knives, as well as spices, medicines, cattle, sheep, pigs, fish, cheese, butter and grain.[34] Sugar bought for the king in 1176 by Ralph Glanvill was probably obtained at Boston fair, while in 1218 the keepers of the fair arrested 6 lbs of pepper.[35] The best early indication of this miscellaneous trade is the existence, around 1210, of 'la mercerie' in Boston fair since mercery at this date was comprised of a wide range of non-bulky goods, including not just fustian, silk and linen but also girdles, ribbons, purses and other accessories, and even spices.[36] The 'mercerie' was perhaps where the crown made its purchases of robes at the fair, including the 20 marks expended by William, the royal tailor, in 1222, whilst miscellaneous purchases made at the fair on behalf of the crown also included the rope sent to Bedford (probably for use in the siege of Bedford castle) and to Ramsey in 1224.[37]

## 4.5. MONASTIC PROPERTY OWNERS IN BOSTON

A final indication of the importance of Boston fair in the twelfth and early thirteenth centuries is provided by the number of monastic houses that obtained property in

Melrose ●

Holm Cultram ●

Durham Priory ●

50 miles

Easby ●

Fountains ●          ● Malton

● Watton

Sallay ●          Meaux ●

Ormsby ●
Louth Park ●     ● Alvingham
Bullington ●
● Barlings
Nocton ●     ● Stixwold
● Kirkstead
Haverholme ● ●
Thurgarton Priory ●     Kyme ●
BOSTON

Croyland ●

*Map 6. Monastic houses with property in Boston, pre-1225.*

the town (Map 6). It is typical of our sources for this period that the activities of these institutions are relatively well documented compared with our lack of information about the individual merchants who bought and sold at the fair. Religious institutions were significant landowners in many medieval English towns and a number of them seem to have been particularly involved in acquiring urban properties in the late thirteenth and early fourteenth centuries, with such acquisitions not being significantly affected, in practice, by the ban on them that was supposedly introduced by the Statute of Mortmain of 1279.[38] In Boston, by contrast, monastic houses were obtaining sites within the town from a much earlier date, with such properties functioning not simply as sources of rent but rather acting as bases from which to conduct business during fair time. For instance, by the early thirteenth century, Ormsby priory (Lincolnshire) owned a house in Boston to which it enjoyed the right of entry and exit with carts and wagons and which it used as lodgings during the fair, where its nuns bought veils and cloaks.[39] Similarly, Louth Park abbey (Lincolnshire) had a plot of land next to the Barditch which was used to store its goods.[40] Malton priory (Yorkshire) was granted land in Boston around 1190 by Walter Bars which came with a stable and a 'grangia', which in this context probably meant a warehouse, to which the priory was to have free ingress and egress from the start to the end of the fair, these facilities being shared with Watton priory, its fellow house of Yorkshire Gilbertines.[41] The Cistercians of Fountains abbey (Yorkshire) had acquired property in Boston by the end of Richard I's reign and the abbey's holdings in the town included not only the mills noted above (section 2.3.) but also a chamber and courtyard specifically granted for use in fair-time with access for wagons, carts and horses. By the fourteenth century one of its messuages was known as 'Fountaynhouses' and by 1562 there was a 'Fountains Lane' in the town. A Fountain Lane is marked on Hall's map of 1741, part of which is the modern street of this name (Map 2, no. 31 and Fig. 31).[42] Likewise, the monks of Durham cathedral priory were granted property in Boston around 1200 and were trading at the fair in this period, although it is only in the late thirteenth and early fourteenth centuries, when accounts survive, that we can see the nature of their purchases.[43] At this date they were buying wax, spices, manufactured goods, foodstuffs, furs and a wide range of textiles at the fair, sending them to Durham via the inland route along the Witham, Trent and Ouse or, in the case of bulkier goods, shipping them along the coast to Newcastle.[44]

Other monasteries that obtained property in Boston in the twelfth and early thirteenth centuries included the Lincolnshire houses of Nocton priory,[45] Kirkstead priory,[46] Bullington priory,[47] Haverholme Priory,[48] Alvingham priory,[49] Stixwold priory,[50] Crowland abbey,[51] Barlings abbey, and Kyme priory,[52] and the Yorkshire abbeys of Easby,[53], Sallay (or Sawley),[54] and Meaux.[55] At some time between 1223 and 1243 Melrose abbey, in the Scottish borders, also acquired property in Boston, which it shared with the Cumberland house of Holm Cultram, for use during the fair, while Thurgarton priory (Nottinghamshire) also obtained a tenement in Boston in the early to mid-thirteenth century.[56] Of these houses, Fountains, Sallay, Meaux, Malton, Ormsby, Alvingham, Louth Park, Kirkstead, Holm Cultram and Melrose were all included in a mid-thirteenth century Flemish list of British monasteries that produced wool for sale. All of these houses also appeared, along also with Easby and Crowland, in Pegolotti's list of monastic wool-producers from c.1340.[57] It is probable that wool from these houses was taken to Boston for sale and that, in return, like Durham priory, they were buying wine, cloth, victuals and other necessities at the fair.

For a fair to prosper to the degree that medieval Boston's did, the permission and assistance of the town's lords were required. It is to the role of Boston's overlords in creating the framework of liberties which encouraged the development of urban life that we now turn.

# Part 5

# Boston as a borough

As towns grew in the twelfth and thirteenth centuries they acquired a range of tenurial, commercial and administrative privileges. It was the possession of these privileges which, in the eyes both of contemporaries and of modern historians, distinguished these communities as 'boroughs', even though what historians now often refer to by the shorthand term of 'borough status' was never a clearly-defined legal concept in the Middle Ages.[1] The role of borough privileges in encouraging urban development in medieval England has been a controversial issue. Here it is argued that the basic tenurial and economic privileges enjoyed by towns such as Boston were a significant factor in promoting urban growth (sections 5.1. to 5.3.). Nevertheless, there was no automatic correlation between a town's size and wealth on the one hand and the extent of its liberties on the other. As Boston itself shows, even important seigneurial boroughs could fail to achieve the degree of self-government often found in the royal boroughs, although the remaining sources make it difficult to discover exactly how the Richmond fee was administered before 1225 (sections 5.4. and 5.5.). Nevertheless, the fact that the townsmen of Boston did not enjoy formal self-government did not mean that they lacked any form of communal organisation or expression (section 5.6.). If the nature of the administration of the Richmond fee is unclear then the situation is even more obscure in Boston's other jurisdictions although, once more, there is no sign that the inhabitants of these parts of the town ever secured self-government (section 5.7.). Nonetheless, the absence of self-government in Boston does not seem to have generated the level of conflict between lords and townsmen that it did in some of England's other towns (section 5.8.).

## 5.1. BOROUGH PRIVILEGES AND URBANISATION

As Richard Britnell argued, a key aspect of the growth of English towns in the twelfth and thirteenth centuries was the recognition by feudal lords that if they were to make the most of the economic opportunities that the commercialisation of the economy was increasingly making available to them, they would also have to accept 'some restrictions on their freedom of action'. For Britnell, it was the acquisition of privileges by urban communities which most clearly exemplified this trend, with lords being prepared to agree to formal limitations on their seigneurial rights in order to draw migrants to the new towns they had founded and to draw trade to the fairs and markets they had set up.[2] The freedom offered by such 'borough' privileges was thus no mere legalistic notion or constitutional nicety that was irrelevant to urban economic development.[3] On the contrary, by reducing the interference of feudal landlords in town-life, these privileges gave merchants and artisans control over their own wealth, time and labour by granting them security of property, freedom from manorial restrictions and impositions, land tenure based on fixed money rents, exemption from labour services, freedom of movement, the right to trade freely, and the power to acquire and to alienate land by sale, gift or bequest. Such liberties also helped to attract the migrants without whom urban populations could not be maintained, let alone increased. They thereby created the essential basis of urban economic development and growth.[4]

The privileges obtained by England's towns in this period did not only minimise the restrictions and burdens imposed by external authorities, they also offered an advantageous trading position to those who were burgesses (i.e. those who held by burgage tenure or who enjoyed full membership of the urban community) against those residents who were non-burgesses as well as against outsiders. For instance, in many towns burgesses were given the right to a share of wholesale goods offered for sale and were granted a favoured access to purchase such goods against those who were not 'in scot and lot' (i.e. who were not fully paid-up members of the community) while outsiders could also be excluded from selling retail or prohibited from dealing with other 'foreigners'.[5] In such cases, where burgage tenure was made available so as to attract migrants and to stimulate urban development, the law did not simply constitute a mere superstructure which was separate from society's economic base; rather law and economics interpenetrated and mutually constituted each other.[6]

It may seem surprising to emphasise the significance of borough privileges for the development of medieval Boston. After all, both Gervase Rosser and Chris Dyer have cited Boston as an example of a town that flourished even though it lacked extensive formal liberties and have used it to show that there was no direct correspondence between the size or prosperity of a town and the extent of its liberties.[7] Certainly, although Boston was one of the leading towns in medieval England, it was rarely referred to as a 'borough' by contemporaries. Indeed, the first known mention of Boston as a '*burgus*' comes from as late as 1280, when the town was so characterised in an extent of the honour of Richmond's lands in Holland, although even here it was also referred to as a 'vill' ('*villata*').[8] Even after this date, Boston was rarely named as a borough but was usually labelled as a 'vill' ('*villa*'), a term with no specifically urban connotations.[9] In 1316, for instance, when the sheriff of Lincoln was asked to provide a list of all the vills within his jurisdiction, he distinguished only the 'city' of Lincoln and the 'borough' of Grimsby from all the other settlements within the county, thus excluding not only Boston but also other sizeable towns, such as Grantham and Stamford, from these categories.[10] It is unlikely that the inhabitants of medieval Boston were interested in the semantic issue of whether or not their town was referred to as a 'borough'. However, they had much more reason to be concerned about the degree to which they enjoyed the privileges which were characteristic of those places which we now describe as boroughs.[11] To what extent, then, did Boston in the twelfth and early thirteenth centuries acquire the tenurial, economic and administrative privileges which were obtained by other English towns in this period?

## 5.2. FREE TENURE

As we have seen, Boston in the twelfth century was the site of both a market and a fair. Nevertheless, if all boroughs held markets as a fundamental economic privilege, the possession of a market or a fair was not, in itself, sufficient for a place to be considered as a borough since many places, including agricultural villages, enjoyed markets even though they were in no sense burghal.[12] Instead, the minimal requirement for a place to be regarded as a borough by modern historians is that it was 'an urban area' in which the tenements were 'small, residential plots' that were suitable for those who made a living from trade, services or manufactures and which were held by burgage tenure or its equivalent, i.e. which were held by payment of low quit-rents in lieu of all services and which were legally 'mobile', i.e. more or less freely transferable by sale, gift and bequest'.[13] Thus, regarding medieval towns as being 'boroughs' is by no means at odds with describing them as 'urban'. On the contrary, the urban nature of a community has long been invoked as one of the defining features of the places which historians have distinguished as boroughs. Medieval Boston was definitely an 'urban area' in the sense that it was 'a relatively dense and permanent concentration of residents engaged in a multiplicity of activities, a substantial proportion of which are non-agrarian'.[14] This was true even though, like other medieval English towns such as Grimsby and Lincoln, the men of Boston had their own fields, meadows and common pasture.[15] But was the 'urban area' of Boston a 'borough' in tenurial terms?

The precise terms on which land in Boston was held is not specified in the surviving sources for the twelfth and early thirteenth centuries but tenements there were certainly held as free tenures which could be defended in the royal court. In 1201, for instance, Abraham de Ria initiated a case of novel disseisin (i.e. for recovery of land which was said to have been recently dispossessed) against Henry de Fley, while two years later Alice, daughter of Duka, brought a case of *mort d'ancestor* (i.e. of disinheritance) about a half of a messuage in Boston against Alan, brother of Alan, and John, son of John.[16] In 1200, Jocelinus, the son of Peter of London, successfully sued Robert Spizirius and two other men who had unjustly disseised him of a free tenement in Boston, and in 1208, Alice, the widow of Reginald Cote, quitclaimed all her right to dower of a free tenement in Boston which had belonged to her husband.[17]

These free tenements owed fixed 'rents of assize' to the lords of the town, as can be seen in the pipe roll for 1199-1200, when the honour of Richmond was in the king's hand, and in 1203–4 when the income of the Croun fee was included in the pipe roll for that year.[18] In the fourteenth century, houses and tenements in Boston were described as being held from the honour of Richmond in 'socage' tenure, rather than as being burgages.[19] In practice, however, this distinction had no real legal significance as burgage tenure was 'no more than a form of socage tenure' (i.e. the standard free, non-military tenure), albeit one which was associated with urban communities.[20] As a result, land held in burgage in undoubted boroughs such as London, Worcester and Bristol could also be described as being held by 'socage' tenure.[21] As late as 1568, over twenty years after Boston's legal incorporation as a borough, land in the town was still said to be held 'in free socage or burgage'.[22]

### 5.3. FREEDOM FROM TOLL

If feudal lords had to accept some limitation on their freedom of action in order to encourage the development of new towns, this self-limitation was not restricted to allowing their tenants to enjoy free, secure tenures, but also took the form of grants of freedom from toll to their burgesses. This privilege might extend only as far as the boundaries of the estate of the lord who granted it but, particularly in the cases of the larger towns and of the royal boroughs, it might also be enjoyed nationally.[23] The rates at which any individual toll was levied seem to have been relatively light for those who traded in bulk. Nevertheless, if tolls had to be 'reasonable', they did fall more heavily on those who dealt in smaller amounts, while even wholesale merchants might face the possibility of paying tolls in a number of different places when goods were in transit, of being charged for a variety of tolls on a particular commodity, or of becoming liable to new charges, such as murage, pontage and pavage, which arose in the thirteenth century.[24]

In the absence of surviving charters to Boston from its lords, we cannot know if a grant of freedom from tolls was ever specifically made to the townsmen as it was, for instance, to the burgesses of Lynn in September 1204.[25] Nevertheless, it is difficult to imagine that the inhabitants of a town of the importance of Boston did not enjoy freedom from tolls. Certainly, in 1281, the abbot of St Mary's, York, claimed that his tenants in Boston were completely exempt from paying tolls.[26] In some towns, exemption from paying tolls could be one of the privileges associated with membership of a guild merchant.[27] In Boston, the Guild of the Blessed Virgin Mary, whose guildhall of c.1390 stands in South Street (Figs 16 and 32), has sometimes been seen as the town's guild merchant. However, there is no evidence that this was actually the case or that the guild's members enjoyed the economic monopolies or privileges that guilds merchant possessed in other towns. Besides, the guild of the Blessed Virgin Mary was only created in 1260.[28]

It is possible that the men of the eastern part of Boston may have possessed some freedom from toll in their capacity as tenants of the honour of Richmond.

In 1257, Peter of Savoy, who was then lord of the honour, maintained that its tenants were, by chartered right, free of tolls in all of England.[29] Nonetheless, this right could not always be maintained. In 1263, for instance, following a dispute over tolls levied in the city of Lincoln which had been simmering since at least 1251, Peter claimed that the men of the honour had been free of toll throughout England since the time of the Norman Conquest. Eventually, after this claim had been contested by the city of Lincoln and a case had been brought before the royal justices in eyre, it was concluded that although the men of the honour were free of tolls in Lincoln for anything bought for their own support or which had been produced or grown in the honour, they should nonetheless pay tolls on produce which was sold as merchandise and on ships coming to city.[30] In 1465, when the honour of Richmond was held by George, duke of Clarence, the king ordered that the men of the honour should be quit of toll nationally 'according to custom', but for how long this exemption had previously been enjoyed is not clear.[31] Grants of the honour by the king usually just specified that the earls should enjoy the liberties which pertained to it without specifying in detail what these liberties actually were.[32]

## 5.4. THE RICHMOND FEE AND THE CHARTER OF 1204

If all medieval towns required the basic tenurial and commercial liberties that made town-life life possible, some urban communities went on to acquire a further level of privilege by which they came to enjoy a substantial degree of self-government. As a result, contemporaries began to associate borough 'status' with the enjoyment of these more advanced liberties, rather than simply with holding land by burgage tenure.[33] This relative administrative independence was most evident in royal towns, such as Lincoln and Grimsby, whose burgesses were able to minimise the interference of the sheriff and other royal officials by obtaining the right to elect their own mayor, bailiffs and other officers who were responsible for running the borough courts, administering the town, and implementing royal writs. These towns often acquired the right to 'farm' their revenues, i.e. to compose them into a fixed, annual lump-sum, for which their elected officials accounted to the crown, with any remaining revenue going into the town's 'common purse'.[34]

By contrast, administrative arrangements within seigneurial boroughs were far more varied, the key difference being that seigneurial towns, even some of the larger and more prosperous ones, did not always acquire the degree of formal self-government which was typical of the royal boroughs. In such cases, the town's lord could retain the right to appoint town officials, or at least to approve the officers chosen by the burgesses, and could collect revenues directly rather than farming them out.[35] Thus the fact that there was no direct correspondence between the size of a town and the extent of its liberties does not mean that such liberties were of minor significance in the development of town life. Rather, whilst all towns required the basic tenurial and commercial privileges which allowed them to attract immigrants and to carry out their economic functions, the degree to which any particular town went on to achieve self-government was, as James Tait long ago showed, dependent upon lordship rather than on its economic significance.[36] What, then, was the situation in Boston in the period before 1225?

The lack of surviving sources means that it is now very hard to establish precisely how Boston was administered in the twelfth and early thirteenth centuries or to assess the extent of its independence from its seigneurial overlords. We are best informed about the position of the townsmen who were tenants of the earldom of Richmond and who therefore shared in the liberties enjoyed by all tenants of the honour. The specific privileges possessed by the honour's tenants before 1225 are unclear but by 1241 they were free of the considerable burden involved in owing suit to the county and wapentake courts. As a result, views of frankpledge (i.e. of the tithing groups that were responsible for policing and the maintenance of order locally) for them were held in the honour's own courts and these courts also had jurisdiction over the assize of bread and ale which regulated the prices of these essential components of the medieval diet. It is likely that these jurisdictional liberties were enjoyed by the honour long before this date.[37] By 1252 Peter of Savoy was also successfully claiming that the honour had customarily enjoyed the right of 'return of writs', which prevented sheriffs and other royal officials from entering the honour to execute royal writs and so further restricted the interference of crown officers within the honour.[38] Given the limited jurisdiction of royal officials within the honour of Richmond, the central issue for the townsmen in the main, eastern part of Boston thus became the degree of freedom they enjoyed in relation to the honour's own administration.

The basic framework of the constitutional history of many medieval English towns is provided by the series of charters of liberties which they received from the crown or from their overlords. For medieval Boston, by contrast, we have only one charter, that which was issued by King John on 30 January 1204 to the tenants of the honour of Richmond in the town. The original charter itself has not survived but its contents have fortunately been preserved for us in the copies which were entered on the charter roll and the pipe roll.[39] As Bärbel Brodt has pointed out, the Boston charter is 'rather unusual' when compared with other borough charters of this period and, as a result, its meaning is rather cryptic.[40] For instance, in contrast to the Lynn charter of 14 September 1204, which was granted to 'the burgesses of Lynn', the Boston charter was granted to the 'men of Boston and of the soke (*hominibus de Sancto Botulfo et de socha*) who are of the honour of Richmond in Holland'.[41] Whereas the Lynn charter consists of a lengthy recitation of the economic and legal privileges the town's burgesses were to enjoy, including freedom from tolls (except in London) and the right to possess a guild merchant, the brief charter to the men of Boston and of the soke granted simply that 'no sheriff or his bailiffs should intermeddle with them, but that they should choose a bailiff from amongst themselves to answer at our exchequer for pleas and issues, as they were accustomed to answer to the count of Brittany when they were in his hand, and for all other things which pertain to us, except for pleas of the crown when they arise, which shall be attached by the sheriff together with their bailiff'.[42]

The granting of this charter was partly a product of the English crown's need to raise money in this period which meant that both Richard I and King John were very willing to sell charters of liberties to towns. Thus, in 1204, the men of the Richmond honour in Boston paid £100 and two palfreys to the king in order to obtain their charter.[43] However, the townsmen themselves may also have pushed for a statement of their liberties because of the position of the honour at this time. As we saw above (in section 2.2.), in September 1203, Guy de Thouars, the widower of Constance, countess of Richmond, had forfeited the honour of Richmond because he had switched his allegiance to the French crown. On 26 September 1203, the honour was granted to Robert de Breteuil, earl of Leicester, although he was only to possess the honour for just over a year, as he died in October 1204.[44] With the honour in the hands of a new lord, the tenants of the honour in Boston perhaps wished to obtain a clarification of their position, just as the proposed construction of a royal castle at Grimsby seems to have been the immediate spur for the burgesses there to obtain two charters of liberties in 1201.[45] That the tenants of the honour of Richmond in Boston had enjoyed some degree of self-government prior to the charter of January 1204 is specified in the charter itself, which confirms to them the privilege of choosing a bailiff from amongst themselves to answer at the Exchequer as they had done when the honour had been in the hands of the 'count of Brittany'.[46] This is probably a reference to Guy de Thouars, who used this title following the death of his wife, Countess Constance, in 1201, and who, as was noted above (page 13), had lost possession of the honour of Richmond only a few months before the charter was granted.[47]

Unfortunately, the charter does not specify the precise nature of the pre-existing relationship between the townsmen and the honour of Richmond, leaving us unclear about the degree to which they had obtained self-government before 1204. The extent to which the townsmen managed to retain the liberties that had been granted in the charter is also now difficult to ascertain. For instance, we have no way of knowing for how long, if at all, the men of the Richmond honour in Boston continued to enjoy the right to elect their own bailiff, which had been granted to them in the charter of 1204. There is, however, no evidence that the charter played any part in the later history of the town or that it was ever invoked after 1204; rather, it seems to have become a dead letter. The situation at Boston thus provides a marked contrast with that in other towns, such as Grimsby, where the burgesses obtained repeated confirmation and extension of the privileges set out in their earlier charters.[48] Without such confirmation and reassertion, it was very difficult for such privileges to be maintained even if, as in the case of those contained in the Boston charter of 1204, they had originally been granted in perpetuity.[49] Thus, although the town of Boston possessed liberties, which in 1272 were taken into the king's hand as a sign of royal displeasure, the absence of charters for the town after 1204 leaves the exact nature of such liberties uncertain.[50] The lack of medieval court rolls for the honour of Richmond's manor in Boston means that we cannot know for sure whether, like the inhabitants of other medieval English boroughs, the men of the honour in Boston obtained their own court, separate from that of the manor, but there is no definite indication that they ever did so.[51] Nor is there any indication that the town ever possessed its own elected mayor prior to its incorporation in 1545, even though the seigneurial borough of Lynn enjoyed this privilege by the end of John's reign.[52]

### 5.5. THE RICHMOND MANOR AT FARM?

For townsmen to obtain the right to farm their town (see page 53, above) was a key step in obtaining self-government as it involved the ability to elect their own representatives, to exclude the lord's officials, and to possess a common purse, which could be used for their own shared purposes. Unfortunately, however, while the charter of 1204 allowed the tenants of the honour of Richmond in Boston to elect their own bailiff, it did not specify whether the bailiff had accounted for a farm of the Richmond manor on behalf of the townsmen prior to 1204 or if he was to do so after this date. It is certainly possible that the honour of Richmond's tenants in Boston had farmed the manor from the honour prior to 1204. After all, the lords of the honour were not hostile to urban self-government in this early period as is shown by the grant made by Alan III, earl of Richmond, to the burgesses of Richmond (Yorkshire), at some point between 1137 and 1145, which gave them the right to farm the borough in return for a yearly render of £29.[53] Indeed, this is one of the earliest examples of the community of burgesses of an English town acquiring the right to farm a borough, although it is often ignored in histories of the subject, which tend to focus on the royal boroughs.[54] Nevertheless, there is no explicit proof that Boston was similarly privileged. Regrettably, although the royal pipe rolls record how much income was received from Boston fair each year from 1172 to 1183, during the minority of Countess Constance (see above, section 4.3.), they give no indication of the other revenues, such as rents, tolls and court fines, which were generated by the town for the honour, or of whether they had been farmed by the townsmen.

The only indication that Boston was farmed during this period comes in 1185 in the *Rotuli de dominabus et pueris et puellis*, a record of widows and wards who were then in the royal gift. Here, as part of her dower, Countess Margaret, the widow of Earl Conan, mother to Countess Constance and the sister of Malcom IV and William I, kings of Scotland, was said to receive £4 from the farm of Boston ('*de firma ville Sancti Botulfi*') via the hands of Richard the Bailiff.[55] Unfortunately, this source does not specify who was responsible for paying the farm. It is possible that, as at the borough of Richmond, the townsmen of Boston themselves accounted for it, which would imply that they already had their own elected officer, as they were explicitly said to have in the 1204 charter. Nevertheless, the manors on many estates were farmed out at this date and so it is also possible that the farm of the town was held by individual lessees or by estate officials rather than by the community of townsmen or that, as was also common, individual sources of income (such as tolls or stallage) was farmed separately.[56]

Moreover, what evidence we have for the period after 1185 does not suggest that the men of Boston were responsible for a single, fixed farm of the revenues levied in the honour of Richmond's manor. Thus, even if the Richmond manor was being farmed in 1185, this may not have been as the result of a grant of a permanent fee-farm but may have been a temporary arrangement. For instance, in 1200, the keeper of the lands of Countess Constance, which were then in the king's hand, accounted separately for £1 4s. 6d. for stall rents and for £8 0s. 5d for rents of assize collected in Boston and distinguished these from the £64 16s of rents of assize which were levied in the honour's soke of Holland.[57] Yet, by 1211, the rents of assize of Boston and those of the soke of Holland had been merged into a total render of £77 16s. 6d. Nor was this a fixed sum as in the following year the rents of assize of the soke of Holland came to £78 10s. 8½d. In 1211 the honour's revenues from the court pleas and perquisites (i.e. profits) of Boston and of the soke of Holland amounted to £18 7s. 8d. In 1212 this court income was composed into a farm of £10, but we cannot know if the surplus over and above this lump sum was kept by the men of Boston and of the soke or by Robert Peverel, who was keeper of the honour at this date.[58] In the same year, an enquiry into fees and tenements held in chief of the crown found that the men of Boston ('homines ville Sancti Botulfi') who were tenants of the honour of Richmond held 70 carucates of land (except for a sixth part, a fifth part and a sixteenth part) for which they rendered £75 14s. 3d. to the crown. It not clear if this sum represented a farm of all the income which was levied in the town for the honour and it seems also to include the revenues of the soke of Holland.[59]

In an inquisition relating to the division of the honour in 1219, the town of Boston and its soke was valued at £103 6s 4½d, excluding the income from the fair, whereas the neighbouring manors of Wyke and Frampton were farmed for the round sums of £24 and £16.[60] The extent of the honour's lands in Holland in 1280 makes no mention of a single farm of the Boston manor but instead lists separate amounts for income received from rents of assize (£8 14s 3½d), from the rents from houses that were leased out between fairs (£20 11s 8d), from the land which John de Wormele had held (£1 10s), from the perquisites of the town court or 'curia ville' (£8) and from the perquisites of the court merchant (£6 4s); as usual the honour's revenues from the fair were listed separately from those of the town.[61] Such revenues continued to fluctuate and by 1294-5, when the first account for the Richmond honour of Boston survives, the income from rents of assize was £8 2s, that from houses leased between fairs was £13 8s 6d, that from the town court was £2 15s 6d, and that from the court merchant was £2 13s.[62] It thus seems unlikely that the men of the honour of Richmond held Boston at a fixed farm during this period.

Indeed, some of the Richmond honour's revenues in Boston were separately farmed to individuals rather than to the community of townsmen. For instance, the honour had the right to levy tronage and pesage for the weighing of wool, lead and other goods in Boston, a right which was also possessed by the Croun and Tattershall lordships.[63] In 1281, John, son of Nicholas, maintained that he possessed half of the tronage and pesage levied in Boston, and from there as far as Dogdyke, along the Witham, on the one side and to 'Normandepe', towards the sea, on the other, claiming this hereditary right on the basis of a charter which had been granted by Earl Conan (d. 1171) to his ancestor, Richard, son of Reiner, of London.[64] As early as 1214, Reiner's grandson, Saier, had complained that he had been unjustly dispossessed of this right, although in 1244 Saier granted it to John de Gisors, of London. Gisors gave his name to Gysors' Hall, which stood in South Square, Boston, until its demolition in 1810 (Map 2, no. 30 and Fig. 33), when some of its stones were used to build Fydell's granary (Fig. 34), which still stands on this site [65]

Thus, there is no clear evidence that the tenants of the Richmond honour in Boston were ever granted the farm of the honour of Richmond's manor or that they ever enjoyed the kind of self-government that such grants entailed. Most of our evidence for the administration of Boston in the Middle Ages relates to the honour of Richmond's manor in the late fourteenth and fifteenth centuries. By this period the town presents a marked contrast with self-governing boroughs such as Lincoln and Grimsby, since instead of being run by annually-elected officials who were responsible to their fellow townsmen, it was being administered by bailiffs and stewards, who were appointed by the lords of the honour, who could serve for a number of years, and for whom local office was often a step on the ladder of promotion within the honorial administration.[66] Thus, whereas the history of many English medieval towns in general is one of growing self-government, the townsmen of Boston, or at least those who were tenants of the honour of Richmond, may have enjoyed more independence in the years immediately before and after the charter of 1204 than they were to do in the later Middle Ages. Nonetheless, we cannot know for certain how long they managed to retain the right to elect their own bailiff that their charter had granted them, or be sure whether they ever obtained the farm of the Richmond manor. Here, the discovery of a single new piece of evidence could radically alter how we see the administration of the town in the period before 1225.

## 5.6. THE COMMUNITY OF TOWNSMEN

If the men of medieval Boston did not achieve formal self-government, this still leaves open the question of how the town was actually administered in its early years. Certainly, even if the townsmen did not obtain the town farm or elect their own officials, this did not mean that they were incapable of acting collectively since some sort of communal organisation was obviously required for them to obtain and pay for the charter of 1204. From 1206, we can see them acting to protect their common rights in Wildmore Fen, nine miles north-west of Boston, where they claimed the right to obtain fodder, to mow hay and to collect reeds in return for a payment of 1d per household, although the ability to act in this way was not confined to urban communities since rural vills also enjoyed similar rights and could organise to defend them.[67]

The creation of the Guild of the Blessed Virgin Mary in Boston in 1260 may reflect the townsmen's desire to have some form of their own organisation.[68] It is even possible that the guild may eventually have functioned as a 'shadow' government for the town, as such guilds did elsewhere.[69] Nevertheless, the surviving sources for the guild emphasise its charitable and religious functions, rather than any political or administrative role, and there is no evidence for the existence of any guilds, whether mercantile, craft or religious, in Boston in the period before 1260.[70]

The tendency for medieval government to be expressed in judicial form and for courts to have broad deliberative and executive functions meant that, even when they lacked formal self-government and their own elected officers, the leading inhabitants of medieval towns could exercise power and influence through their role as officers and jurors of the local court.[71] Thus, even where courts were nominally supervised by the lords' appointed stewards, townsmen could formulate by-laws, decide which offences or individuals were to be prosecuted, could choose which punishments to impose, and could determine the level of money-fines, thereby adapting general laws to local needs and priorities.[72] It is extremely likely that this was the case at Boston although, once more, the lack of court rolls means that we cannot see this arrangement in operation. The extent of the Richmond honour in 1280 refers to the courts of the town, fair and market whilst an account of 1295-6 notes the courts of the town and market held by the honour.[73] By the fifteenth century, accounts of the honour refer to annual or bi-annual views of frankpledge held in the town along with the market court, fair court and court of the brewers.[74]

Finally, communal organisation was not necessarily the result of the assertion of autonomy from below. After all, being a 'community' involved duties and shared burdens, as well as rights, as can be seen in the sessions held before royal commissioners in the late thirteenth- and early fourteenth-century inquisitions in which the obligations of the men of Boston to maintain the sewers and streams flowing into the Witham were set out, obligations which implied some sort of communal administrative and financial organisation.[75]

## 5.7. BOSTON'S DIVIDED ADMINISTRATION

As we saw above (in sections 2.2. and 2.6.), medieval Boston was divided between four separate lordships: the Richmond fee and the soke of St Mary's abbey on the east side of the River Witham, and the Croun and Tattershall fees to the west. Each of these lordships had its own courts, officers and revenues. In 1274, the Hundred Roll jurors for the wapentake of Skirbeck listed the abbot of St Mary's, York, amongst those landowners who claimed to have the right to a three-weekly court and who exercised the assize of bread and ale within their fees in the wapentake.[76] They also returned that a great court with view of frankpledge was held by Simon son of Simon, who was then a life-tenant of what had originally been the Croun fee, which he held by the gift of John de Vaux.[77] By 1293, when the Croun fee was held by William de Roos, it was said that there were two courts held there, a three-weekly court baron and a court in the time of the fair, whilst by 1478-79 the Roos fee held two views of frankpledge, nine fair courts and twenty-five market courts.[78] For the Tattershall fee, the Hundred Roll jurors reported that a weekly market court was held there and in the fifteenth century the manor held two annual views of frankpledge as well as other 'courts' and 'market courts'.[79] With four separate jurisdictions, there was no single lord who could grant a borough charter that would provide all the inhabitants of the town with the same privileges or create a single unified administration.

At first sight, the situation at Boston may seem unusual but, in fact, many medieval English towns possessed divided administrations of this type. At Coventry, for instance, the town was divided in the period before c.1250 between the 'Earl's half' and the 'Prior's half', each with its own court, view of frankpledge and officials.[80] At Tamworth, one half of the town lay in Staffordshire while the other was in Warwickshire, with each again having its own courts and officials.[81] In the small town of Durham, there were six separate miniature administrations, each with its own court, while in the London suburb of Southwark there were five main manors, each of which possessed its own court and officials.[82] Even in Lincoln, which was a model of a chartered, self-governing borough, the constable of the castle and the dean and chapter of the cathedral claimed their own jurisdictions, with separate courts, revenues, officers and markets.[83] Quarrels between such neighbouring jurisdictions are a commonplace of medieval urban history. At York, for instance, the existence of the liberty of the abbey of St Mary's,

*Top: Fig. 1.* The Hussey Tower. The tower probably dates from the 1450s but material from as early as the Roman period has been found at the site. *Bottom: Fig. 2.* St Nicholas's parish church, Skirbeck. The parish of Boston was probably carved out of the parish of Skirbeck. The present building dates to the thirteenth century but it was much altered in the nineteenth century.

*Above*: *Fig. 3*. St Botolph's church. Boston is often identified as the site of the minster founded by Botolph in 653/4 but Botolph's church was probably at Iken in Suffolk.

*Opposite: Bottom Left: Fig. 4*. St Mary's Abbey, York. The abbey was one of the wealthiest in the north and included St Botolph's church among its possessions. Its remains date mainly from the late thirteenth and early fourteenth centuries. *Top: Fig. 5.* The south side of St Botolph's church. In the eighteenth century William Stukeley referred to the discovery of the remains of vast stone walls on this side of the church. *Bottom rght: Fig. 6.* Lion's head knocker on the south door of the tower of St Botolph's. The knocker is the only remnant above ground of the church that preceded the fourteenth- and fifteenth-century building which now stands on the site.

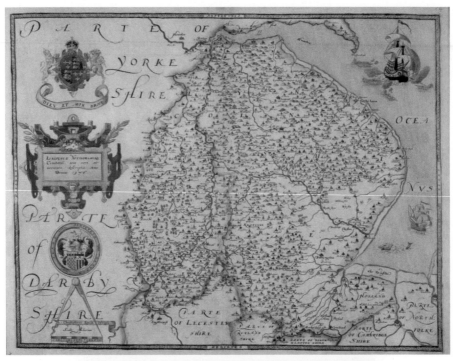

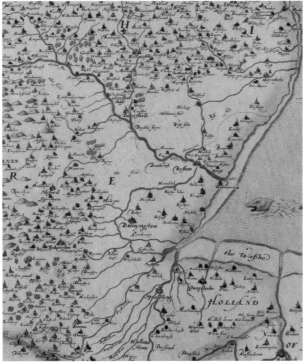

*Fig. 7. Top:* Christopher Saxton's 1576 map of Lincolnshire and Nottinghamshire. The map clearly shows the line of settlements on the 'townlands' between the fenland to the west and the coastal marshland to the east. *Bottom:* Extract showing the area around Boston.

*Fig. 8.* Flood markers at the base of the Stump. Boston remains in danger of tidal flooding, as is shown by the line indicating the level reached by the tidal surge of 5 December 2013.

*Fig. 9.* The view upstream from Town Bridge. Boston's medieval bridge may have stood slightly upstream of the current crossing.

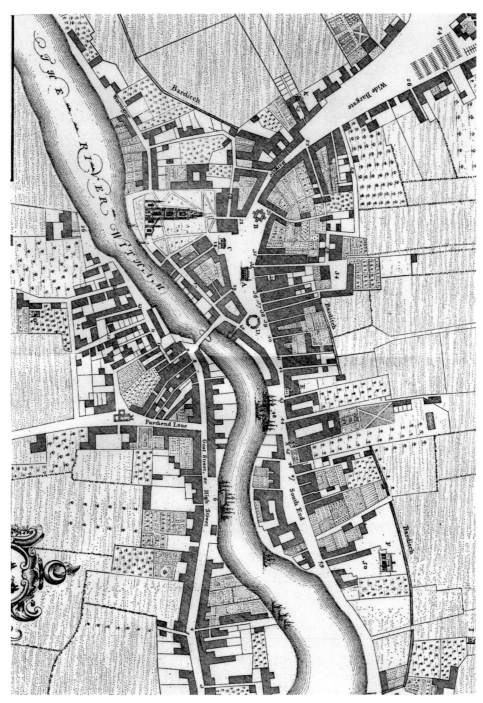

*Fig. 10.* Robert Hall's 1741 map of Boston. The map clearly shows the line of the Barditch, which has since been covered over.

*Top: Fig. 11.* Strait Bargate, where the street crosses the Barditch. Few modern shoppers realise that this grid-cover on Bargate indicates the line of the medieval Barditch. *Bottom: Fig. 12.* Fydell House, South Square. The house was built in the early eighteenth century but eleventh-century pottery found in its grounds helps date the Barditch to the earliest days of the new town of Boston.

*Top: Fig. 13.* Market Place. This was the site of Boston's medieval fair and is still used as a market today. *Bottom: Fig. 14.* The River Witham and the south end of the Market Place from the Stump. St Botolph's church, the marketplace and the bridge, which was slightly closer to the church than the modern road bridge, formed the central core of medieval Boston.

*Top Left: Fig. 15.* Wormgate from the south. The street's name dates back at least as far as the twelfth century and evidence of lead-working from this period has been found there. *Top Right: Fig. 16.* South Street, the Guildhall. The southern part of the town was not intensively occupied in the period before 1225. *Bottom: Fig. 17.* South Street, Shodfriars Hall. This early fifteenth-century timber-framed house, which may have been the guildhall of the Corpus Christi guild, was much altered in the 1870s.

*Top: Fig. 18.* The Dominican friary. Of the four Boston houses of friars, only that of the Dominicans has standing remains. They date from the period of the friary's rebuilding, which followed the fire that devastated the town in 1288. *Bottom: Fig. 19.* The Market Place from the Stump. This view clearly shows the triangular shape of the marketplace, although this is slightly obscured by later infill.

*Top: Fig. 20.* The east side of the Market Place. This view shows one of the surviving double tenements, with its alleys down either side running to the back of the plots, a layout which also developed on the Bergen waterfront in the twelfth century. *Bottom: Fig. 21.* The Sessions House, built between 1841 and 1843. A house called 'The Priory' previously occupied this site but there is no evidence that medieval Boston possessed a monastery or a nunnery.

*Top: Fig. 22.* The site of the Skirbeck hospital of St John at the east end of Norfolk Street, at the junction with Grand Sluice Lane. *Bottom: Fig. 23.* Jerusalem House, which once stood at the site of the Skirbeck hospital of St John at the east end of Norfolk Street. Pishey Thompson suggested that the house was constructed from materials taken from the hospital rather than forming part of its original buildings.

*Top: Fig. 24.* 'The Barracks', 124-136 High Street. This building was perhaps originally an eighteenth-century warehouse but was converted to domestic use in the early nineteenth century. It may possibly have been the site of the Boston hospital of St Leonard. *Bottom: Fig. 25.* Freiston priory. The priory was founded in 1114 by Alan de Croun who held a manor on the west side of Boston.

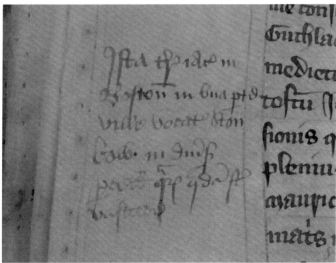

*Top: Fig. 26.* 35 High Street from the south, showing fifteenth-century timbering. It was probably High Street to which Leland was referring, around 1544, when he described the west side of Boston as consisting of 'one long street'. *Bottom: Fig. 27.* The Wrest Park Cartulary of Crowland abbey. This entry, in abbreviated Latin, which refers to land 'in Boston' in the part of the town called 'Stonbow' suggests the close connections between Boston and Lincoln.

*Fig. 28*. A view from the Stump, looking upstream towards Lincoln. The River Witham has been much straightened since the medieval period. The Grand Sluice, built in 1764–66, was well upstream of the medieval sluice.

*Top: Fig. 29.* Quays along the River Witham, looking northwards towards Shodfriars Hall. The eighteenth-century quays and warehouses on the east bank of the river are a reminder that the waterfront as we see it today is very different from its original form. *Bottom: Fig. 30.* The Grammar School and Mart Yard, off South Street. In the sixteenth century the Mart Yard, next to the Grammar School (of 1567), was a privileged site for shops and trading, but Boston's medieval fair seems to have been more centrally located.

*Fig. 31.* The junction of Wormgate and Fountain Lane. The lane takes its name from Fountains abbey, which held property here.

*Fig. 32.* St Mary's Guildhall, South Street. The guild was founded in 1260 but its guildhall dates from *c.* 1390.

*Above: Fig. 33.* Gysors' Hall, South Square. The hall took its name from a London merchant who, in 1244, obtained the right to collect tronage in Boston. *Left: Fig. 34.* Fydell's warehouse, South Square. This granary was built in 1810 using stone from the thirteenth-century Gysors' Hall.

which had its own court and officials, led to clashes with the city's administration on a number of occasions in the thirteenth and fourteenth centuries; similarly, at Lincoln the rights of the castle and of the cathedral were a source of conflict with the mayor and citizens.[84] At Boston, by contrast, there is no sign that the abbey's soke gave rise to quarrels with the townsmen or with the holders of the other local fees. Nor is there any evidence for disputes between the Richmond, Croun and Tattershall fees in the period before 1225.

The first sign of conflict between Boston's jurisdictions comes in 1256 when there was violence in the town between the men of Robert de Tattershall and those of Peter of Savoy.[85] This violence probably related to disagreements about the division of tolls, rents and court fines and about the administration of justice during the time of the fair, which were eventually resolved in 1261. Although it comes from after the period which is our focus here, the agreement that settled these differences provides a fascinating glimpse into the way that Boston was administered in the thirteenth century. The source of the conflict was Robert de Tattershall's complaint that Peter of Savoy did not allow him to take tronage and pesage during the fair, as was his right (see above, page 58), and prevented him from collecting fines for offences committed by merchants on his fee during the fair. In response, Peter agreed not to hinder Robert in this way, saving the 'ancient customs' that determined where different merchants should deposit their goods on the Richmond fee. He further agreed that Robert could receive a half of the tronage and pesage levied on the Tattershall fee, that he could take a half of the fines paid by merchants in his court and that Robert's officer could make attachments 'bearing a rod' (i.e. carrying a rod of office) during fair time. However, Peter's officials were to receive the other half of the tronage and pessage and of the court fines levied on the Tattershall fee, while his bailiffs were to retain the right to approve Robert's officer as suitable and were to receive the oath from him that he would defend Peter's liberties. A fair court was to be held on the Tattershall fee but it was to be overseen by Peter's bailiff sitting alongside Robert's officer and clerk.[86] The 1261 agreement indicates the power that the Richmond lordship could exert over the other lords within Boston. The honour's influence can also be seen in the fact that in 1280 it was receiving £10 a year from the men of Lincoln for permission to trade on the Croun and Tattershall fees during fair time even though, as we saw above (section 1.2.), the fair had been held on the Croun fee from a very early date.

In some towns with divided lordship, a certain degree of administrative unity was eventually achieved. At Coventry, for instance, the prior of Coventry obtained the Earl's half of the city in 1249 and then seems to have tried to merge the town's two separate jurisdictions by holding a single portmoot (i.e. court) for both, although the problems generated by the town's division were only finally resolved in 1355 when the mayor, bailiffs and community acquired control over the whole town.[87] In Tamworth, despite the existence of the two parts of the town with their own separate courts and officials, there was a community of burgesses with a common seal, a common chest and a common hall.[88] At Boston, however, no single lord ever acquired control over the entire town and a unified government under the mayor, aldermen and common councillors was only created when the town was incorporated in 1545.[89] Nor do the separate parts of the town seem to have possessed their own farms and elected officials, which allowed the creation of a unified community of burgesses at Tamworth. At Durham, the potential difficulties created by the town's fragmented administration were overcome by agreements between the prior and bishop, which created standardised weights and measures and a hierarchy of courts; it is likely that some similar form of agreement, like that over the administration of the fair, which was reached between the Richmond and Tattershall fees in 1261, existed at Boston.[90]

It is probable that, as the most powerful of Boston's overlords, and as the authority that controlled the largest part of the town, the honour of Richmond took the initiative in co-ordinating the administration of the town and of its fair.[91] Thus, in 1281 and 1285, it was the intercession of John of Brittany, earl of Richmond, which secured royal grants of pavage to the 'bailiffs, burgesses and good men' of Boston, while in 1305 John successfully petitioned in parliament for a grant of pontage for 'his town of Boston', although these grants do not specify whether they applied only to the Richmond manor within the town.[92] However, we need not assume that references to the 'good men' of the town in 1281 and 1285, along with that in 1301 when the 'bailiffs and good men' of Boston were to send a ship to Berwick for service against the Scots, were a sign of any particular degree of urban communal organisation or corporate identity.[93] After all, the 1301 order about ships for Berwick was sent to the 'good men' of many other places which were not self-governing boroughs, including Great Shelford (Cornwall) and Aldrington (Sussex), just as a royal writ had been addressed to the 'good men' of all the king's manors and demesnes in 1236.[94]

If, as we saw above, the nature of the government of the Richmond manor in Boston before 1225 is rather unclear, then the administrative arrangements in the other lordships which made up the town are even more obscure. Whether the tenants of the abbot of St Mary's or of the Croun-Vaux-Roos and Tattershall fees enjoyed any degree of self-government in the twelfth and thirteenth centuries is impossible to know. However, the fact that the rents of assize of the Croun fee were accounted for at the Exchequer in 1204 does not suggest that the revenues of this manor had been composed into a fixed farm at this date.[95] Tronage was levied on the Croun fee before the end of the twelfth century and by 1227 it had, like that on the Richmond manor, been farmed out to an individual rather than to the tenants of the manor as a community.[96] In the later Middle Ages, both the Croun and Tattershall fees were, like the Richmond manor in Boston, administered by appointed bailiffs and stewards rather than by elected representatives and it is likely that this was also the case in the period before 1225.[97]

## 5.8. LORDS AND TOWNSMEN: CONFLICT AND CO-OPERATION

The basic tenurial and economic privileges enjoyed by towns such as Boston played an important part in encouraging urban growth in the twelfth and thirteenth centuries even though there was no direct correlation between the size and wealth of a town and the extent of the liberties that it obtained. This view of towns in medieval England as being, in certain respects, islands of 'privileged autonomy set in a feudal sea' is by no means at odds with a recognition that they were also an integral part of the wider society to which they were inseparably linked.[98] Indeed, it was precisely the relative freedom that medieval towns enjoyed that enabled them to carry out their essential functions for contemporary society. Nevertheless, as Rosser has argued, it would be wrong for an emphasis on the importance of borough liberties to lead to the conclusion that manorial lordship was 'totally unacceptable' to medieval townspeople.[99] After all, in England, as in medieval Europe in general, most towns were themselves seigneurial foundations and profited from the support and patronage of their manorial lords.[100] This was certainly the case at Boston where, as we have seen, it was the lords of the honour of Richmond and of the Croun fee who seem to have founded and laid out the town, where it was Alan de Croun who built the sluice which helped to improve the port, and where the earls of Richmond obtained grants of pontage and pavage on behalf of the townsmen.

Nevertheless, if the inhabitants of English medieval towns were perfectly happy to accept the benefits of manorial lordship in terms of the protection and patronage which it offered, they also sought, where possible, to minimise the burdens and restrictions which such lordship potentially entailed. In some towns, particularly in towns with monastic overlords, such as Bury St Edmunds or St Albans, this could result in a long history of conflict between townsmen and lords – conflict in which the lords usually emerged triumphant.[101] By contrast, at Boston, as in other seigneurial boroughs such as Leicester and Tewkesbury, and even in some of the monastic boroughs, including Durham and Westminster, peaceful coexistence between lords and townspeople, rather than conflict, seems to have been the norm.[102] Boston was hit by disturbances in 1347 when rebels elected their own mayor and issued their 'quasi-royal proclamations', but this outbreak of violence, which seems to have been occasioned by the high grain prices of this year, was an isolated incident in the history of the town.[103] The lack of sources means that any conclusions must be very tentative but it seems that in general the inhabitants of Boston, particularly in the town's early period of growth, assumed that they had more to gain by co-operation with the town's overlords than they did from conflict.

# Part 6

# Conclusion: Boston's early growth

The rise of Boston in the century and a half after Domesday Book has to be understood in the context of the growth of population and the expansion of trade which England experienced in this period. Traditionally, population growth has been seen as the key determinant of English economic change between the late eleventh and the early fourteenth centuries.[1] In this perspective, the commercialisation of the economy in these years, along with other changes such as the colonisation of the fens, is explained by a two- to three-fold increase in national population, with this demographic growth largely being taken as a given in the absence of positive checks such as famine and epidemic disease.[2] Yet, more recent studies have argued that commercialisation was not simply a response to increased population but rather itself constituted a key stimulus, which encouraged family formation and population growth. If so, the growth of towns such as Boston was not simply the passive reflection of colonisation and of national population growth but was itself an active agent that helped to encourage these processes. Despite the evident symbiosis and interaction between trade and population, it seems plausible that an expansion of trade and entrepreneurial activity preceded and enabled the sustained growth of population that England experienced in the thirteenth century, even if this take-off in commercialisation is easier to describe than to explain.[3]

Whilst there is a historiographical consensus about the expansion of trade and the growth of towns in England between the eleventh and the thirteenth centuries, the precise chronology of such change is a more controversial issue. For some historians England was already highly commercialised and urbanised even before the Norman Conquest; for some, urban growth took off in the late tenth and eleventh centuries; for some it was 1066 that was the turning point in the growth of a market economy; for others these trends were part of a cumulative expansion of the economy, which took place between the tenth and the early fourteenth centuries.[4] Certainly, there can be no doubting the expansion of towns and trade and the development of a money economy that England experienced in the tenth and eleventh centuries.[5] Nevertheless, it still seems likely that the scale of commercial growth was relatively modest until the middle of the twelfth century, having perhaps even suffered short-term set-backs after 1066 and during the disturbances of Stephen's reign, and that the key period of sustained economic expansion may have begun as late as 1165 or even 1175.[6]

If this was the case, then Boston, whose growth seems to have begun in the early years of the twelfth century, can be counted among those towns that were to enjoy the benefits of having an early start in the process of urbanisation and commercialisation. Indeed, from the tenth or eleventh centuries onwards, eastern England and the Danelaw may have been ahead of Wessex and Mercia in the process whereby boroughs ceased to be primarily military, ecclesiastical and administrative settlements and centres of aristocratic residence and were transformed into genuinely urban communities that were reliant upon commerce and industry.[7] In the late eleventh and early twelfth centuries, the east coast ports, including Berwick, Newcastle and, Lynn, seem to have particularly benefited from the growth of overseas trade.[8] The foundation of Boston itself as an urban centre, the creation of its fair, the reopening of the Foss Dyke, and the construction of the sluice and improvement of the River Witham in the period before 1150 all anticipated the wider expansion of the market, the development of the material infrastructure of trade, and the proliferation of new towns, which characterised the English economy in the second half of the twelfth century and the first half of the thirteenth century.[9] The scale and timing of Boston's growth was the outcome of multiple factors, including its position as the out-port for Lincoln, the shift of overseas trade from inland to estuarine and coastal ports, the growth of the wool export trade, the availability of woollen textiles from Lincoln and the other cloth-producing towns of eastern England, the port's access to the markets of Scandinavia, Germany and the Low Countries, the expansion of Derbyshire lead-mining, the prosperity of the wine trade, the colonisation of the fens, and the encouragement of its lords who founded the town and allowed its inhabitants the liberties that made town life possible. In turn, these factors often had a positive impact on each other, as when the reopening of the Foss Dyke or the improvement of Boston's port facilities were both a response to commercial growth and also a further stimulus to such growth, or when the development of the international stockfish trade not only encouraged urban growth but was itself a response to the increase in consumer demand caused by the expansion of urban populations.[10]

As we have seen, our surviving sources help to document the remarkable growth that Boston experienced in the century and a half after Domesday Book. Nonetheless, much of the town's economic, social, political and cultural life in this period, including its local trade and industrial production, the nature of its local administration, the social position of women, and the history of its parish church and of the piety of its parishioners, remains shrouded in mystery. It is unlikely that new documentary evidence will come to light that would allow us to fill these gaps in our knowledge. One possibility for future development is archaeological excavation since Boston, and in particular its early history, has been relatively neglected by archaeologists.[11] Nevertheless, like the documentary sources, archaeological evidence has limitations of its own, at least when it is used to answer the kinds of questions in which historians tend to be interested. For instance, it has often been difficult to date material finds from Boston with the precision that an historical account of the town's evolution requires, as when a pottery sherd is said to be from the 'twelfth to the fourteenth century', a gold brooch is dated as from the 'late twelfth to the fourteenth century', or when the deposits within a particular layer are said to be of the 'thirteenth century or earlier'.[12]

Finally, it should be emphasised that, for all the precocity of Boston's development between the late eleventh and early thirteenth centuries, the town continued to expand after 1225 as part of the wider growth and commercialisation of the English economy. Boston's success in the thirteenth century is best illustrated by the extension and development of its fair. At the start of the century, the fair ran for eight days from 17 June. Then, in 1218 it was lengthened by another eight days from the 24 June, while by 1232 its further extension was said to be affecting the fair at Lynn, which began on 13 July.[13] By 1288, when fire swept through Boston, the fair was being held on 26 July, while by 1331 it was claimed that in previous years it had lasted until as late as 13 October, i.e. for almost four months.[14] Inevitably, the extension of the fair led to an increase in the revenues it generated. Thus, while the maximum figure we have for the income generated by Boston fair for the Richmond honour in the years between 1172 to 1212 is £106 6s 4d in 1209, an extent of the honour made in 1280 valued the fair at £289 13s 4d.[15] During this later phase of the town's growth, the documentary evidence for Boston becomes much richer and this period of the town's history, not to mention the fluctuations in fortunes it experienced in the fourteenth century and the eventual decline of its national economic significance in the fifteenth and early sixteenth centuries, is worthy of separate detailed study of its own.[16]

# Notes and references

## PART ONE: THE EARLY HISTORY OF BOSTON

1. M. Bonney, *Lordship and the urban community: Durham and its overlords, 1250–1540* (Cambridge, 1990), pp. 34-5; C. Dyer, *Making a living in the Middle Ages: the people of Britain, 8501520* (New Haven, 2002), p. 103.

2. For an excellent study of Boston in the thirteenth century see H. Summerson, 'Calamity and commerce: the burning of Boston fair in 1288', in C. M. Barron and A. F. Sutton, eds, *The medieval merchant: proceedings of the 2012 Harlaxton symposium* (Donington, 2014), pp. 146-165. For studies of Boston in the later Middle Ages see W. I. Haward, 'The trade of Boston in the fifteenth century', *Associated Architectural Societies Reports and Papers*, 41 (1932–33), pp. 169-178; E. M. Carus-Wilson, 'The medieval trade of the ports of the Wash', *Medieval Archaeology*, VI-VII (1962–3), pp. 182-201; S. H. Rigby, 'Boston and Grimsby in the Middle Ages' (unpublished University of London PhD thesis, 1983), (cited below as Rigby, 'Boston and Grimsby in the Middle Ages'); S. H. Rigby, 'Boston and Grimsby in the Middle Ages: an administrative contrast', *Journal of Medieval History*, 10 (1984), pp. 51-66 (cited below as Rigby, 'An administrative contrast'); S. H. Rigby, '"Sore decay" and "fair dwellings": Boston and urban decline in the later Middle Ages', *Midland History*, 10 (1985), pp. 47-61; S. H. Rigby, 'The customs administration at Boston in the reign of Richard II', *Bulletin of the Institute of Historical Research*, 58 (1985), pp. 12-24; S. H. Rigby, 'Urban society in the early fourteenth century: the evidence of the lay subsidies', *Bulletin of the John Rylands Library*, 72 (1990), pp. 169-184; *The overseas trade of Boston in the reign of Richard II*, ed. S. H. Rigby (LRS, 93 (2005)); S. H. Rigby, 'Medieval Boston: economy, society and administration', in S. Badham and P. Cockerham, eds., *'The beste and fayrest of al Lincolnshire': the church of St Botolph's, Boston, Lincolnshire, and its medieval monuments* (British Archaeological Reports, British Series, 554 (2012), pp. 6-28.

3. S. Jenks, *England, Die Hanse und Preußen: Handel und Diplomatie, 1377–1474* (three volumes; Koln, 1992); J. D. Fudge, *Cargoes, embargoes and emissaries: the commercial and political interaction of England and the German Hanse, 1450–1510* (Toronto, 1995); M. Burkhardt, 'One hundred years of thriving commerce at a major English sea port: the Hanseatic trade at Boston between 1370 and 1470', in H. Brand and L. Muller, eds, *The dynamics of European culture in the North Sea and Baltic region* (Hilversum, 2007), pp. 65-85; M. Burkhardt, 'The German Hanse and Bergen: new perspectives on an old subject', *Scandinavian Economic History Review*, 58 (2010), pp. 60-79, especially pp. 64-5.

4. See Badham and Cockerham, '*The beste and fayrest of al Lincolnshire*', chapters 3 to 10; C. Cross, 'Communal piety in sixteenth century Boston', *Lincolnshire History and Archaeology*, 25 (1990), pp. 33-38; W. M. Ormrod, ed., *The guilds in Boston* (Boston, 1993); K. Giles and J. Clark, 'St Mary's Guildhall, Boston, Lincolnshire: the archaeology of a medieval "public" building', *Medieval Archaeology*, 55 (2011), pp. 226-256; K. Giles, '"A table of alabaster with the story of the Doom": the religious objects and spaces of the Guild f Our Blessed Virgin, Boston (Lincs)', in T. Hamling and C. Richardson, eds, *Everyday objects: medieval and early modern material culture and its meanings* (Farnham, 2010), pp. 267–85; G. Rosser, *The art of solidarity in the Middle Ages: guilds in England, 1250–1550* (Oxford, 2015), pp. 84, 113n., 126-7, 129-30, 132, 136, 204, 224. See also the entries for Boston in the index to R. N. Swanson, *Indulgences in late medieval England: passports to paradise?* (Cambridge, 2007).

5. P. Thompson, *The history and antiquities of Boston, and the villages of Skirbeck, Fishtoft, Freiston, Butterwick, Benington, Leverton, Leake and Wrangle; comprising the hundred of Skirbeck in the County of Lincoln* (Sleaford, 1997; first published 1856). This work was an enlarged version of Thompson's earlier *Collections for a topographical and historical account of Boston and the hundred of Skirbeck in the County of Lincoln* (London, 1820). See also P. Thompson, 'On the early commerce of Boston', *Associated Architectural Societies Reports and Papers*, 2 (1852–53), pp. 362-381. On Thompson see I. Bailey, *Pishey Thompson: man of two worlds* (Boston, 1991).

6. D. M. Owen, 'The beginnings of the port of Boston', in N. Field and A. White, eds, *A prospect of Lincolnshire, being collected articles on the history and traditions of Lincolnshire in honour of Ethel H. Rudkin* (Lincoln, 1984), pp. 42-5.

7. L. Pezzolo, 'The *via italiana* to capitalism', in L. Neal and J. G. Williamson, eds, *The Cambridge history of capitalism, volume I: the rise of capitalism from ancient origins to 1848* (Cambridge, 2014), pp. 267-313, at pp. 269-70. For an excellent survey of England, see R. H. Britnell, *The commercialisation of English society, 1000–1500* (second edition; Manchester, 1996), chapters 1-6. For bibliography, see M. Bailey, 'The commercialisation of the English economy, 1086–1500', *Journal of Medieval History*, 24 (1998), pp. 297–311.

8. E. Miller and J. Hatcher, *Medieval England: towns, commerce and crafts, 1086–1348* (London, 1995), pp. 393-4; Dyer, *Making a living*, pp. 95, 233, 235; S. Broadberry, B. M. S. Campbell, A. Klein, M. Overton and B. van Leeuwen, *British economic growth, 1270–1280* (Cambridge, 2015), pp. 20-1.

9. For references see M. Bailey, 'Trade and towns in medieval England: new insights from familiar sources', *The Local Historian*, 29 (1999), pp. 194-211, at p. 199; S. H. Rigby, 'Urban population in late medieval England: the evidence of the lay subsidies', *Economic History Review*, 63 (2010), pp. 393-417, at p. 393; S. H. Rigby, 'Social structure and economic change in late medieval England', in R. Horrox and M. Ormrod, eds, *A social history of England, 1200–1500* (Cambridge, 2006), pp. 13, 25. For earlier dobts about an increase in the proportion of the total population living in towns in this period see J. C. Russell, *British medieval population* (Albuquerque, 1948), pp. 304-5 and E. Miller and J. Hatcher, *Medieval England: rural society and economic change, 1086–1348* (London, 1978), p. 74.

10. M. Beresford, *New towns of the Middle Ages: town plantation in England, Wales and Gascony* (London, 1967), pp. 327-338; M. W. Beresford and H. P. R. Finberg, 'English medieval boroughs: a hand-list' (Totowa, 1973), pp. 37-40 (and see also M. Beresford, 'English medieval boroughs: a handlist': revisions, 1973–1981', *Urban History Yearbook 1982*, pp. 59-64); *The Lincolnshire Domesday and the Lindsey survey*, eds C. W. Foster and T. Longley (LRS, 19 (1921)), p. lxxiii.

11. Beresford, *New towns*, pp. 270, 467-8; Carus-Wilson, 'The medieval trade of the ports of the Wash', pp. 182-3; V. Parker, *The making of King's Lynn* (London, 1971), pp. 1-5; D. M. Owen , 'Bishop's Lynn: the first century of a new town?', in R. A. Brown, ed., *Proceedings of the Battle Conference on Anglo-Norman studies*, volume II (Woodbridge, 1979), pp. 141-153; *The making of King's Lynn*, ed. D. M. Owen (London, 1984), pp. 5-12; P. Richards, 'The hinterland and overseas trade of King's Lynn, 1205–1537; an introduction', in K. Friedland and P. Richards, eds, *Essays in Hanseatic trade:the King's Lynn symposium, 1998* (Dereham, 2005), pp. 10-21, at pp. 10-11.

12. A. Rogers, *A history of Lincolnshire* (Chichester, 1985), p. 51.

13. TNA, Pipe Rolls, E.372/50, m. 17d; *Pipe Roll, 6 John*, p. 218. No returns survive for the west coast ports, including Bristol and Chester. We do not know which merchants paid the duty, on which goods, or during which period. The period covered by the pipe roll account is also uncertain although it may be from 20 July 1203 to 30 November 1204. (T. H. Lloyd, *The English wool trade in the Middle Ages* (Cambridge, 1977), pp. 9-10; Miller and Hatcher, *Medieval England: towns, commerce and crafts*, pp. 195-7).

14. M. Kowaleski, 'Port towns: England and Wales, 1300–1540', in D. M. Palliser, ed., *The Cambridge urban history of Britain*, volume I (Cambridge, 2000), pp. 467-494, at p. 477.

15. Rigby, 'Social structure and economic change', pp. 14-15. For the Black Death in Lincolnshire see A. Hamilton Thompson, 'Registers of John Gynewell, bshop of Lincoln for the 1347–1350', *Archaeological Jornal*, 68 (1911), pp. 301-60. Boston is omitted from the account of the spread of the plague in the county in O. Benedictow, *The Black Death, 1346–1353: a complete history* (Woodbridge, 2004), pp. 138-40.

16. As a result of Topham's pioneering transcription of the enrolled poll tax returns, Thompson (and, following him, Dover) claimed that there were 814 poll tax payers in Boston in 1377 (J. Topham, 'Subsidy roll of 51 Edward III', *Archaeologia*, 7 (1785), pp. 337-347, at p. 341; Thompson, *The history and antiquities of Boston*, p. 57; P. Dover, *The early medieval history of Boston, AD 1086–1400* (second edition; Boston, 1972), p. 13). In fact both of the Exchequer enrolments of the poll tax refer to 2,871 taxpayers in Boston (TNA, Enrolled Lay Subsidies, E.359/8B, m. 18; E.359/8C. See also *The poll taxes*

*of 1377, 1379 and 1381, part 2: Lincolnshire-Westmoreland* ed. C. Fenwick (Oxford, 2001), p. 3). For the problem of calculating total populations from the numbers of taxpayers in 1377 see the references in Rigby, 'Urban population', pp. 398-9. For urban population in 1377 see A. Dyer, 'Ranking lists of English medieval towns', in Palliser, *The Cambridge urban history*, volume I, pp. 747-70, at p. 758.

17. Rigby, 'Medieval Boston', pp. 16-19.

18. Dyer, 'Ranking lists', p. 755. In 1334 some towns paid taxation at the rate of a tenth whilst others, including Boston, paid at a fifteenth. If we compare towns in terms of their actual tax payments instead of by their valuations, Boston would be ranked around thirteenth in the urban hierarchy.

19. For town friaries see S. Reynolds, *An introduction to the history of English medieval towns* (Oxford, 1977), pp. 62-3. For Boston's friaries see below, part 2, notes 53-56 and 133. Beresford and St Joseph refer to 'nineteen religious houses and three friaries' in late medieval Boston but presumably this should be read as a reference to the property owned in Boston by nineteen religious houses and three friaries, which was granted to the borough of Boston after the dissolution (M. W. Beresford and J. K. S. St Joseph, *Medieval England: an aerial survey* (second edition; Cambridge, 1979), p. 218; Beresford, *New towns*, p. 464; Thompson, *The history and antiquities of Boston*, p. 64; LAO, BB1/1/1, Receipt by the Treasurer of Augmentations for property obtained by the borough of Boston).

20. W. Marrat, *The history of Lincolnshire, topographical, historical and descriptive* (two volumes; Boston, 1814), volume I, pp. 1-3; T. H. Allen, *The history of the county of Lincoln, from the earliest period to the present time*, volume I (London, 1834), pp. 211-12; Thompson, *The history and antiquities of Boston*, pp. 16-18; S. B. J. Skertchly, *The geology of the fenland* (London, 1877), pp. 11-13; J. B. Whitwell, *Roman Lincolnshire* (Lincoln, 1970), pp. 13, 96; G. Harden, *Medieval Boston and its archaeological implications* (Sleaford, 1978), pp. 7-9; LHER, MLI13351, A Middle Saxon settlement at Church Road, Boston; J. Rylatt, *Report on a programme of archaeological fieldwork at Boston Grammar School, Boston, Lincolnshire* (2002), p. 4 (Library of Unpublished Fieldwork Reports [data-set]. York Archaeology Data Service [distributor] (doi: 10.5284/1014344)).

21. A. Thomas, 'Rivers of gold? The coastal zone between the Humber and the Wash in the mid-Saxon period', in H. Hamerow, ed., *Anglo-Saxon Studies in Archaeology and History*, 18 (2013), pp. 97-118, at p. 101; P. Cope-Faulkner, J. Hambly and J. Young, *Boston town historic environment baseline study* (Heckington, 2007), pp. 6-7; *The big dig: Boston marketplace, Boston, Lincolnshire. Community excavation* (Network Archaeology for Lincolnshire County Council, report no. 591 (May, 2012), p. 3; J. Minnis, K. Carmichael, C. Fletcher and M. Anderson, *Boston, Lincolnshire: historic North Sea port and market town* (Swindon, 2015), p. 5. For the Hussey Tower see T. P. Smith, 'Hussey Tower, Boston: a late medieval tower-house', *Lincolnshire History and Archaeology*, 14 (1979), pp. 31-7.

22. For these variant forms of Boston's placename see 'Petri Blesensis Continuatio' in *Rerum Anglicarum scriptorum veterum*, volume I, ed. W. Fulman (Oxford, 1684), p. 261; *The great roll of the pipe for the thirty-first year of the reign of King Henry I, Michaelmas 1130 (Pipe Roll I)*, ed. J. A. Green (Pipe Roll Society, n.s., 57 (2012)), p. 95; *Early Yorkshire charters, volume IV: the honour of Richmond, part I*, ed. C. T. Clay (Yorkshire Archaeological Society Record Series, extra series, 1 (1935)), pp. 14, 34-6, 76; *Memorials of the abbey of St Mary of Fountains*, volume II, part I, ed. J. R. Walbran (Surtees Society, 67 (1876)), pp. 15, 19n; 'Dame Sirith', line 77, in *Early Middle English verse and prose*, eds J. A. W. Bennett and G. V. Smithers (Oxford, 1966), pp. 77-95.

23. The Gough map, which dates from 1355–66, labels the town as 'Boston' (N. Millea, *The Gough Map: the earliest road map of Great Britain* (Oxford, 2007), pp. 12-13, 66-7. An entry in John of Gaunt's register refers to 'la ville de Boston' in 1373 (*John of Gaunt's register*, volume II, ed. S. Armitage-Smith (Camden Society, third series, 21 (1911), no. 1213). The Wrest Park cartulary of Crowland Abbey, which was compiled after 1343, includes a reference to land in 'Boston' (Spalding Gentlemen's Society, Wrest Park cartulary, f. 138v; G. R. C. Davis, Medieval cartularies of Great Britain (revised edition; London, 2010), p. 61)0. For a transcription of the Crowland cartulary see Reading University Library, RUL MS 1148/14/12. For other early uses of 'Boston' and 'Bostane' see BL, Additional MS 40008, Cartulary of Bridlington priory, ff.1v 278; Cotton MS Vespasian, Cartulary of Kirkstead priory, ff. 183-184v. Kerling's edition of the cartulary of St Bartholemew's Hospital claims to give place-names in their original spelling (*Cartulary of St Bartholemew's Hospital, founded 1123*, ed. N. J. M. Kerling (London, 1973), p. 14) and includes references to 'Boston' from *c.*1190 (nos. 1664, 1671), *c.*1224–46 (no. 1668),

*c.*1250 (no. 1661), and 1371 (no. 1667) but the cartulary itself (as well as the deeds on which it is based) refers to 'Sanctus Botulphus' rather than to 'Boston' (SBHAO, Cartulary of St Bartholemew's Hospital, SBHB.HC.2/1, ff. 592v, 593, 593v-594; SBHAO, St Bartholemew's Hospital Deeds, SBHB.HC.1, nos. 57, 307, 413, 456. The hospital's cartulary and deeds do include references to 'Boston' and 'Botston' but these are from the fifteenth century (SBHAO, Cartulary of St Bartholemew's Hospital, SBHB. HC.2/1, ff. 591v, 592; SBHAO, St Bartholemew's Hospital Deeds, SBHB.HC.1, nos. 1321, 1322). The cartulary of Stixwould priory, which was originally compiled in the late thirteenth century, includes entries 'De terra Boston' but this phrase has been added in a later medieval hand (BL, Additional MS 46701, f. 37. The printed edition of the cartulary of Fountains abbey gives 'Boston', Bustona' and 'Bustun' as surnames, but these references are probably to members of the 'Roston' or 'Rustun' family (*Chartulary of Fountains*, volume II, pp. 629-30; D. Crouch, 'Urban government and oligarchy in medieval Scarborough', in D. Crouch and T. Pearson, eds., *Medieval Scarborough: studies in trade and civic life* (Yorkshire Archaeological Society Occasional Paper, 1 (2002), pp. 41-7, at pp. 45-6). For the use of 'Boston' as a surname in 1195, see *Feet of fines of the reign of Henry II and of the first seven years of the reign of Richard I, A.D. 1182 to A.D. 1196* (Pipe Roll Society, 17 (1894), p. 50.

24.  *The Anglo-Saxon chronicle: a revised translation*, eds D. Whitelock, D. C. Douglas and S. I. Tucker (London, 1961), p. 20; *The Peterborough chronicle (The Bodleian manuscript Laud Misc.636)*, ed. D. Whitelock (Copenhagen, 1964), plate 27; *The Peterborough chronicle*, ed. H. A. Rositzke (New York, 1951), p. 41; 'Chronicle of Florence of Worcester', in *The church historians of England*, volume II, part I, ed. J. Stevenson (London, 1853), pp. 171-372, at p. 181; *Matthaei Parisiensis, monarchi Sancti Albani, Chronica majora, volume I: the Creation to A.D. 1066*, ed. H. R. Luard (London: Rolls Series, 1872), p. 290; J. Blair, 'Botwulf (*fl.* 654–*c.*670)', *Oxford Dictionary of National Biography*, online edition [http://www.oxforddnb.com/view/article/2963, accessed 25 March 2015]. The main account of Botolph's life is that by Folcard (*c.*1070) and there are also mentions of him in the *Slesvig Breviary* as well as later lives of him by John Capgrave and John of Tynemouth (see S. E. West, N. Scarfe and R. Cramp, 'Iken, St Botolph and the coming of East Anglian Christianity', *Proceedings of the Suffolk Institute of Archaeology and History*, 35 (1984), pp. 279-301, at pp. 297-8; *Acta sanctorum Junii, tomus III* (Antwerp, 1701), pp. 398-403; John of Tynemouth, *Explicit (Nova legenda Anglie)* (London: printed by Wynkyn de Worde,1515/16), f. 42; Thompson, *The history and antiquities of Boston*, pp. 369-72).

25.  *St Botolph's church, Boston Stump, parish of Boston* (n.p., n.d.), p. 2. See also W. Stukeley, *Itinerarium curiosum: or, an account of the antiquities and remarkable curiosities in nature or art observed in travels through Great Britain* (second edition; two volumes; London, 1776), volume I, p. 31; Allen, *The history of the county of Lincoln*, volume I, pp. 212-13; Thompson, *The history and antiquities of Boston*, pp. 25-27, 108, 460 n.1; W. H. Wheeler, *A history of the fens of south Lincolnshire* (second edition; Boston, 1896), appendix, p. 5; G. Jebb, *A guide to the church of St Botolph with notes on the history and antiquities of Boston and Skirbeck* (Boston, 1896), p. 35; 'Boston, Lincolnshire', in *Encyclopaedia Britannica, Volume IV* (eleventh edition; Cambridge, 1910), pp. 289-90, at p. 290; P. H. Ditchfield, 'Proceedings of the congress', *Journal of the British Archaeological Association*, n.s., 27 (1921), pp. 8-60, at p. 50; Sister Elspeth, 'The monastery of Ikanho', in W. Page, ed., *The Victoria history of the county of Lincoln*, volume II (London, 1988; first published 1906), pp. 96-7; M. R. Lambert and R. Walker, *Boston, Tattershall and Croyland* (Oxford, 1930), pp. 26-7.

26.  F. Bond, *Dedications and patron saints of English churches: ecclesiastical symbolism; saints and their emblems* (London, 1914), pp. 67, 90; F. S. Stevenson, 'St Botolph (Botwulf) and Iken', *Proceedings of the Suffolk Institute of Archaeology and Natural History*, 18 (1922–4), pp. 29-51; W. T. Whitley, 'Botulph's Ycean-ho', *Journal of the British Archaeological Association*, n.s., 36 (1930), pp. 233-8; West, Scarfe and Cramp, 'Iken, St Botolph and the coming of East Anglian Christianity' pp. 279-301; A. Vince, 'Lincoln in the Viking Age', in J. Graham-Campbell, R. Hall, J. Jesch and D. N. Parsons, eds, *Vikings and the Danelaw: select papers from the proceedings of the thirteenth Viking congress, Nottingham and York, 21-30 August 1997* (Oxford, 1997), pp. 157-79, at p. 161.

27.  *The Lincolnshire Domesday*, pp. xiv-xv; *Documents illustrative of the social and economic history of the Danelaw from various collections*, ed. F. M. Stenton (London, 1920), pp. lxiii-lxix; *Inquisitions and assessments relating to feudal aids; with other analogous documents preserved in the Public Record Office, 1284–1431, volume III: Kent-Norfolk* (London, 1904), p. 184; BL, Harley MS 742, Cartulary of Spalding priory, f. 244v.

28. https://hydra.hull.ac.uk/assets/hull:510/content; *The Lincolnshire Domesday*, pp. lxxi, 68; *Liber Feodorum: the book of fees commonly called Testa de Nevill reformed from the earliest MSS* (three volumes; London: 1920, 1923, 1931), volume I, p. 195.

29. *The Lincolnshire Domesday*, 12/67, 29/33.

30. *The complete peerage*, volume X, pp. 783-5; K. S. B. Keats-Rohan, 'Alan Rufus (*d.* 1093)', *Oxford Dictionary of National Biography* online edition http://www.oxforddnb.com/view/article/article/52358, accessed 24 February 2013; K. S. B. Keats-Rohan, *Domesday people: a prosopography of persons occurring in English documents, 1066–1166. I: Domesday Book* (Woodbridge, 1999), pp. 127-8; K. S. B. Keats-Rohan, 'The Bretons and the Normans of England, 1066–1154: the family, the fief and the feudal monarchy', *Nottingham Medieval Studies*, 36 (1992), pp. 42-78, at p. 46; P. Dalton, *Conquest, anarchy and lordship: Yorkshire, 1066–1154* (Cambridge, 1994), pp. 66-7. On the role of Bretons in the 'Norman' Conquest see K. S. B. Keats-Rohan, 'William I and the Breton contingent in the non-Norman Conquest, 1066–1087', *Anglo-Norman Studies*, 13 (1991), pp. 157-72; K. S. B. Keats-Rohan, 'Le rôle des Bretons dans la colonisation normande de l'Angleterre (vers 1042–1135)', *Memoires de la Société d'histoire et d'archaeologie de Bretagne*, 74 (1996), pp. 181-215.

31. Rogers, *A history of Lincolnshire*, p. 51; H. C. Darby, *The Domesday geography of eastern England* (Cambridge, 1952), p. 34; R. Welldon Finn, *Domesday Book: a guide* (Chichester, 1973), pp. 6-8; P. H. Sawyer, 'Medieval English settlement: new interpretations', in P. H. Sawyer, ed., *English medieval settlement* (London, 1979), pp. 1-8, at p. 1-3; W. G. Hoskins, *The making of the English landscape* (London, 1955), p. 69.

32. *The Lincolnshire Domesday*, 12/67; 57/38; P. Sawyer, *Anglo-Saxon Lincolnshire* (Lincoln, 1998), p. 197.

33. Harden, *Medieval Boston*, p. 9; N. Wright, *Boston: a history and celebration* (Salisbury, 2005), p. 16; Marrat, *The history of Lincolnshire*, volume I, p. 83; Thompson, *The history and antiquities of Boston*, pp. 27, 199; F. H. Molyneux and N. R. Wright, *An atlas of Boston* (Boston, 1974), pp. 14, 31. See also John Rocque's plan of Boston, indicating Skirbeck Quarter, in A. Dury, *A collection of the plans of the principal cities of Great Britain and Ireland* (London, 1764). For the carving out of parishes from larger, Anglo-Saxon ones, see R. Goddard, *Lordship and medieval urbanization: Coventry, 1043–1355* (Woodbridge, 2004), pp. 25-6.

34. BL, Additional MS 38816, Miscellaneous volume including charters of St Mary's abbey, York, ff. 29v-34v; W. Dugdale, *Monasticon Anglicanum* (six volumes; London, 1817–1830), volume III: 544-6; *Early Yorkshire charters, volume IV*, pp. 3-4, 10; A. B. Whittingham, 'St Mary's abbey, York: an interpretation of its plan', *Archaeological Journal*, 120 (1971), pp. 118-146, at p. 119; C. Norton, 'The buildings of St Mary's abbey, York, and their destruction', *Antiquaries Journal*, 74 (1994), pp. 256-288, at pp. 256-7, 280-2; D. Palliser, *Domesday York* (York: Borthwick Paper, 78 (1990)), pp. 3, 15; D. M. Palliser, *Medieval York, 600–1540* (Oxford 2014), pp. 64-5, 93, 98-9, 124; C. Wilson and J. Burton, *St Mary's abbey, York*, (York, 1988), pp. 1-3; J. Burton, *St Mary's abbey and the city of York* (York, 1989), pp. 2-4, 7; J. Burton, 'The monastic revival in Yorkshire' in D. Rollason, M. Harvey and M. Prestwich, eds, *Anglo-Norman Durham, 1093–1193* (Woodbridge, 1994), pp. 41-51; J. Burton, *The monastic order in Yorkshire, 1069–1215* (Cambridge, 1999), pp. xvii, 3-4, 13-14, 35-44, 85, 273, 289, 298; S. Rees Jones, *York: the making of a city, 1068–1350* (Oxford, 2013), pp. 50, 158-162; Dalton, *Conquest, anarchy and lordship*, pp. 136-41. Alan Rufus's *obit* was observed at St Mary's, as were those of his younger brothers Alan Niger and Stephen (*The chronicle of St Mary's abbey, York, from Bodley MS. 39*, eds H. H. E. Craster and M. E. Thornton (Surtees Society, 148 (1933)), pp. 112-13).

35. *Regesta regum Anglo-Normannorum, 1066–1154*, volume I, eds H. W. C. Davis and R. J. Whitwell (Oxford, 1913), no. 313.

36. BL, Additional MS 38816, Miscellaneous volume including charters of St Mary's abbey, York, ff. 21-22; Dugdale, *Monasticon Anglicanum*, volume III, p. 547; *Early Yorkshire charters, volume I*, p. 265. The charter, whose authenticity is, as we have seen, problematic, was witnessed by Count Alan, who died in 1093 (see below, part 2, note 15). Thompson ascribed it to the second year of William II's reign, i.e. 1088–89, but refers to this as '1090' (Thompson, *The history and antiquities of Boston*, p.461); Harden gives it as 1089 (*Medieval Boston*, p. 9) ; and Owen dates it to 1091 (Owen, 'The beginnings of the port of Boston', p. 42). For later royal confirmations, see BL, Additional MS 38816, Miscellaneous

volume including charters of St Mary's abbey, York, ff. 23, 25v; *Monasticon Anglicanum*, volume III, pp. 548-50; *Early Yorkshire charters, volume I*, p. 270; *CChR 1300–26*, p. 113; *CPR 1301–07*, p. 488 (for the text of the latter, see TNA, Patent Rolls, C.66/128, m. 41).

37. *Early Yorkshire charters, volume I*, pp. 265, 269-70; *Early Yorkshire charters, volume IV*, pp. 3, 10; CChR 1300–26, p. 113; *Liber feodorum*, volume I, p. 195; *Liber feodorum*, volume II, pp. 1010, 1477; Owen, 'The beginnings of the port of Boston', p. 42.

38. *Early Yorkshire charters, volume IV*, pp. 3-4.

39. *CPR 1476–85*, pp. 182, 230, 241; *CCR 1476–85*, nos. 733, 734, 741; *Rotuli parliamentorum*, six volumes; London, 1783), volume VI, pp. 209-15; G. O'Malley, *The Knights Hospitaller of the English langue, 1460–1565* (Oxford, 2010), pp. 75, 139.

40. *Rotuli Hugonis de Welles, episcopi Lincolniensis, A.D. MCCIX–MCCXXXV, volume III*, ed, ed. F. N. Davies (LRS, 9 (1914)), p. 164.

41. Stukeley, *Itinerarium curiosum*, volume I, p. 31; Thompson, *The history and antiquities of Boston*, pp. 161n., 168; Jebb, *A guide to the church of St Botolph*, p. 33.

42. L. Monckton, '"The beste and fayrest of al Lincolnshire": the parish church of St Botolph, Boston', in Badham and Cockerham, *'The beste and fayrest of al Lincolnshire'*, pp. 29-48, at pp. 34-5.

43. Sawyer, *Anglo-Saxon Lincolnshire*, p. 198; Cope-Faulkner *et al.*, *Boston town historic environment baseline study*, p. 7; E. Gillett and K. A. MacMahon, *The early history of Hull* (Oxford, 1980), p. 1.

44. *The Lincolnshire Domesday*, 12/67, 29/33. Some of the tenants on the land of Wido de Croun in Wyberton should perhaps also be added to this total (see below, section 2.6).

45. A. Hinde, *England's population: a history since the Domesday survey* (London, 2003), pp. 16-19, 66-9.

46. *The Lincolnshire Domesday*, 12/60, 12/63-79; A. Williams, 'Ralph the Staller, earl of East Anglia (d. 1068x70)', *Oxford Dictionary of National Biography*, Oxford University Press, 2004 [http://www. oxforddnb.com/view/article/52354, accessed 7 June 2016].

47. H. C. Darby, Domesday England (Cambridge, 1977), p. 289; J. McDonald and G. D. Snooks, *Domesday economy: a new approach to Anglo-Norman history* (Oxford, 1986), p. 19; R. H. C. Davis, *The early history of Coventry* (Dugdale Society Occasional Papers, 24 (1976)), pp. 17-18; Goddard, *Lordship and medieval urbanization*, pp. 29-31. For a more optimistic view of the Domesday evidence about towns see D. Roffe, *Decoding Domesday* (Woodbridge, 2007), pp. 111-12, 118-19.

48. *The Lincolnshire Domesday*, 12/67.

49. C. Platt, *The English medieval town* (London, 1976), p. 21; Reynolds, *An introduction to the history of English medieval towns*, pp. 43, 72; R. H. Britnell, 'The economy of English towns, 600–1300', in Palliser, *The Cambridge urban history*, volume I, pp. 58-69; D. Nicholas, *The growth of the medieval city: from late antiquity to the early fourteenth century* (London, 1997), pp. 57-64, 67-8, 110. For a recent, alternative view of the impact of the Norman Conquest see C. Eisenberg, *The rise of market society in England, 1066–1800* (New York, 2013), pp. 5, 23-35, 118. For the earlier debate on the Conquest and urbanisation, see the critique of Carl Stephenson's views in J. Tait, *The medieval English borough: studies on its origins and constitutional history* (Manchester, 1936), pp. 68-108, 130-8.

50. F. M. Stenton, *The first century of English feudalism, 1066–1166* (Oxford, 1932), p. 26; Carus-Wilson, 'The medieval trade of the ports of the Wash', p. 182.

51. *The complete peerage*, volume X, pp. 786, 788, 791, 794. For Breton connections see *Sibton abbey cartularies and charters*, ed. P. Brown (four parts, Suffolk Records Society, Suffolk Charters, 7-10 (1985-88), part I, p. 83; part IV, p. 3; *Early Yorkshire charters, volume IV*, pp. ix-x, 78; *Early Yorkshire charters, volume V: the honour of Richmond, part II*, ed. C. T. Clay (Yorkshire Archaeological Society, Record Series, extra series 2 (1936)), pp. 351-2.

52. *Early Yorkshire charters, volume IV*, pp. 35-8; *The complete peerage*, volume X, pp. 791-3; M. Jones, 'Conan (IV), duke of Brittany (c.1135–1171)', *Oxford Dictionary of National Biography*, online edition [http://www.oxforddnb.com/view/article/59576, accessed 13 Oct 2015]. On the loyalty of the Bretons to their *patria* see Keats-Rohan, 'William I and the Breton contingent in the non-Norman Conquest, 1066–1987', p. 159.

53. For Villeneuve see *The charters of Duchess Constance of Brittany and her family, 1171–1221*, eds J. Everard and M. Jones (Woodbridge, 1999), p. 79; *Early Yorkshire charters, volume IV*, p. 78; M. Jones, 'Constance, duchess of Brittany (c.1161–1201)', *Oxford Dictionary of National Biography*, online edition [http://www.oxforddnb.com/view/article/46701, accessed 24 July 2015]. For confirmations that the abbey of Villeneuve should receive these payments, some of which specify that they were to be made from the issues of the fair, rather than merely at the time of the fair, see *Rotuli literarum clausarum in Turri Londinensi asservati*, ed. T. D. Hardy (two volumes; London, 1833, 1844), volume I, pp. 141, 215, 363, 392, 418. For Bégard see *The complete peerage*, volume X, p. 787; *The charters of Duchess Constance*, pp. 74-5; *Rotuli literarum clausarum*, volume I pp. 418, 498, 543; *Rotuli literarum clausarum*, volume II (London, 1844), pp. 128, 184; Jones, 'Conan (IV), duke of Brittany (c.1135–1171)'. See also J. A. Everard, *Brittany and the Angevins: province and empire, 1158–1203* (Oxford, 2000), pp. 150-1.

54. 'Ingulfi Croylandensis Historia', in *Rerum Anglicarum scriptorum veterum*, Volume I, ed. W. Fulman (Oxford, 1684), p. 101; *Ingulph's chronicle of the abbey of Croyland with the continations of Peter of Blois and anonymous writers*, ed. H. T. Riley (London, 1854), p. 208.

55. Owen, 'The beginnings of the port of Boston', p. 43.

56. Dover, *The early medieval history of Boston*, p. 21; Sawyer, *Anglo-Saxon Lincolnshire*, p. 198; Rigby, 'Medieval Boston', p. 9; S. Letters, *et al.*, eds, *Gazetteer of markets and fairs in England and Wales to 1516* (two parts: List and Index Society, Special Series, 32-3, (2003)), part I, p. 212; P. Fleet, 'Markets in medieval Lincolnshire', *East Midland Historian*, 3 (1993), pp. 7-14, at p. 12; Summerson, 'Calamity and commerce', p. 147. For the text of the charter see *Early Yorkshire charters, volume IV*, pp. 8-11; *Monasticon Anglicanum*, volume III, p. 547.

57. *The complete peerage, volume VI: N to R*, by G. E. C[okayne] (first edtion; London, 1895), p. 344; M. Maynard, 'Honour and castle of Richmond', in W. Page, ed., *The Victoria county history of the county of York: North Riding*, volume I (London, 1914), pp. 1-16, at p. 2; *Early Yorkshire charters, volume IV*, pp. 10-11, 84-8; *The complete peerage*, volume X (new edition), pp. 786-7.

58. Everard, *Brittany and the Angevins*, p. 189; Keats-Rohan, 'The Bretons and the Normans of England, 1066–1154', pp. 48, 70. A date of 1138 or earlier for this charter means that the fair was not founded 'in 1200' (E. Lipson, *The economic history of England, volume I: the Middle Ages* (eleventh edition; London, 1956), p. 231; *Records of early english drama: Lincolnshire*, volume II, ed. J. Stokes (Toronto, 2009), p. 386). The annual fair referred to in Count Stephen's charter should be distinguished from the town's weekly market (Cope-Faulkner, *et al.*, *Boston town historic env5ronent baseline study*, p. 9).

59. *Early Yorkshire charters, volume IV*, p. 10. See also the confirmation of the abbey's liberties in the time of the fair by the bishop of Lincoln, dated dated 1161x1166 (*English episcopal acta, 1: Lincoln 1067–1185*, ed. D. M. Smith (Oxford, 1980), no. 284).

60. 'Petri Blesensis Continuatio', p. 126; *Ingulph's Chronicle*, p. 261. The chronicle and its continuations date from the late fourteenth or fifteenth centuries but draw on earlier sources. For an assessment of their reliability see D. Roffe, 'The *Historia Croylandensis*: a plea for reassessment', *EHR*, 110 (1995), pp. 95-108.

61. A. F. L. Beeston, 'Idrisi's account of the British Isles', *Bulletin of the School of African and Oriental Studies*, 13 (1950), pp. 265-81, at pp. 277-9; K. Miller, *Mappa Arabicae*, volume II (Stuttgart, 1927), p. 146. I am grateful to Caitlin Green and Neil Wright for drawing my attention to this source.

## PART TWO: LORDSHIP AND TOPOGRAPHY

1. Minnis *et al.*, *Boston, Lincolnshire*, pp. 13-20; Ditchfield, 'Proceedings of the congress', pp. 51-2; N. Pevsner, J. Harris and N. Antram, *The buildings of England: Lincolnshire* (second edition; London, 1989), p. 159. For the Dominicans in Boston, see note 54, below.

2. T. Williamson, *England's landscape: East Anglia* (London, 2006), pp. 18-12; Molyneux and Wright, *An atlas of Boston*, pp. 2-7; N. Wright, *Boston: a pictorial history* (Chichester, 1994), p. 1; Wright, *Boston: a history and celebration*, pp. 10-11; N. R. Wright, *The book of Boston* (Buckingham, 1986), pp. 12-14; A. Mattinson, 'Topography and society in Boston, 1086-1400' (Unpublished University of Nottingham M.Phil. thesis, 1996), pp. 12-19. For Saxton, see *Christopher Saxton's 16th century maps: the counties of England and Wales*, ed. W. Ravenhill (Shrewsbury, 1992), pp. 72-3; *Saxton's survey of*

*England and Wales with a facsimile of Saxton's wall map of 1583*, ed. R. A. Skelton (Amsterdam, 1974), pp. 8, 11, 18.

3. *Historia Anglicanae scriptores, X* (London, 1652), column 1117; *Chronicon Petroburgense*, ed T. Stapleton (Camden Society, 1849), p. 4; *Historiae Anglicanae scriptores varii et codicibus manuscriptis nunc primum editi* (London, 1723), p. 83; H. E. Hallam, *Settlement and society: a study of the early agrarian history of south Lincolnshire* (Cambridge, 1965), p. 126. For later floods, see *Ibid.*, pp. 127-32 and *The big dig*, pp. 21, 28.

4. *The Boston assembly minutes, 1545-1575*, ed. P. Clark and J. Clark (L.R.S., 77 (1986)), nos 498, 517; A. Young, *General view of the agriculture of Lincolnshire* (second edition; London, 1813), pp. 16-17; Marrat, *The history of Lincolnshire*, volume I, pp. 77-8; Thompson, *The history and antiquities of Boston*, pp. 66-7, 96-99, 102, 666-73, 787.

5. *CPR 1327-30*, p. 182; A. G. Little, 'Black friars of Boston', in Page, *The Victoria history of the county of Lincoln*, volume II, p. 214.

6. *The itinerary of John Leland in or about the years 1535-1543, parts I-III*, ed. L. Toulmin Smith (London, 1907), p. 29; *The itinerary of John Leland in or about the years 1535-1543, parts IX, X, XI*, ed. L. Toulmin Smith (London, 1910), p. 34. For the date of Leland's visit, see John Chandler, 'Introduction' in *John Leland's Itinerary: travels in Tudor England* (Stroud, 1993), pp. xi-xxxvi, at p. xxx.

7. *CPR 1301-07*, p. 322; *Records of the parliament holden at Westminster on the twenty-eighth day of February in the thirty-third year of the reign of King Edward I (A.D. 1305)*, ed. F. W. Maitland (London: Rolls Series, 1893), p. 94; Thompson, *The history and antiquities of Boston*, p. 249; M. W. Barley, 'Lincolnshire rivers in the Middle Ages', *Architectural and Archaeological Society of Lincolnshire, Reports and Papers*, volume I, part I (1936), pp. 1-21; Wright, *Boston: a history and celebration*, p. 13; Beresford, *New towns*, p. 464.

8. SBHAO, Cartulary of St Bartholomew's Hospital, SBHB.HC.2/1, f. 593; SBHAO, St Bartholomew's Hospital Deeds, SBHB.HC.1, no. 875; *Cartulary of St Bartholomew's Hospital*, no. 1665. Owen claims that the existence of the bridge is shown by an '1191' grant by Roger, son of William Huntingfield, of plot of land at 'Bridgend' in Boston to Alexander the Clerk (Owen 'The beginnings of the port of Boston', pp. 43, 44) but this grant was actually made in 1291 (LAO, 3 ANC 2/1, Huntingfield cartulary, f. 1). On the Huntingfield cartulary, see *Lincolnshire Archives Committee, Archivists' Report*, no. 7 (1955-56), pp. 23-7). For a calendar of the cartulary, see Reading University Library, RUL MS 1148/14/14.

9. SBHAO, Cartulary of St Bartholomew's Hospital, SBHB.HC.2/1, f. 593v-594; SBHAO, St Bartholomew's Hospital Deeds, SBHB.HC.1, no. 307; *Cartulary of St Bartholomew's Hospital*, no. 1668. On Bridge Street, see also page 41, above.

10. Harden, *Medieval Boston*, p. 20.

11. Thompson, *The history and antiquities of Boston*, pp. 249-53; *The itinerary of John Leland, parts IX, X and XI*, p. 34; Molyneux and Wright, *An atlas of Boston*, pp. 14-15. For the building of the 1500 sluice, see M. Jones, 'Lady Margaret Beaufort, the royal council and an early fenland drainage scheme', *Lincolnshire History and Archaeology*, 21 (1986), pp. 11-18.

12. *Liber feodorum*, volume II, p. 1010. See also *Ibid.*, pp. 1477-8.

13. *Liber feodorum*, volume I, p. 195.

14. *Liber feodorum*, volume II, p. 1010.

15. Alan Rufus's death has traditionally been assigned to 1089 and Alan Niger's to 1093 but 1093 and 1098 now seem the more likely dates (*The complete peerage*, volume X, p. 785; I. J. Sanders, *English baronies: a study of their origin and descent, 1086-1327* (Oxford, 1960), p. 140; Keats-Rohan, 'Alan Rufus (*d.* 1093)'; Keats-Rohan, *Domesday people*, pp. 127-8; Keats-Rohan, 'Le rôle des Bretons dans la colonisation normande de l'Angleterre', p. 189).

16. See part 1, notes 56-8.

17. *The charters of Duchess Constance*, p. 33; *The complete peerage*, volume X, p. 788-9; *Early Yorkshire charters, volume IV*, p. 100. Strictly speaking, therefore, Alan Rufus, who granted St Botolph's church

to St Mary's abbey, was not the 'earl of Richmond' even though he was lord of the honour (Owen, 'The beginnings of the port of Boston', p. 42; Thompson, *The history and antiquities of Boston*, p. 461; Minnis *et al.*, *Boston, Lincolnshire*, p. 5).

18. *The complete peerage*, volume X, pp. 788, 791; Jones, 'Conan (IV), duke of Brittany (*c*.1135–1171)'; *Ancient charters, royal and private, prior to A.D.1200, part 1*, ed. J. H. Round (Pipe Roll Society, 1888), pp. 54, 56; *Pipe Roll, 22 Henry II*, p. 121; *Pipe Roll, 24 Henry II*, p. 23; *Pipe Roll, 3 Richard I*, p. 191.

19. *The complete peerage*, volume X, pp. 794-6; *The complete peerage*, volume III, p. 168; *The charters of Duchess Constance*, *passim*; Jones, 'Constance, duchess of Brittany (*c*.1161–1201)'; Y. Hilton, 'La Bretagne et la rivalité Capétiens-Plantagenets. *Un exemple: la duchesse Constance* (1186-1202)', *Annales de Bretagne*, 92 (1985), pp. 111-44; R. Eales, 'Ranulf (III) , sixth earl of Chester and first earl of Lincoln (1170–1232)', *Oxford Dictionary of National Biography*, online edition http://www.oxforddnb.com/view/article/2716, accessed 27 July 2015]; A. L. Poole, *From Domesday Book to Magna Carta, 1087-1216* (second edition; Oxford 1955), p. 337n; Sanders, *English baronies*, p. 140; Everard, *Brittany and the Angevins*, pp. 29-33, 39-43, 93-100, 130-40, 150-1, 157-8, 171-2. Constance was not the 'duchess of Richmond' (S. M. Johns, *Noblewomen, aristocracy and power in the twelfth-century Anglo-Norman realm* (Manchester, 2003), p. 66).

20. See, for instance, *The charters of Duchess Constance*, p. 118.

21. *The charters of Duchess Constance*, pp. 109-11; M. Jones, 'Arthur, duke of Brittany (1187–1203)', *Oxford Dictionary of National Biography*, online edition [http://www.oxforddnb.com/view/article/704, accessed 27 July 2015]; Everard, *Brittany and the Angevins*, pp. 153-4, 157, 169-75.

22. *Pipe Roll, 2 John*, p. 88.

23. *The charters of Duchess Constance*, pp. 111, 135; *Rotuli litterarum patentium in Turri Londinensi asservati*, volume I, part I, ed. T. D. Hardy (London, 1835), pp. 4, 27; Everard, *Brittany and the Angevins*, pp. 172-5.

24. *Rotuli litterarum patentium*, volume I, part I, pp. 34, 47, 105; *The complete peerage*, volume VII, p. 535; D. Crouch, 'Breteuil, Robert de, fourth earl of Leicester (*d.* 1204)', *Oxford Dictionary of National Biography*, online edition [http://www.oxforddnb.com/view/article/47202, accessed 5 Aug 2015].

25. *The charters of Duchess Constance*, pp. 149, 153, 164-5, 171; M. Jones, 'Eleanor, *suo jure* duchess of Brittany (1182x4–1241)', *Oxford Dictionary of National Biography*, online edition [http://www.oxforddnb.com/view/article/46702, accessed 5 Aug 2015].

26. *The charters of Duchess Constance*, pp. 166-72.

27. *The charters of Duchess Constance, 1171-1221*, pp. 100, 166; *Rotuli litterarum patentium*, volume I, part I, p. 152; *CPR 1216-25*, pp. 68, 96, 120, 158, 197; S. Painter, *The scourge of the clergy: Peter of Dreux, duke of Brittany* (Baltimore, 1937), pp. 9, 12, 14-15; *Rotuli litterarum clausarum*, volume I, p. 350.

28. *Rolls of the justices in eyre, being the rolls of pleas and assizes for Lincolnshire, 1218-19, and Worcestershire, 1221*, ed. D. M. Stenton (Selden Society, 53 (1934)), pp. l-li; *CPR 1216-25*, p. 174; *Calendar of fine rolls of the reign of Henry III preserved in The National Archives, volume I: 1 to 8 Henry III*, eds P. Dryburgh and B. Hartland (Woodbridge, 2007), p. 57; *Registrum honoris de Richmond*, ed. R. Gale (London, 1722), appendix, pp. 107-8; Painter, *The scourge of the clergy*, pp. 16-17; *Rotuli litterarum clausarum*, volume I, pp. 360, 361, 379, 394, 404, 418; *Rotuli litterarum clausarum*, volume II, pp. 121,128.

29. *The complete peerage*, volume X, pp. 802-3; Maynard, 'Honour and castle of Richmond', pp. 5-6; *Rotuli litterarum clausarum*, volume I, p. 566; *Rotuli litterarum clausarum*, volume II, pp. 4, 26, 36, 186, 202; *CPR 1232-47*, pp. 96, 176; *CCR 1227-31*, pp. 224, 410-11; Painter, *The scourge of the clergy*, pp. 33-6, 41-2, 47-8, 65, 87-9.

30. *The complete peerage*, volume X, pp. 805-7; *CChR 1226-57*, p. 252; *CPR 1232-47*, p. 251; N. Vincent, 'Savoy, Peter of, count of Savoy and de facto earl of Richmond (1203?–1268)', *Oxford Dictionary of National Biography*, online edition [http://www.oxforddnb.com/view/article/22016, accessed 5 Aug 2015]; Sanders, *English baronies*, pp. 120, 141; E. L. Cox, *The eagles of Savoy: the house of Savoy in thirteenth-century Europe* (Princeton, 1974), pp. 107-9].

31. Molyneux and Wright, *An atlas of Boston*, pp. 14-15, 20; Rylatt, *Report on a programme of archaeological fieldwork*, p. 5.

32. Wright, *Boston: a history and celebration*, pp. 13-15. For places where the line of the Barditch is problematic, see Minnis *et al.*, *Boston, Lincolnshire*, pp. 6-7.

33. *The Boston assembly minutes*, no. 592; Thompson, *The history and antiquities of Boston*, p. 241.

34. *CChR 1226-57*, p. 259; *Chartulary of Fountains*, volume I, pp. 116, 121. For Deppol, see also Thompson, *The history and antiquities of Boston*, p. 43.

35. BL, Cotton MS Vespasian E.XX, Cartulary of Bardney abbey, f. 238. This grant does not mention 'abbot Walter' (Owen, 'The beginnings of the port of Boston', p. 45). See also the reference to the 'Barredich' in the confirmation of Eudo's grant by Robert de Tattershall (BL, Cotton MS Vespasian E.XX, Cartulary of Bardney abbey, f. 238-238v). For other late twelfth- and thirteenth-century references to the Barditch (le barredik', 'la Barredic', 'Barredyk', 'fossatum barre'), see BL Cotton MS Faustina B.I, Cartulary of Barlings Abbey, f. 66v; BL Cotton MS Vespasian E.XVIII, Cartulary of Kirkstead abbey, ff. 182v-184v; LAO, 3 ANC 2/1, Huntingfield cartulary, ff. 28, 30v, 31, 32v, 34v; Owen, 'The beginnings of the port of Boston', pp. 44-5; JRLM, Latin MS 221, Cartulary of St Mary's abbey, f. 385; *Transcripts of the charters relating to the Gilbertine houses of Sixle, Ormsby, Catley, Bullington and Alvingham*, ed. F. M. Stenton (L.R.S., 18 (1920)), p. 99; *The Registrum Antiquissimum of the cathedral church of Lincoln, part VII*, ed. K. Major (L.R.S., 46, 1950)), p. 26; *Chartulary of Fountains*, volume I, pp. 115-17.

36. Owen, 'The beginnings of the port of Boston', p. 43; D. M. Wilson and J. G. Hurst, 'Medieval Britain in 1960', *Medieval Archaeology*, 5 (1961), pp. 309-39, at p. 323. See also Wright, *Boston: a pictorial history*, p. 2.

37. M. W. Barley, 'Town defences in England and Wales after 1066', in M. W. Barley, ed., *The plans and topography of medieval towns in England and Wales* (Council for British Archaeology Research Report no., 14 (1976)), pp. 57-71, at p. 60; *The big dig*, p. 4.

38. *CChR 1327-41*, p. 416; G. Harden. 'Four dagger sheaths from the Barditch, Boston', *Lincolnshire History and Archaeology*, 18 (1983), pp. 108-110, at p. 110.

39. *The Boston assembly minutes*, no. 429.

40. L. Butler, 'The evolution of towns: planted towns after 1066', in Barley, *The plans and topography of medieval towns*, pp. 32-48 at pp. 42, 46.

41. C. Platt, 'The evolution of towns: natural growth', in Barley, *The plans and topography of medieval towns*, pp. 48-56, at p. 55; *Early Yorkshire charters, volume IV*, p. 10.

42. Platt, 'The evolution of towns', p. 56; J. W. F. Hill, *Medieval Lincoln* (Stamford, 1990; first published 1948), p. 147; J. Hutchinson and D. M. Palliser, *York* (Edinburgh, 1980), p. 32; J. Barrow, 'Urban planning', in J. Crick and E. Van Houts, eds, *A social history of England, 900-1200* (Cambridge, 2011), pp. 188-97, at p. 196. See also below, notes 134-5.

43. *CChR 1300-26*, pp. 122-3. A grant of a market to Crowland abbey in 1257 related to the abbey's Lincolnshire manor of Baston, not to Boston ('Boston, Lincolnshire', in *Encyclopedia Britannica, Volume IV*, p. 290; *CChR 1226-57*, p. 476), a similarity of spelling which has generated confusion on other occasions.

44. J. Davis, *Medieval market morality: life, law and ethics in the medieval marketplace, 1200-1500* (Cambridge, 2012), pp. 44, 279-80, 285.

45. *Transcripts of the charters relating to the Gilbertine houses*, pp. 109-10; J. E. Redford, 'An edition of the cartulary of Alvingham priory (Oxford, Bodleian Library Laud Misc. 642)' (Unpublished University of York Ph.D. thesis, 2010), pp. 64, 1060-63. This reference is earlier than the first reference (from 1241) to a market at Boston given in Letters, *et al.*, *Gazetteer of markets and fairs*, part I, p. 212, on the basis of *CChR 1226-57*, p. 259. Transcriptions of some of the deeds of St Bartholomew's Hospital, London, from the early thirteenth century, sent by 'Miss Stokes' to M. W. Barley in 1957, which are preserved at the Lincolnshire Archives Office, include a number of references to the 'marketplace' in Boston (LAO, MCD 234, Notes on the deeds of St Bartholomew's Hospital, London, relating to Boston, nos 212, 307, 624, 875) but the deeds themselves refer to the '*nundine*' (i.e., to the fair) of Boston (SBHAO, Cartulary of St Bartholomew's Hospital, SBHB.HC.2/1, ff. 591v-594; SBHAO, St Bartholomew's Hospital Deeds, SBHB.HC.1, nos 57; 212; 307; 1320. For Reiner of Waxham, see also part 4, note 23, below.

46. See below, section 4.1.

47. For the importance of seigneurial initiative in town foundations and layouts, see Goddard, *Lordship and medieval urbanization*, pp. 3, 43-5, 90, 290-2 and T. R. Slater, 'Lordship, economy and society in English medieval marketplaces', in A. Simms and H. B. Clarke, eds, *Lords and towns in medieval Europe: the European Historic Towns Atlas project* (Farnham, 2015), pp. 213-31, at pp. 214-5.

48. Beresford, *New towns*, pp. 149-61; Butler, 'The evolution of towns', pp. 32-45; A. E. J. Morris, *History of urban form before the industrial revolution* (third edition; Harlow, 1994), p. 102.

49. Thompson, *The history and antiquities of Boston*, pp. 207, 211; *The Boston assembly minutes*, nos 397, 748, 808; Wright, *The Book of Boston*, p. 27.

50. BL, Cotton MS Claudius D.XI, Register of Malton priory, f. 216; Owen, 'The beginnings of the port of Boston', p. 45; R. Gurnham, *The story of Boston* (Stroud, 2014), p. 17; Thompson, *The history and antiquities of Boston*, p. 211; R. Thorpe, *Excavations at Wormgate, Boston, Lincolnshire* (1989) (*Library of Unpublished Fieldwork Reports* [data-set]. York: Archaeology Data Service [distributor] (doi:10.5284/1012869)). For Deppol, see also above, note 34. Golding reads 'Wrmgate' as 'Wrinegate' (B. Golding, *Gilbert of Sempringham and the Gilbertine order, c.1130-c.1300* (Oxford, 1995), p. 440).

51. *Registrum Antiquissimum, part VII*, pp. 21-3, 26. As late as 1531, Stephen Woodhouse of Boston bequeathed a house in Bargate in the 'Horse Market' to his wife (*Lincoln wills registered in the diocesan probate at Lincoln, volume III: A.D. 1530 to 1532*, ed. C. W. Foster (L.R.S., 24 (1930)), p. 161).

52. Barrow, 'Urban planning', p. 191; Minnis *et al.*, *Boston, Lincolnshire*, p. 12; Molyneux and Wright, *An atlas of Boston*, pp. 19, 21, 23; . H. Shinn, *Boston through time* (Stroud, 2014), pp. 52-3.

53. The Franciscans arrived in England in 1224 (J. Röhrkasten, 'The origin and development of the London mendicant houses', in T. R. Slater and G. Rosser, eds, *The church in the medieval town* (Aldershot, 1998), pp. 76-99, at p. 77), but the earliest reference to the Boston Franciscans comes in 1268 (*Placitorum in domo capitulari Westmonastriensi asservatorum abbreviatio, temporibus regum Ric. I, Johann., Henr. III, Edw. I, Edw. II* (London, 1811), p. 176).

54. The Dominicans were in England from 1221 (Röhrkasten, 'The origin and development of the London mendicant houses', p. 77), but we first hear of them in Boston only in 1288, when their friary was destroyed in the great fire of that year (*The chronicle of Bury St Edmunds*, ed. A. Gransden (London, 1964), p. 91; S. Moorhouse, 'Finds in the refectory at the Dominican friary, Boston', *Lincolnshire History and Archaeology*, 7 (1972), pp. 21-53).

55. The order of Austin friars was formed in 1256 although one of its predecessors, the Hermits of St Augustine, had arrived in England in 1249 (Röhrkasten, 'The origin and development of the London mendicant houses', p. 79). Land in London was donated to the Austins in aid of the foundation of their Boston house in 1316 (*CIM*, volume II, no. 833) and in November 1317 this house was described as having been recently built (TNA, Inquisitions Post-Mortem, C.133/130/8; *CPR 1313-17*, p. 607; *Calendar of Patent Rolls 1317-21*, pp. 79, 326; *CCR 1318-23*, pp. 124-5). Although it was located in the southern part of the town, its exact site has been the subject of some disagreement, see Cope-Faulkner *et al.*, *Boston town historic environment baseline study*, p. 10.

56. Wright, *The book of Boston*, p. 28. For the Boston friaries, see the articles by A. G. Little in Page, *The Victoria history of the county of Lincoln*, volume II, pp. 213-7 and D. O'Sullivan, *In the company of preachers: the archaeology of medieval friaries in England and Wales* (Leicester Archaeology Monograph, no. 23 (2013)), pp. 53-57. For the location of the houses, see Harden, *Medieval Boston*, pp. 18, 22-5; Thompson, *The history and Antiquities of Boston*, pp. 108-9, 111-12; LHER, MLI12695, The Augustinian friary at Boston. For the Carmelites in Boston, see note 133, below. For other friaries built on the edge of the built-up area of medieval towns, see N. Baker and R. Holt, *Urban growth and the medieval church: Gloucester and Worcester* (Aldershot, 2005), pp. 315-6.

57. LHER, MLI89035, Occupation deposits at South Square, Boston.

58. Molyneux and Wright, *An atlas of Boston*, pp. 19, 23.

59. Gurnham, *The story of Boston*, p. 17; B. Ayers, 'Cities, cogs and commerce: archaeological approaches to the material culture of the North Sea world', in D. Bates and R. Liddiard, eds, *East Anglia and its North Sea world in the Middle Ages* (Woodbridge, 2013), pp. 63-81, at p. 68.

60.  *CCR 1279-88*, p. 154; *The chronicle of St Mary's abbey, York*, p. 20. This may be the fire which Walter of Guisborough's chronicle dates to 1281 (*The chronicle of Walter of Guisborough previously edited as the chronicle of Walter of Hemingford or Hemingburgh*, ed. H. Rothwell (Camden Society, third series, 89 (1957)), pp. 217-8).

61.  For the 1288 fire, see Summerson, 'Calamity and commerce', pp. 146-65. For other references to the fire and its aftermath, see Rigby, 'Boston and Grimsby in the Middle Ages', p. 201.

62.  For other examples of plots which were 24 feet wide, see BL, Harley MS 742, Cartulary of Spalding priory, f. 244v; *Chartulary of Fountains*, volume I, pp. 114, 117; BL, Cotton MS Vespasian E.XX, Cartulary of Bardney abbey, ff. 239, 239v; LAO, 3 ANC 2/1, Huntingfield cartulary, ff. 1, 27, 27v.

63.  LAO, 3 ANC 2/1, Huntingfield cartulary, ff. 28-28v; Owen, 'The beginnings of the port of Boston'. p. 44.

64.  Thompson, *Collections for a topographical and historical account of Boston*, p. 32; Thompson, *The history and antiquities of Boston*, pp. 43-4; Beresford, *New towns*, p. 464; Jebb, *A guide to the church of S. Botolph*, pp. 9-10; Lambert and Walker, *Boston, Tattershall and Croyland*, pp. 30, 33; A. M. Cook, *Boston (Botolph's Town)* (second edition; Boston, 1948), p. 20; Dover, *The early medieval history of Boston*, pp. 12-13; G. S. Bagley, *Boston: its story and people* (Boston, 1986), p. 6; B. P. Hindle, *Medieval town plans* (Prince Risborough, 1990), p. 35; *Records of early English drama: Lincolnshire*, volume II, p. 385; Gurnham, *The story of Boston*, pp. 16-17; LHER, MLI12644, Barditch and Bargate, Boston; *The big dig*, p. 4. Beresford and St Joseph state both that Boston 'lacked substantial defences' and that town walls were placed alongside the Barditch from 1285 (Beresford and St Joseph, *Medieval England*, pp. 191, 218).

65.  TNA, Patent Rolls, C.66/104, m. 20; *CPR 1281-92*, p. 165. For an earlier grant of pavage, see *CPR 1272-81*, p. 462.

66.  For claims that the western side of Boston was walled, see above, page 26.

67.  Beeston, 'Idrisi's account of the British Isles', pp. 277-80 (I am grateful to Mustapha Sheikh for advice on the translation of this source); C. Green, 'Islamic gold dinars in eleventh- and twelfth-century England', http://www.caitlingreen.org/2016/04/islamic-gold-dinars-anglo-norman.html; Minnis *et al.*, *Boston, Lincolnshire*, pp. 4, 6; Millea, *The Gough Map*, pp. 66-7.

68.  *Archaeological watching brief and survey report: 3 New Street, Boston, Lincolnshire*, p.12; H. L. Turner, *Town defences in England and Wales: an architectural and documentary study, A.D. 900-1500* (London, 1971), pp. 118, 126-9; Barley 'Town defences', pp. 58, 60; Beresford and St Joseph, *Medieval England*, p. 191; D. M. Palliser, 'Town defences in medieval England and Wales', in D. M. Palliser, *Towns and local communities in medieval and early modern England* (Aldershot, 2006), V: 105-21, at pp. 107, 109; *The making of King's Lynn*, pp. 21-2

69.  Wilson and Hurst, 'Medieval Britain in 1960', p. 323; D. M. Wilson and J. G. Hurst, 'Medieval Britain in 1957', *Medieval Archaeology*, 2 (1958), pp. 183-213, at p. 200. See also the evidence of walls along the line of the Barditch, which were associated with twelfth- or early thirteenth century pottery, at the northern end of the Barditch circuit, in New Street, although these could be the remains of a high-status building (LHER, MLI12644, Barditch and Bargate, Boston; LHER, MLI13360, Medieval remains, 3 New Street, Boston; *Archaeological watching brief and survey report: 3 New Street, Boston, Lincolnshire* (*Library of Unpublished Fieldwork Reports* [data-set]. York: Archaeology Data Service [distributor] (doi:10.5284/1015283)).

70.  Rylatt, *Report on a programme of archaeological fieldwork*, pp. 6-7.

71.  Wheeler, *A history of the fens*, p. 67; *The Boston assembly minutes*, nos. 322, 444, 589-82.

72.  Beresford, *New towns*, pp. 61, 125-30, 332-6; Britnell, 'The economy of English towns', p. 107; M. Maynard, 'The borough of Richmond', in Page, *The Victoria county history of the county of York: North Riding*, volume I, pp. 17-35, at p. 24;

73.  *The Boston assembly minutes*, no. 633.

74.  Thompson, *The history and antiquities of Boston*, pp. 39, 318. See also Allen, *The history of the county of Lincoln*, volume I, p. 215. Boston is also given as the location of Ranulf's castle in the printed editions of Knighton's chronicle in *Historia Anglicanae scriptores, X*, column 2430 and *Chronicon*

*Henrici Knighton vel Cnitthon, monachi Leycestrensis*, volume I, ed. J. R Lumby (London: Rolls Series, 1889), pp. 209-10.

75. *A summarie of the chronicles of England, diligently collected, abridged and continued unto this present yere of Christ, 1598 by John Stow* (London, 1598), p. 89; *Annales or a general chronicle of England, begun by John Stow: continued and augmented with matters foraigne and domestique, ancient and moderne, unto the end of this present yeere, 1631, by Edmund Howes, gent.* (London, 1631), p. 172. The construction of Beeston Castle actually began in 1225 (P. Morgan, 'Medieval settlement and society', in A. D. M. Phillips and C. B. Phillips, *A new historical atlas of Cheshire* (Chester, 2002), pp. 32-3, at p. 32). For the complicated relationship between Ranulph and the honour of Richmond, see *The charters of Duchess Constance, 1171-1221*, pp. 99-100.

76. *Feet of fines of the tenth year of the reign of King Richard I, A.D. 1198 to A.D. 1199* (Pipe Roll Society, 24 (1900)), p. 11; *Early Yorkshire charters, volume V*, pp. 256-7, 316; *CRR* volume IV, p. 181; *CRR* volume V, p. 181; *CRR* volume VI, p. 17; *Placitorum in domo capitulari Westmonastriensi asservatorum abbreviatio*, p. 59.

77. Thompson, *The history and antiquities of Boston*, pp. 63, 238; *Letters and papers, foreign and domestic, of the reign of Henry VIII*, volume 20, part 1, eds J. Gairdner and R. Brodie (London, 1905), no. 846/87. A grammar school had been founded in Boston by 1329. Its original site is unknown. By 1554, there was a grammar school in Wormgate End but a new school was built in the Mart Yard in 1567 (A. F. Leach, 'Boston Grammar School', *Associated Architectural Societies Reports and Papers*, 26/2 (1902), pp. 398-405; Thompson, *The history and antiquities of Boston*, pp. 213, 238-40, 284).

78. Beresford, *New towns*, pp. 130-2, 326-7, 333.

79 Stukeley, *Itinerarium curiosum*, volume I, p. 31; Jebb, *A guide to the church of St Botolph*, pp. 1, 14, 36; Thompson, *The history and antiquities of Boston*, p. 113; Wright, *Boston; a history and celebration*, p. 18; Wright, *The book of Boston*, p. 14; D. M. Owen, *Church and society in medieval Lincolnshire* (Lincoln, 1971), p. 147; G. Platts, *Land and people in medieval Lincolnshire* (Lincoln, 1985), p. 210; N. Bennett, 'Religious houses', in S. Bennett and N. Bennett, eds, *An historical atlas of Lincolnshire* (Hull, 1993), pp. 48-9, at p. 49; Cope-Faulkner *et al.*, *Boston town historic environment baseline study*, pp. 9, 11.

80. Thompson, *The history and antiquities of Boston*, p. 108; Bagley, *Boston*, p. 277; Minnis *et al.*, *Boston, Lincolnshire*, p. 51. Marrat suggested this as the site of one of the Boston hospitals but the reference he cites is probably to St John's, which was located in Skirbeck Road (Marrat, *The history of Lincolnshire*, volume I, p. 34).

81 D. Knowles and R. N. Hadcock, *Medieval religious houses, England and Wales* (second edition; Harlow, 1971), pp. 52, 60; Burton, *The monastic order in Yorkshire*, pp. 4, 43; Hill, *Medieval Lincoln*, pp. 33, 118, 364. Jebb claimed that Leland refers to a priory at Boston but Leland may actually have been referring to the cell of St Mary's Abbey, York, on the east side of Lincoln (Jebb, *A guide to the church of St Botolph*, p. 36; Thompson, *The history and antiquities of Boston*, p. 126; *Joannis Lelandi antiquarii, De rebus Britannicis collectanea*, ed. T. Hearne (six volumes; Oxford, 1715), volume III, p. 33; Hill, *Medieval Lincoln* pp. 338-9).

82. Thompson, *The history and antiquities of Boston*, p. 113; N. Canfield, 'The guilds of St Botolph's', in W. M. Ormrod, ed., *The guilds in Boston* (Boston, 1993), pp. 25-34, at p. 28; Gurnham, *The story of Boston*, p. 52. See also Jebb, *A guide to the church of St Botolph*, p. 14.

83. For Boston's friaries, see above, part 2, notes 53-56, and below, part 2, note 133.

84. *The itinerary of John Leland, parts IX, X, XI*, p. 33. St John's was presumably the 'hospital for poor men' to which Leland also refers (*Ibid.*, p. 34). Pevsner and Harris claim that Boston was a chapel of ease of Skirbeck until the fourteenth century (Pevsner, Harris and Antram, *The buildings of England: Lincolnshire*, p. 153).

85. See note 96, below

86. JRLM, Latin MS 221, Cartulary of St Mary's abbey, f. 385.

87. Thompson, *The history and antiquities of Boston*, pp. 164, 241-; Bagley, *Boston*, pp. 72-3.

88. Molyneux and Wright, *An atlas of Boston*, pp. 14-15; Wright, *The book of Boston*, p. 28.

89. *The register of Henry Burghersh, 1320-1342, volume I,* ed. N. Bennett (L.R.S., 87 (1999)), no. 662; *CPR 1476-85,* pp. 230, 235, 241. See also above, part 1, note 39. The Hospitallers did not possess St John's in 1281 (Wright, *Boston: a history and celebration,* p. 21).

90. Sister Elspeth, 'The hospital of St John the Baptist without Boston', in Page, *The Victoria history of the county of Lincoln,* volume II, p. 233; T. Tanner, *Notitia monastica* (London, 1744), p. 283; Thompson, *The history and antiquities of Boston,* pp. 241-2; Knowles and Hadcock, *Medieval religious houses,* pp. 315, 344. This is much earlier than the date given in M. Jurkowski, N. Ramsay and S. Renton, *English monastic estates, 1066-1540: a list of manors, chapels and churches* (three parts; List and Index Society, special series, 40-42 (2007)), part III, p. 566.

91. *Rotuli Hugonis de Welles, episcopi Lincolniensis, A.D. MCCIX-MCCXXXV,* volume I, ed. W. P. W. Phillimore (L.R.S., 3 (1912)), pp. 115-16, 171-2; *The acta of Hugh of Wells, bishop of Lincoln, 1209-1235,* ed. D. M. Smith (L.R.S., 88 (2000)), no. 103; Rigby, 'Medieval Boston' p. 8; Gurnham, *The story of Boston,* p. 37.

92. S. Watson, 'City as charter: charity and the lordship of English towns, 1170-1250', in C. Goodson, E. Lester and C. Symes, eds, *Cities, texts and social networks: experiences and perceptions of medieval urban space* (Farnham, 2010), pp. 235-62, at pp. 239-40. For the hospital 'outside' Boston, see also *Rotuli hundredorum,* volume I (London, 1812), p. 349. The church of the Hospitallers' Skirbeck house was described as 'juxta Sanctum Botolphum' in 1305 (*The charters of the Cistercian abbey of St Mary of Sallay in Craven,* volume I, ed. J. McNulty, (Yorkshire Archaeological Record Society Record Series, 87 (1933)), no. 251). The unspecified 'hospital' of Boston which is referred to in the 1270s and 1280s could thus be either St Leonard's or St John's (*Registrum honoris de Richmond,* appendix, pp. 32-3; *CIPM,* volume II, p. 217).

93. Tanner, *Notitia monastica,* p. 281; Dugdale, *Monasticon Anglicanum,* volume VI, part II, p. 804; Marrat, *The history of Lincolnshire,* volume I, p. 84; Thompson, *The history and antiquities of Boston,* pp. 466-7; *The Knights Hospitaller in England: being the report of Prior Philip de Thame to the Grand Master, Elyan de Villa Nova for A.D. 1338,* eds L. B. Larking and J. M. Kemble (Camden Society, 65 (1857)), pp. 60-2, 228; *CIPM,* volume VI, no. 331; *CIPM,* volume VII, no. 628; Knowles and Hadcock, *Medieval religious houses,* pp. 300, 306, 392; W. T. Whitley, 'In the palmy days of Boston: the Hospitallers of St John and the men of St Botolph at Skirbeck', *Journal of the British Archaeological Association,* n.s., 37 (1932), pp. 225-42, at pp. 231, 233; *A terrier of Fleet, Lincolnshire, from a manuscript in the British Museum,* ed. N. Neilson (London, 1920), pp. 101-2; *The complete peerage,* volume IX, p. 401; R. V. Turner, *Men raised from the dust: administrative service and upward mobility in Angevin England* (Philadelphia, 1988), p. 187. For Multon, see *Ibid.,* pp. 107-19 and C. L. Kingsford, 'Moulton, Sir Thomas of (d. 1240)', rev. Ralph V. Turner, *Oxford Dictionary of National Biography,* online edition [http://www.oxforddnb.com/view/article/19521, accessed 9 Oct 2015].

94. Whitley, 'In the palmy days of Boston', p. 241; Harden, *Medieval Boston,* p. 25; Gurnham, *The story of Boston,* p. 37.

95. Stukeley, *Itinerarium curiosum,* volume I, p. 25; Thompson, *The history and antiquities of Boston,* pp. 200-2, 469; *The Boston assembly minutes,* no. 526; Molyneux and Wright, *An atlas of Boston,* p. 23.

96. JRLM, Latin MS 221, Cartulary of St Mary's abbey, f. 385. A later grant refers simply to the 'brothers' of the hospital (*Ibid.,* f. 399). For Huntingfield, see R. V. Turner, 'Huntingfield, William of (d. in or before 1225)', *Oxford Dictionary of National Biography,* online edition [http://www.oxforddnb.com/view/article/14238, accessed 26 Aug 2014].

97. *Registrum Antiquissimum, part VII,* p. 26; *The earliest Lincolnshire assize rolls, A.D. 1202-1209,* ed. D. M. Stenton (L.R.S., 22 (1926)), nos 390, 1088; *Pipe Roll, 6 John,* p. 76; *Pleas before the king or his justices, 1198-1212,* volume IV, ed. D. M. Stenton (Selden Society, 84 (1967)), no. 4597. Alexander Gernun, who was the brother of Roger Gernun and the father of Thomas, also appears amongst the undated lists of witnesses to grants in the Huntingfield cartulary (LAO, 3 ANC 2/1, Huntingfield cartulary, ff. 27,27v, 28, 28v, 29v, 30), to grants of land in Boston to Fountains abbey (*Chartulary of Fountains,* volume I, pp. 114-5, 117), to Kirkstead abbey (BL, Cotton MS Vespasian E.XVIII, Cartulary of Kirkstead abbey, ff. 182v-183v), and to the Hospital of St John the Baptist in Boston and was an owner of land in Boston (JRLM, Latin MS 221, Cartulary of St Mary's abbey, ff. 385, 385v). He was both

a witness to a grant of land in Boston to Alvingham priory and himself gave a plot of land to the priory which was 42 feet square in his '*curia*' which was 'outside the bar' in Boston (Redford, 'An edition of the cartulary of Alvingham priory', pp. 64, 918, 1062, 1064).

98.  Watson, 'City as charter', pp. 235-62; S. Sweetinburgh, *The role of the hospital in medieval England: gift-giving and the spiritual economy* (Dublin, 2004), pp. 29-30, 241-7; Goddard, *Lordship and medieval urbanization*, pp. 62-3.

99.  *CRR*, volume X, p. 313.

100.  Sweetinburgh, *The role of the hospital*,  pp. 29-30; Watson, 'City as charter', p. 238; P. H. Cullum, 'Leper houses and borough status in the thirteenth century', in P. R. Coss and S. D. Lloyd, eds, *Thirteenth century England, volume III: proceedings of the Newcastle upon Tyne conference, 1989* (Woodbridge, 1991), pp. 37-46, at p. 38.

101.  C. Rawcliffe, 'The earthly and spiritual topography of suburban hospitals', in K. Giles and C. Dyer, eds, *Town and country in the Middle Ages: contrasts, contacts and connections, 1100-1500* (Leeds, 2005), pp. 251-74, at p. 252; Cullum, 'Leper houses', p. 44; Baker and Holt, *Urban growth*, p. 320; R. Gilchrist, 'Christian bodies and souls: the archaeology of life and death in late medieval hospitals', in S. Bassett, ed., *Death in towns: urban responses to the dying and the dead, 100-1600* (Leicester, 1992), pp. 101-18, at pp. 113-16.

102.  Thompson, *The history and antiquities of Boston*, pp. 155, 263; Minnis *et al.*, *Boston, Lincolnshire*, pp. 28-9. This site was not the location of St John's Hospital (LHER, MLI12691, St John's the Baptist's Hospital, Boston). Wills from the 1520s mention places called 'The Hospital' and 'the hospytall ende', although these could refer to the Hospital of St John (*Lincoln wills registered in the diocesan probate at Lincoln, volume II: A.D. 1505 to May 1530*, ed. C. W. Foster (L.R.S., 10 (1918 for 1914)), pp. 72, 100.

103.  Baker and Holt, *Urban growth*, p. 320; *Lincoln wills registered in the diocesan probate at Lincoln, volume I: A.D. 1271 to 1526*, ed. C. W. Foster (L.R.S., 5 (1914)), p. 43.

104.  *The Lincolnshire Domesday*, 57/27; Thompson, *The history and antiquities of Boston*, pp. 496, 504-5; S. Raban, *The estates of Thorney and Crowland: a study in medieval monastic tenure* (Cambridge, 1973), p. 34.

105.  'Petri Blesensis Continuatio', pp. 112, 117, 118-20, 125-6; *Ingulph's Chronicle*, pp. 233-4, 245-6, 250, 260-1; E. M. Poynton, 'The fee of Creon', *The Genealogist*, n.s., 18 (1901), pp. 162-66, 219-25, at pp. 162-3; Sister Elspeth, 'The priory of Freiston', in Page, *The Victoria history of the county of Lincoln*, volume II, pp. 128-9; Thompson, *The history and antiquities of Boston*, p. 505. It is not clear if this was the Alan de Creon who held land in Leicestershire in the 1120s and who gave land to Nostell Priory (Yorkshire) in 1121-22 (J. H. Round, *Feudal England: historical studies in the XIth and XIIth centuries* (London, 1895), p. 202; W. Farrer, 'An outline itinerary of King Henry the First', *EHR*, 34 (1919), pp. 303-82, 505-79, at p. 517.

106.  Petri Blesensis Continuatio', pp. 118, 119; 125-6; *Ingulph's Chronicle*, pp. 245-6.

107.  Marrat, *The history of Lincolnshire*, volume II, p. 169. An Alan de Creon acted as a witness at some point in 1136-41 (*Regesta regum Anglo-Normannorum, 1066-1154*, volume III, eds H. A. Cronne and R. H. C. Davis (Oxford, 1956), no. 656. For the sluice of 1142, see section 3.1., below. An alternative view is that the succession was simply from the Domesday Guy, through Alan, then Maurice, Guy II and Petronilla (Sanders, *English baronies*, p. 47).

108.  LAO, 3 ANC 2/1, Huntingfield cartulary, ff. 9v, 10; *Regesta regum Anglo-Normannorum*, volume III, nos 412-14.  Maurice appears regularly in the pipe rolls from 1158-9 onwards (*Pipe Roll, 5 Henry II*, pp. 64, 65).

109.  LAO, 3 ANC 2/1, Huntingfield cartulary, ff. 5, 7, 28v, 31v; *Final concords of the county of Lincoln, A.D. 1242-1272, with additions A.D. 1176-1250*, volume II, ed. C. W. Foster (L.R.S., 17 (1920)), pp. 307-8; Poynton, 'The fee of Creon', pp. 165-6.

110.  LAO, 3 ANC 2/1, Huntingfield cartulary, ff. 5-5v, 11, 28v, 30; Poynton, 'The fee of Creon', p. 219; Thompson, *The history and antiquities of Boston*, p. 505; *Pipe Roll, 34 Henry II*, p. 81. Guy II appears regularly in the pipe rolls from 1167-8 (*Pipe Roll, 14  Henry II*, p. 185). Some of the pipe rolls give Guy as Maurice's nephew but this error was eventually corrected (*Pipe Roll, 25 Henry II*, p. 114; *Pipe Roll, 26 Henry II*, p. 104; *Pipe Roll, 27 Henry II*, p. 78).

111. Poynton, 'The fee of Creon', p. 219; Thompson, *The history and antiquities of Boston,* p. 505; *English episcopal acta, 31: Ely, 1109-1197,* ed. N. Karn (Oxford, 2005), pp. lxxxix, 184-5; Sanders, *English baronies,* p. 47.

112. *Pipe Roll, 13 John,* p. 1; Poynton, 'The fee of Creon', p. 219; *Liber feodorum,* volume I, pp. 68, 285, 363; *Liber feodorum,* volume II, p. 1367; Thompson, *The history and antiquities of Boston,* p. 505; T. C. Banks, *The dormant and extinct baronage of England,* volume I (London, 1807), pp. 63, 189; *Liber feodorum,* volume I, p. 75; Sanders, *English baronies,* p. 47.

113. Banks, *The dormant and extinct baronage,* volume I, pp. 63, 189, 384; T. C. Banks, *The dormant and extinct baronage of England,* volume II (London, 1808), pp. 443-4; *The complete peerage,* volume XI, pp. 96-7; *CCR 1279-88,* pp. 530-1; Poynton, 'The fee of Creon', pp. 222-4; *CIPM,* volume II, no. 653.

114. *The complete peerage,* volume XI, pp. 98-107.

115. *Records of the parliament holden at Westminster,* p. 94. Robert de Tattershall V had died in 1303 and his son, Robert VI, was a minor in 1305 (*The complete peerage,* volume XII, part I, pp. 651-3; *CPR 1301-07,* p. 206; *CIPM,* volume IV, nos 163, 391).

116. *The Lincolnshire Domesday,* 29/33; Keats-Rohan, *Domesday people,* p. 195; *The complete peerage,* volume XII, part I, p. 645. For descent of the Tattershall fee, see also Sanders, *English baronies,* pp. 2, 69, 88.

117. W. H. B. B., 'The Kirkstead chartulary', *The Genealogist,* n.s. 18 (1902), pp. 89-92, at p. 89; Sister Elspeth, 'The abbey of Kirkstead', in Page, *The Victoria history of the county of Lincoln,* volume II, pp. 135-8, at p. 135; *The complete peerage,* volume XII, part I, pp. 645-6.

118. Sister Elspeth, 'The abbey of Kirkstead', p. 135; *The complete peerage,* volume XII, part I, pp. 645-7.

119. *The complete peerage,* volume XII, part I, pp. 647-53.

120. *The complete peerage,* volume III, p. 551-2; *The complete peerage,* volume XII, part I, p. 653; *CIPM,* volume IV, no. 391; *CIPM,* volume VI, no. 48; *CIPM,* volume XII, nos. 25, 50; *CIPM,* volume XV, no. 572; *CIPM,* volume XVI, no. 676.

121. *The itinerary of John Leland, parts IX, X, XI,* pp. 33-4.

122. Molyneux and Wright, *An atlas of Boston,* p. 15; Thompson, *The history and antiquities of Boston,* p. 256.

123. Owen, 'The beginnings of the port of Boston', p. 43; Gurnham, *The story of Boston,* pp. 16-18; Cope-Faulkner *et al., Boston town historic environment baseline study,* p. 19; Minnis *et al., Boston, Lincolnshire,* p. 8. It is also assumed that the sluice and bridge were built together in *Ibid.,* p. 9 and *The big dig,* p. 4. See also Rigby, 'Medieval Boston', p. 8.

124. *Pipe Roll, 2 John,* p. 88; *Pipe Roll, 6 John,* p. 256.

125. For the sluice of 1142, see section 3.1., below.

126. Thompson, *The history and antiquities of Boston,* pp. 253-4; *The Boston assembly minutes,* p. xv; nos 201, 237, 284, 352, 949. For the 'manor of Hall Garth' see *Ibid.,* no. 330.

127. Thompson, *The history and antiquities of Boston,* p. 257. The street is labelled 'Furthend Lane' on Hall's map (see Fig. 10).

128. *Placitorum abbreviatio,* pp. 155-6; *CPR 1258-66,* pp. 481-2; Hill, *Medieval Lincoln,* p. 319; Thompson, *The history and antiquities of Boston,* p. 505.

129. *Rotuli hundredorum,* volume I, pp. 313, 320; *Registrum honoris de Richmond,* appendix, p. 39; TNA, Inquisitions Post-Mortem, C.133/26/6; Hill, *Medieval Lincoln,* pp. 319-20; *The complete peerage,* volume X, p. 808. This payment is given as £20 in *CIPM,* volume II, p. 211.

130. Hill, *Medieval Lincoln,* pp. 318, 392-3; Golding, *Gilbert of Sempringham,* p. 244.

131. Molyneux and Wright, *An atlas of Boston,* pp. 14-15; Thompson, *The history and antiquities of Boston,* pp. 128-9, 254. See also *Early registers of writs,* eds E. De Haas and G. D. G. Hall (Selden Society, 87 (1990)), pp. 214-5.

132. Molyneux and Wright, *An atlas of Boston,* pp. 14-15; Thompson, *The history and antiquities of Boston,* p. 253; Spalding Gentlemen's Society, Wrest Park cartulary, f. 138v; F. M. Page, *The estates of Crowland abbey: a study in manorial organization* (Cambridge, 1934), p. 139.

133. The Carmelites probably founded their first house in England in 1247 (Röhrkasten, 'The origin and development of the London mendicant houses', p. 77) and were present in Boston by 1293. The location of their first house in Boston is not known but it may have been on the west side of the river as in 1305 they obtained a messuage which Robert de Wellebek had held of William de Roos, who was the lord of what had originally been the Croun fee on the west side of Boston bridge. In 1307, they obtained a new site on land granted to them by William de Roos (A. G. Little, 'The White friars of Boston', in Page, *The Victoria history of the county of Lincoln*, volume II, pp. 216-17; *The rolls and register of Bishop Oliver Sutton, 1280-1299, volume IV.* ed. R. M. T. Hill (L.R.S., 52 (1958)), pp. 113, 127-8; *Calendar of entries in the papal registers relating to Great Britain and Ireland, volume II: A.D. 1305-1342*, ed. W. H. Bliss (London, 1895), p. 30; *CPR 1307-13*, p. 17; TNA, Inquisitions Ad Quod Damnum, C.143/66/14; C.143/52/1). For the site of their house see Thompson, *The history and antiquities of Boston*, p. 110; Minnis *et al.*, *Boston, Lincolnshire*, p. 10; LHER, MLI12688, The Carmelite friary at Boston. For archaeological evidence, see LHER, MLI83896. Medieval wall and associated deposits, 71 High Street, Boston; LHER, MLI13313, Medieval masonry, 35 Paddock Grove, Boston. The Whitefriars' house was not originally in Skirbeck (LHER, MLI12688, The Carmelite friary of Boston).

134. Owen, 'The beginnings of the port of Boston', p. 42.

135. Thompson, *The history and antiquities of Boston*, pp. 263-4.

136. *Pipe Roll, 14 John*, p. 7; see also notes 128-9, above.

137. Dover, *The early medieval history of Boston, A.D. 1086-1400*, p. 13. See also the discssion in Cope-Faulkner *et al.*, *Boston town historic environment baseline study*, p. 9.

138. *CPR 1354-8*, p. 345; see also *Ibid.*, p. 526.

139. Beresford, *New towns*, pp. 335-6

## PART THREE: BOSTON'S EARLY TRADE

1. H. Swanson, *Medieval British towns* (Basingstoke, 1999), p. 23; Nicholas, *The growth of the medieval city*, pp. 113-14.

2. The honour of Richmond was in the king's hand at this date (*CPR 1216-25*, p. 157; TNA, Patent Rolls, C.66/18, m. 3; *Calendar of fine rolls of the reign of Henry III, volume I*, p. 29). See also Part 4, note 4, below.

3. See above, section 1.1., note 13.

4. S. H. Rigby, *English society in the later Middle Ages: class, status and gender* (Basingstoke, 1995), p. 148; E. T. Jones, 'River navigation in medieval England', *Journal of Historical Geography*, 26 (2000), pp. 60-75, at p. 61; J. Bond, 'Canal construction in the early Middle Ages: an introductory review', in J. Blair, ed., *Waterways and canal-building in medieval England* (Oxford, 2007), pp. 153-206, at pp. 204-5.

5. J. Patten, *English towns 1500-1700* (Folkestone, 1978), pp. 227, 229-30.

6. D. A. Hinton, 'The large towns, 600-1300', in Palliser, *The Cambridge urban history*, volume I, pp. 217-43, at p. 240; Kowaleski, 'Port towns', p. 467; Dyer, 'Ranking lists', p. 755.

7. J. Langdon, 'The efficiency of inland water transport in medieval England', in Blair, *Waterways and canal-building in medieval England*, pp. 110-30, at pp. 114, 130.

8. Owen, 'The beginnings of the port of Boston', pp. 42-4; Hill, *Medieval Lincoln*, pp. 53-4, 63, 182-3; R. Holt, 'Urban transformation in England, 900-1100', *Anglo-Norman* Studies, 32 (2010), pp. 57-78, at pp. 76-7; Vince, 'Lincoln and the Viking Age', pp. 157, 160-1, 170, 176-8; L. ten Harkel, 'Urban identity and material culture: a case study of Viking-age Lincoln, *c.* A.D. 850-1000', in Hamerow, *Anglo-Saxon studies in archaeology and history*, pp. 157-73, at pp. 159-61; *Pipe Roll, 4 John*, p. xx; Dyer, 'Ranking lists', pp. 750-4, 755, 758; Miller and Hatcher, *Medieval England: towns, commerce and crafts*, p . 100.

9. *The earliest Lincolnshire assize rolls*, no. 972. For the assize of wine, see Davis, *Medieval market morality*, pp. 248-9.

10. BL, Cotton MS Claudius D. XI, Register of Malton priory, f. 216.

11. C. Roth, *A history of the Jews in England* (second edition; London, 1949), pp. 91-2; H. G. Richardson, *The English Jewry under the Angevin kings* (London, 1960), pp. 6-19.

12. W. Stukeley, *An account of Richard of Cirencester, monk of Westminster, and of his work* (London, 1757), pp. 27-8; Skertchly, *The geology of the fenland*, pp. 12-13, 106-7; S. H. Miller and S. B. J. Skertchly, *The fenland, past and present* (London, 1878), pp. 180-2; A. J. Jukes-Browne, *The geology of the south-west part of Lincolnshire, with parts of Leicestershire and Nottinghamshire* (London, 1885), pp. 110-11; Wheeler, *A history of the fens*, pp. 136, 138; J. S. Alexander, 'Building stone from east Midland quarries: sources, transportation and usage', *Medieval Archaeology*, 39 (1995), pp. 107-35, at p. 125.

13. T. W. Lane, *et al.*, *The Fenland project, number 8: Lincolnshire survey, the northern fen edge* (East Anglian Archaeology Report, 66 (1993)), pp. 16-20, 88.

14. Hallam, *Settlement and society*, pp. 41, 105, 219-20; H. E. Hallam, *The new lands of Elloe* (Department of English Local History, University College of Leicester, Occasional Papers 6. (1954)), p. 4; Marrat, *The history of Lincolnshire*, volume I, p. 176; Lewis, 'The trade and shipping of Boston', pp. 1-2; Rigby, 'An administrative contrast', p. 63; Bagley, *Boston*, p. 2; M. Chisholm, 'Water management in the Fens before the introduction of pumps', *Landscape History*, 33 (2012), pp. 45-68; H. Healey, 'A medieval salt-making site in Bicker Haven, Lincolnshire', in A. Bell, D. Gurney and H. Healey, *Lincolnshire salterns: excavations at Helpringham, Holbeach and Bicker Haven* (East Anglian Archaeology Report, 89 (1999)), pp. 82-101, at 82; P. P. Hayes and T. W. Lane, *The Fenland project, number 5: the south-west fens* (East Anglian Archaeology Report, 55 (1992)), p. 31.

15. See, for instance, 'Boston, Lincolnshire', https://en.wikipedia.org/wiki/Boston,_Lincolnshire, accessed 6 June 2016; Shinn, *Boston through time*, p. 3; C. J. Gardner, 'The behaviour and ecology of adult common bream *Abramis brama* (L.) in a heavily modified lowland river' (Unpublished University of Lincoln Ph.D. thesis, 2013), p. 37.

16. *The Peterborough chronicle*, ed. Rositzke, p. 92; *William of Malmesbury, Historia regum Anglorum. The history of the English kings*, volume I, eds R. A. B. Mynors, R. M. Thomson and M. Winterbottom (Oxford, 1998), pp. 310-11.

17. S. K. Haslett, 'Historic tsunami in Britain since AD 1000: a review', *Natural Hazards and Earth System Sciences*, 8 (2008), pp. 587-601, at 594-5; M. Baillie, 'The case for significant numbers of extraterrestrial impacts through the late Holocene', *Journal of Quaternary Science*, 22 (2007), pp. 101-9, at 107-8; M. Baillie, *New light on the Black Death: the cosmic connection* (Stroud, 2006), pp. 116-25. I am grateful to Cathy Delaney for her bibliographical guidance on this issue.

18. Owen, 'The beginnings of the port of Boston', p. 43; Harden, *Medieval Boston*, pp. 5, 7; Cope-Faulkner *et al.*, *Boston town historic environment baseline study*, p. 6. For a detailed analysis of the course of the River Witham within Boston, see N. Wright, 'Grand deviations: the course of the River Witham in Boston', *Lincolnshire History and Archaeology*, 44 (2009), pp. 48-53.

19. The inquisition was not held in 1316 (Rigby, 'Medieval Boston', p. 9) but was actually held on the Tuesday after the feast of the Exaltation of the Holy Cross, 9 Edward II, i.e. 16 September, 1315 (LAO, Spalding Sewers, 503/55; 503/56). For other returns for sessions held by these commissioners at Boston on the same day, see BL, Additional MS 35296, Cartulary of Spalding priory, ff. 254-256; W. Dugdale, *The history of imbanking and draining* (second edition; London, 1772), pp. 199-201, 227-9.

20. *The records of the commissioners of sewers in the parts of Holland, 1547-1603*, ed. A. Mary Kirkus (L.R.S., 54 (1959)), p. xix.

21. For the 'Black Book', see LAO, Spalding Sewers, 505/2. For early modern copies of the 1315 return, see note 25, below.

22. LAO, Spalding Sewers, 503/40-41.

23. *CPR 1313-17*, p. 410. For a list of the jurors at the 1315 sessions of the commissioners, see LAO, Spalding Sewers, 505/2.

24. Baker and Holt, *Urban growth and the medieval church*, pp. 118-19. I am grateful to Richard Holt for this reference.

25. For early modern copies and translations of the 1315 return, see LAO, Monson 7/27, Miscellaneous Book relating to the sluice at Boston, f.1; LAO, Spalding Sewers, 503/54; 503/55; 503/56. Lincoln

Central Library, L Fens 9, L.A22.9, Joseph Banks, 'Fens Antiquities: a collection of documents relating to the history and antiquities of the East, West and Wildmore Fens in the parts of Lindsey and the county of Lincoln', pp. 88-9. For secondary works, see Thompson, *The history and antiquities of Boston*, pp. 249-50; Hallam, *Settlement and society*, pp. 219-20; H. E. Hallam, 'Drainage techniques', in H. E Hallam, ed., *The agrarian history of England and Wales, volume II: 1042-1350* (Cambridge, 1988), pp. 497-507, p. 501. The sluice was not built by the earl of Richmond (Rigby, 'Boston and Grimsby in the Middle Ages', p. 170).

26. LAO, Monson 7.27, f. 2; LAO, Spalding Sewers, 503/54; 503/55; 503/56. The sluice of 1142 has sometimes been conflated with that of 1500 (Wheeler, *A history of the fens*, pp. 26-7; Owen, 'The beginnings of the port of Boston', p. 43).

27. Lewis, 'The trade and shipping of Boston', p. 2.

28. Wheeler, *A history of the fens*, pp. 157-61; Jones, 'Lady Margaret Beaufort'. p. 15; Marrat, *The history of Lincolnshire*, volume I, pp. 66-7.

29. G. Hutchinson, *Medieval ships and shipping* (London, 1994), pp. 15-20, 104-5; H. Clarke, 'The archaeology, history and architecture of the medieval ports of the east coast, with special reference to King's Lynn, Norfolk', in S. McGrail, ed., *The archaeology of medieval ships and harbours in northern Europe* (British Archaeological Reports, International Series, 66 (1979)), pp. 155-65, at p. 158; R. W. Unger, *The ship in the medieval economy, 600-1600* (London, 1980), p. 147; R. W. Unger, 'Changes in ship design and construction: England in the European mould', in R Gorski, ed., *Roles of the sea in medieval England* (Woodbridge, 2012), pp. 25-39, at pp. 27-31; I. Friel, *Maritime History of Britain and Ireland, c. 400-2001* (London, 2003), p. 79; G. Milne and B. Hobley, *Waterfront archaeology in Britain and northern Europe* (Council for British Archaeology Research Report, 41 (1981)), p. 19; Ayers, 'Cities, cogs and commerce', pp. 68-9; E. Okansen, 'Economic relations between East Anglia and Flanders in the Anglo-Norman period', in Bates and Liddiard, *East Anglia and its North Sea world*, pp. 174-203, at p. 178; E. Okansen, *Flanders and the Anglo-Norman world, 1066-1216* (Cambridge, 2012), pp. 156, 161.

30. Hutchinson, *Medieval ships*, pp. 104-115; Unger, *The ship in the medieval economy*, pp. 133-48; Milne and Hobley, *Waterfront archaeology*, pp. 2, 7, 14, 19, 21, 24, 3, 82; C. O'Brien, L. Bown, S. Dixon, R. Nicholson, *et al.*, *The origins of the Newcastle quayside: excavations at Queen Street and Dog Bank* (Newcastle, 1988), pp. 5, 156-8; D. Meier, *Seafarers, merchants and pirates in the Middle Ages* (Woodbridge, 2006), pp. 22, 33-5; Ayers, 'Cities, cogs and commerce', pp. 72-3.

31. LAO, 3 ANC 2/1, Huntingfield cartulary, ff. 32, 33; Owen, 'The beginnings of the port of Boston', p.44.

32. *Chartulary of Fountains*, volume I, p. 115.

33. Hill, *Medieval Lincoln*, pp. 13-14, 173, 307-8; Whitwell, *Roman Lincolnshire*, pp. 42, 57-8; Vince, 'Lincoln in the Viking Age', pp. 173-4; Sawyer, *Anglo-Saxon Lincolnshire*, p. 197; F. M. Stenton, 'Introduction' in *The Lincolnshire Domesday* , p. xxxv; Bond, 'Canal construction in the early Middle Ages', pp. 167, 175-6; *Symeonis Monachi opera omnia*, volume II, ed. T. Arnold (London: Rolls Series, 1885), p. 260.

34. K. J. Allison, 'Medieval Hull', in K. J. Allison and P. M. Tillott, eds, *The Victoria history of the county of York: East Riding, volume I: the city of Kingston-upon-Hull* (Oxford, 1969), pp. 11-89, at pp. 11-14.

35. J. Langdon and J. Masschaele, 'Commercial activity and population growth in medieval England', *Past and Present*, 190 (2006), pp. 35-82, at pp. 50-2; D. Harrison, *The bridges of medieval England: transport and society, 400-1800* (Oxford, 2007), pp. 43-7.

36. P. Spufford, *Power and profit: the merchant in medieval Europe* (London, 2002), pp. 192-6.

37. J. Masschaele, 'The English economy in the era of Magna Carta', in J. S. Loengard, ed., *Magna Carta and the England of King John* (Woodbridge, 2010), pp. 151-67, at pp. 161-3; Harrison, *The bridges of medieval England*, pp. 43-7, 52-4.

38. BL, MS Harley 742, Cartulary of Spalding priory, f. 244v; BL, Cotton MS Vespasian E.xx, Cartulary of Bardney abbey, f. 238. See also LAO, 3 ANC 2/1, Huntingfield cartulary, ff. 28, 28v. See also below, part 4, notes 39 and 42.

39. Hill, *Medieval Lincoln*, pp. 304-5; Hoskins, *The making of the English landscape*, pp. 76-9; Hallam, *Settlement and society*, pp. 93-4; Millea, *The Gough Map*, pp. 13, 67, 86; Cope-Faulkner *et al.*, *Boston town historic environment baseline study*, p. 8; Golding, *Gilbert of Sempringham*, p. 244; Summerson, 'Calamity and commerce', pp. 146, 152; *Rotuli litterarum patentium*, volume I, part I, p. 198.

40. Henry II's grant survives only in a confirmation by Edward I (*British borough charters, 1042-1216*, ed. A. Ballard (Cambridge, 1913), p. 178; *The royal charters of the city of Lincoln, Henry II to William III*, ed. W. de Gray Birch (Cambridge, 1911), p. 18; *Historical Manuscripts Commission, fourteenth report, appendix, part VIII* (London, 1895), p. 7).

41. Sawyer, *Anglo-Saxon Lincolnshire* p. 182; Platts, *Land and people in medieval Lincolnshire*, p. 126; S. Maritt, 'Drogo the sheriff: a neglected lost romance tradition and Anglo-Norwegian relations in the twelfth century', *History*, 80 (2007), pp. 157-84, at pp. 166, 170-1; A. Nedkvitne, 'The development of the Norwegian long-distance stockfish trade', in J. H. Barrett and D. C. Orton, eds. *Cod and herring: the archaeology and history of medieval sea fishing* (Oxford, 2016), pp. 50-9, at pp. 50-4; S. H. Rigby, *Medieval Grimsby: growth and decline* (Hull, 1993), pp. 7-9; *The saga of King Sverri of Norway*, trans. J. Sephton (London, 1899), pp. 128-31; *The making of King's Lynn*, p. 42.

42. A. Nedkvitne, *The German Hansa and Bergen, 1100-1600* (Cologne, 2014), pp. 26-31, 55, 65-6, 75-6, 79; Nedkvitne, 'The development of the Norwegian long-distance stockfish trade', p. 51.

43. *Pipe Roll, 21 Henry II*, p. 144; *Pipe Roll, 22 Henry II*, p. 77; Hill, *Medieval Lincoln*, pp. 174-5.

44. *Rotuli litterarum clausarum*, volume I, pp. 85, 136, 206; *Pipe Roll, 16 John*, p. 146. See also *CPR 1216-25*, p. 332.

45. R. S. Oggins, *The kings and their hawks: falconry in medieval England* (New Haven, pp. 30, 57-9, 62, 65, 67, 69-74, 79-80, 88-9, 91-2, 96-7, 105.

46. *CIPM*, volume I, nos 281, 337, 685, 756; *CIPM*, volume IV, no. 109. The Hauvills also held the lastage of Lynn, Yarmouth and Ipswich (N. S. B. Gras, *The early English customs system* (Cambridge, Mass., 1918), p. 29; *Placitorum abbreviatio*, p 280). For a 1225 dispute involving lastage levied in Boston and Lynn by Henry Hauvill, which he claimed to possess by hereditary right, see *CRR*, volume XII, no. 2108. For lastage in Boston, see also Gras, *The early English customs system*, pp. 207-10; *Registrum honoris de Richmond*, appendix, p. 39; *CIPM*, volume II, p. 211; TNA, Inquisitions Post-Mortem, C.133/26/6.

47. J. P. Huffman, *Family, commerce and religion in London and Cologne: Anglo-German emigrants c.1000-c.1300* (Cambridge, 1998), pp. 9-26

48. *Pipe Roll, 23 Henry II*, pp. 116-7; *Rotuli litterarum clausarum*, volume I, pp. 137, 603; Huffman, *Family, commerce and religion*, pp. 180, 186-9. See also the house in Boston belonging to the men of Cologne in 1280 (*Registrum honoris de Richmond*, appendix, p. 39; *CIPM*, volume II, p. 211; TNA, Inquisitions Post-Mortem, C.133/26/6).

49. Nedkvitne, *The German Hansa and Bergen*, pp. 55, 65-6, 75-6; Burkhardt, 'One hundred years of thriving commerce', pp. 65-85; J. Wubs-Mrozewicz, '"Alle goede coeplyden...": strategies in the Scandinavian trade politics of Amsterdam and Lübeck, *c.*1440-1560', in Brand and Müller, *The Dynamics of European culture in the North Sea and Baltic region*, pp. 86-101, at pp. 87-9; Rigby, 'Medieval Boston', pp. 14-19, 23-6.

50. Huffman, *Family, commerce and religion*, pp. 23-39, 163-4; P. Dollinger, *The German Hansa* (London, 1970), pp. 39-40.

51. *Rotuli litterarum clausarum*, volume I, p. 502; *CRR*, volume XII, no 2108; T. H. Lloyd, *England and the German Hanse, 1157-1611: a study of their trade and commercial diplomacy* (Cambridge, 1991), p. 17; Dollinger, *The German Hansa*, pp. 24-6; E. M. Veale, *The English fur trade in the later Middle Ages* (Oxford, 1966), pp. 63, 67.

52. A. R. Bell, C. Brooks and P. R. Dryburgh, *The English wool market, c.1230-1327* (Cambridge, 2007), pp. 55-7; E. M. Carus-Wilson and O. Coleman, *England's export trade, 1275-1547* (Oxford, 1963), pp. 36-7; P. Nightingale, *A medieval mercantile community: the Grocers' Company and the politics and trade of London, 1000-1485* (New Haven, 1995), pp. 10, 13, 19, 21, 103-4. For the wool contracts, see *Advance*

*contracts for the sale of wool, c.1200-c.1327*, eds A. Bell, C. Brooks and P. Dryburgh (List and Index Society, 315 (2006)).

53.  P. D. A. Harvey, 'The English trade in wool and cloth, 1150-1250: some problems and suggestions', in M. Spallanzani, ed., *Produzione, commercio e consumo dei panni di lana (nei secoli XII-XVIII)* (Florence, 1976), pp. 369-75, at p. 372; M. M. Postan, *Medieval economy and society: an economic history of Britain in the Middle Ages* (London, 1972), pp. 190-1; Lloyd, *The English wool trade*, p. 6; D. Nicholas, *Medieval Flanders* (London, 1992), pp. 112-17; D. Nicholas, 'Of poverty and primacy: demand, liquidity and the Flemish economic miracle, 1050-1200', *American Historical Review*, 96 (1991), pp. 17-41, at pp. 24, 28, 31, 33-6; Nightingale, *A medieval mercantile community*, pp. 10, 19, 59, 63; Okansen, 'Economic relations between East Anglia and Flanders', pp. 174, 179, 184; Okansen, *Flanders and the Anglo-Norman world*, 146, 153-4, 163, 168, 172; Langdon and Masschaele, 'Commercial activity and population growth', pp. 48-50; Masschaele, 'The English economy', p. 164; L. V. D. Owen, 'Lincolnshire and the wool trade in the Middle Ages', *Reports and Papers of the Architectural Societies of the County of Lincoln, County of York, Archdeaconries of Northampton and Oakham and County of Leicester*, 39 (1928-9), pp. 259-63. For references to wool exports in the early twelfth century, see *Henry, archdeaon of Huntingdon, Historia Anglorum: The history of the English people*, ed. D. Greenway (Oxford, 1996), p. 10; Herman of Laon, 'De Miraculis S. Mariae Laudunensis', in *Patrologia Latina*, 156 (Paris, 1853), cols 962-1018, at col. 975.

54.  Nicholas, *Medieval Flanders*, pp. 116-17; Okansen, *Flanders and the Anglo-Norman world*, p. 154.

55.  See part 1, note 13, above.

56.  R. Britnell, 'Commerce and markets', in Crick and Van Houts, *A social history of England*, pp. 179-87, at p. 184; Nightingale, *A medieval mercantile community*, pp. 9, 14-15, 20, 62-3, 103-4.

57.  *Liber Albus: the White Book of the city of London*, ed. H. T. Riley (London, 1861), p. 278; *Munimenta Gildhallae Londoniensis: Liber Albus, Liber Custumarum et Liber Horn*, volume I, ed. H. T. Riley (London, 1859), p. 321. However, Nightingale has suggested that it was only from the 1270s that the Husting Court was closed during fair-time (Nightingale, *A medieval mercantile community*, pp. 97-8). This part of the assize was repealed in 1416 on the grounds that Boston fair had not been held for many years (*Memorials of London and London life in the XIIIth, XIVth and XVth centuries*, ed. H. T. Riley (London, 1868), pp. 637-8; *Calendar of letter-books preserved among the archives of the corporation of the city of London. Letter Book I, circa A.D. 1400-1422*, ed. R. R. Sharpe (London, 1909), p. 159). For Londoners at the fair, see also *Rotuli litterarum clausarum*, volume I, p. 135 and below, Part 4, notes 11 and 32.

58.  SBHAO, Cartulary of St Bartholomew's Hospital, SBHB.HC.2/1, f. 593; SBHAO, St Bartholomew's Hospital Deeds, SBHB.HC.1, no. 875; *Cartulary of St Bartholomew's hospital,* no. 1665; *Curia Regis Rolls,* volume I, p. 271.

59.  Sawyer, *Anglo-Saxon Lincolnshire*, p. 181; A. E. B. Owen, 'Beyond the sea bank: sheep on the Huttoft outmarsh in the early thirteenth century', *Lincolnshire History and Archaeology*, 28 (1993), pp. 39-41; R. Faith, 'The structure of the market for wool in early medieval Lincolnshire', *EcHR*, 65 (2012), pp. 674-700; P. Sawyer, *The wealth of Anglo-Saxon England* (Oxford, 2013), pp. 15-17, 19-20, 26, 104-5.

60.  Rigby, 'Boston and Grimsby in the Middle Ages', pp. 173-6, 195-7; Bell, Brooks and Dryburgh, *The English wool market*, pp. 55-6, 61.

61.  Lloyd, *The English wool trade*, pp. 2-24; Rigby, 'Boston and Grimsby in the Middle Ages', pp. 174-5, 180. For Ypres men at Boston fair in 1222, see *Rotuli litterarum clausarum*, volume I, p. 501. For the house of the men of Ypres at Boston in 1280, see *Registrum honoris de Richmond*, appendix, p. 39; TNA, Inquisitions Post-Mortem, C.133/26/6; *CIPM*, volume II, p. 211.

62.  Nightingale, *A medieval mercantile community*, pp. 3, 19-21, 62-3; *Pipe Roll, 3 Henry III*, p. 128; *Calendar of fine rolls of the reign of Henry III, volume I*, p. 35; Golding, *Gilbert of Sempringham*, p. 425.

63.  Lloyd, *The English wool trade*, pp. 708; *Pipe Roll, 8 Richard I*, pp. 19, 248-9; *Pipe Roll, 9 Richard I*, pp. 93, 111; *Pipe Roll, 10 Richard I*, pp. 45, 61, 63. Simon was eventually pardoned £200 of the fine for this offence (*Pipe Roll, 9 Richard I*, p. 115). This incident may also explain the need for the iron chains which were sent to Boston fair in 1195-6 (*Pipe Roll, 9 Richard I*, p. 94).

64. *Rotuli litterarum clausarum*, volume II, pp. 129, 188.

65. *Chronica Magistri Rogeri de Houedene*, volume IV, ed. W. Stubbs (London, 1871: Rolls Series), p. 172. For the assize itself, see *Ibid.*, pp. 33-4.

66. Thompson, *The history and antiquities of Boston*, p. 37. The trade in raw wool of monastic houses at Boston should also be distinguished from the production of textiles (Cope-Faulkner *et al.*, *Boston town historic environment baseline study*, p. 11).

67. The introduction to the printed edition of the pipe roll for this year names 28 towns which were fined but this list omits Sleaford in Lincolnshire (*Pipe Roll, 4 John*, pp. xx, 239).

68. Miller and Hatcher, *Medieval England: towns, commerce and crafts*, pp. 97, 100, 104, 105, 116; Rigby, 'Boston and Grimsby in the Middle Ages', pp. 178-9.

69 *Calendar of fine rolls of the reign of Henry III preserved in The National Archives, volume II: 9 to 18 Henry III*, eds P. Dryburgh and B. Hartland (Woodbridge, 2008), pp. 91, 92, 107, 110; *Rotuli litterarum clausarum*, volume II, pp. 131, 135, 138, 187. For Leicester men at Boston fair in 1226 and 1227, see *Records of the borough of Leicester, volume I, 1103-1327*, ed. M. Bateson (London, 1899), pp, 29, 31.

70. *Calendar of fine rolls of the reign of Henry III, volume I*, p.38.

71. A. R. Bridbury, *Medieval English clothmaking: an economic survey* (London, 1982), pp. 106-7; Miller and Hatcher, *Medieval England: towns, commerce and crafts*, p. 100, n. 111.

72. *Rotuli litterarum clausarum*, volume II, pp. 191, 207.

73. Nicholas, *Medieval Flanders*, p. 117; Harvey, 'The English trade in wool and cloth', pp. 373-5; Rigby, 'Boston and Grimsby in the Middle Ages', pp. 177-8.

74. J. H. Lander and C. H. Vellacott, 'Lead mining', in W. Page, ed., *The Victoria history of the county of Derby*, volume II (London, 1907), pp. 323-49, at pp. 323-5; I. S. W. Blanchard, 'Derbyshire lead production, 1195-1505', *Derbyshire Archaeological Journal*, 91 (1971), pp. 119-40, at pp. 122-4; I. Blanchard, *Mining, metallurgy and minting in the Middle Ages*, (three volumes; Stuttgart, 2001-5), volume I, pp. 532-3; volume II, pp. 797, 806-9.

75. *Pipe Roll, 26 Henry II*, p. 137; R. C. Fowler, 'Abbey of Waltham Holy Cross', in W. Page and J. H. Round, eds, *The Victoria history of the county of Essex*, volume II (London, 1907), pp. 166-70, at pp. 166-7. Becket himself had passed through Boston, *en route* to Kent and the Continent, when fleeing from Henry II in 1164 (*Materials for the history of Thomas Becket, archbishop of Canterbury*, volume III, ed. J. C. Robertson (London: Rolls Series, 1877), pp. 323-5; Hallam, *Settlement and society*, p. 69n; Golding, *Gilbert of Sempringham*, pp. 38-9).

76. *Pipe Roll, 30 Henry II*, p. 29; W. L. Warren, *Henry II* (Berkeley, 1973), pp. 32, 128, 179; *Pipe Roll, 2 John*, p. 89; *Building accounts of King Henry III*, ed. H. M. Colvin (Oxford, 1971), pp. 124, 154.

77. Rigby, 'Boston and Grimsby in the Middle Ages', pp. 182-3.

78. *Sibton abbey cartularies*, part I, p. 83; part IV, p. 3; *Early Yorkshire charters, volume V*, pp. 351-2; *Sir Christopher Hatton's book of seals*, eds L. C. Loyd and D. M. Stenton (Oxford, 1950), no. 352; *The charters of Duchess Constance*, pp. 54-5; LAO, 3 ANC 2/1, Huntingfield cartulary f. 9. For a later confirmation, see *Calendar of Charter Rolls 1257-1300*, p. 95; R. A. Brown, 'Early charters of Sibton Abbey, Suffolk', in P. M. Barnes and C. F. Slade, eds, *A medieval miscellany for D. M. Stenton* (London, 1962), pp. 65-76, at p. 65; *The complete peerage*, volume X, p. 791. By 1289-90, the right to empty casks was once more being claimed by the earl of Richmond (Summerson, 'Calamity and commerce', p. 162).

79. *Sibton abbey cartularies*, part IV, pp. 4-5; LAO, 3 ANC 2/1, Huntingfield cartulary, ff. 9, 34.

80. *Pipe Roll, 30 Henry II*, p. 14; *Pipe Roll, 2 John*, p. 8.

81. *Pipe Roll, 9 John*, p. 126; *Pipe Roll, 14 John*, pp. 169-70; *Rotuli litterarum clausarum*, volume I, pp. 14, 39, 90, 93, 606, 610, 612, 635, 637; *Pipe Roll, 8 Henry III*, p. 50.

82. R. Allen Brown and H. M. Colvin, 'The Angevin kings, 1154-1216', in R. Allen Brown, H. M. Colvin and J. Taylor, eds, *The history of the king's works*, volume I (London, 1963), pp. 51-91, at pp. 83-5.

83. *The earliest Lincolnshire assize rolls*, no. 972. For the assize of wine at the fair, see also *Calendar of Patent Rolls, 1216-25*, p. 293.

84. A. L. Simon, *The history of the wine trade in England*, volume I (London, 1964), pp. 30-1, 60-4, 67, 84, 92-3, 98-9, 274; S. Rose, *The wine trade in medieval Europe, 1000-1500* (London, 2011), pp. 61-4; *Rotuli litterarum clausarum*, volume I, pp. 608, 610. For a Rouen man in Boston in 1225, see *Rotuli litterarum clausarum*, volume II, p. 45.

85. *Pipe Roll, 2 John*, p. 89.

86. *CLR 1245-51*, p. 366; TNA, Particular Customs Accounts, E.122/7/4.

87. Gurnham, *The story of Boston*, p. 20; Huffman, *Family, commerce and religion*, pp. 14-19.

88. R. S. Lopez, *The commercial revolution of the Middle Ages, 950-1350* (Cambridge, 1976), pp. 91-7; Nedkvitne, *The German Hansa and Bergen*, p. 24; Ayers, 'Cites, cogs and commerce', p. 67; Masschaele, 'The English economy', p. 164.

89. Okansen, 'Economic relations between East Anglia and Flanders', p. 184; *Pipe Roll, 10 Richard I*, pp. 92-3, 137-8, 209-10; *The making of King's Lynn*, p. 42.

90. *Rotuli litterarum clausaum*, volume I, p. 124a; *Ibid.*, volume II, pp. 108, 170.

91. A. R. Bridbury, *England and the salt trade in the Middle Ages* (London, 1955), pp. 20-1; Rigby, 'Boston and Grimsby in the Middle Ages', p. 199; Thomas, 'Rivers of gold?', p. 113; F. T. Baker, 'The Iron Age salt industry in Lincolnshire', *Lincolnshire Architectural and Archaeological Society Reports and Papers*, n.s., 8 (1959-60), pp. 26-34; S. J. Hallam, 'The Romano-British salt industry in south Lincolnshire', *Ibid.*, pp. 35-75; E. H. Rudkin and D. M. Owen, 'The medieval salt industry in the Lindsey marshland', *Ibid.*, pp. 76-84; H. E. Hallam, 'Salt making in the Lincolnshire fenland during the Middle Ages', *Ibid.*, pp. 85-112; Sawyer, *Anglo-Saxon Lincolnshire*, pp. 21-2; Platts, *Land and people in medieval Lincolnshire*, pp. 134-5, 144; H. C. Darby, *The medieval fenland*, (Newton Abbot, 1974; first published 1940), pp. 37-42; Darby, *The Domesday geography of eastern England*, pp. 69-70. For salt-making at Boston itself in 1298, see Thompson, *The history and antiquities of Boston*, p. 45.

92. *Matthaei Parisiensis monachi Sancti Albani, Chronica majora, volume V: A.D. 1238 to A.D. 1259*, ed. H. R. Luard (London: Rolls Series, 1880), p. 570; Hoskins, *The making of the English landscape*, pp. 78-9; Darby, *The medieval fenland*, p. 52; Carus-Wilson, 'The medieval trade of the ports of the Wash', p. 184.

93. Darby, *The medieval fenland*, pp. 141-2; Darby, *The Domesday geography of eastern England*, pp. 53, 55, 95; H. C. Darby, *The changing fenland* (Cambridge, 1983), pp. 10-20; Hallam, *The new lands of Elloe*, p. 41; H. E Hallam, 'New settlement: eastern England', in Hallam, *The agrarian history of England and Wales, volume II: 1042-1350*, pp. 139-74, at pp. 139, 143, 151-2; H. E. Hallam, 'Some thirteenth century censuses', *EcHR*, second series, 10 (1957-8), pp. 340-61; H. E. Hallam, 'Population density in the medieval fenland', *EcHR*, second series, 14 (1961-2), pp. 71-81; R. E. Glasscock, 'The lay subsidy of 1334 for Lincolnshire', *Lincolnshire Architectural and Archaeological Society Reports and Papers*, 10/2 (1964), pp. 115-33; R. E. Glasscock, 'The distribution of wealth in East Anglia in the early fourteenth century', *Transactions of the Institute of British Geographers*, 32 (1963), pp. 113-23; J. V. Beckett, *The east Midlands from A.D. 1000* (London, 1988), pp. 16-18; B. M. S. Campbell and K. Bartley, *England on the eve of the Black Death: an atlas of lay lordship, land and wealth* (Manchester, 2006), maps 18.5-18.16.

94. Hallam, *Settlement and society*, map 1; Darby, *The changing fenland*, pp. 7-8; Darby, *The medieval fenland*, p. 15; M. J. T. Lewis, 'The trade and shipping of Boston', in M. J. T. Lewis and N. R Wright, *Boston as a port (Proceedings of the seventh East Midlands industrial archaeology conference: Lincolnshire Industrial Archaeology special issue, 8/4 (1973))*, pp. 1-22, at pp. 1-2.

95. Hallam, *Settlement and society*, pp. 195-6.

96. Goddard, *Lordship and medieval urbanization*, pp. 156, 160, 188. See also below, part 5, note 14.

97. M. R. Evans, '"A far from aristocratic affair": poor and non-combatant crusaders from the Midlands, c.1160-1300', *Midland History*, 21 (1996), pp. 23-36, at p. 27; *Historical Manuscripts Commission: report on manuscripts in various collections, volume I* (London, 1901), p. 235.

98. Spalding Gentlemen's Society, Wrest Park cartulary, f. 138v; *Final concords of the county of Lincoln*, volume II, pp. 307-8; LAO, 3 ANC 2/1, Huntingfield cartulary, f. 31v. For a bakehouse in Boston, see *Ibid.*, f. 31.

99. Harden, 'Four dagger sheaths', p. 110.

100. Rigby, 'Urban society', pp. 179-182.

## PART FOUR: BOSTON FAIR

1. Langdon and Masschaele, 'Commercial activity and population growth', pp. 43-4; Masschaele, 'The English economy', pp. 159-60.

2. Moore, *The fairs of medieval England*, pp. 9-23.

3. *Rotuli chartarum in Turri Londinensi asservati* (London, 1837), pp. 77, 135.

4. *CPR 1216-25*, p. 157; TNA, Patent Rolls, C.66/18, m. 3; *Calendar of fine rolls of the reign of Henry III, volume I*, p. 29. Moore interprets this reference to mean that the fair was extended 'to' eight days and that it began on 24 June (Moore, *The fairs of medieval England*, p. 16; see also Wright, *Boston: a history and a celebration*, p. 19).

5. Owen, 'The beginnings of the port of Boston'. p. 43; Bagley, *Boston*, p. 12; Gurnham, *The story of Boston*, p. 23; Cope-Faulkner *et al.*, *Boston town historic environment baseline study*, p. 9.

6. *The complete peerage*, volume X, pp. 793-4; *Pipe Roll, 18 Henry II*, p. 5; *Pipe Roll, 19 Henry II*, p. 10; *Pipe Roll, 21 Henry II*, p. 4; *Pipe Roll, 22 Henry II*, p. 121; *Pipe Roll, 23 Henry II*, p. 80; *Pipe Roll, 24 Henry II*, p. 74; *Pipe Roll, 25 Henry II*, p. 24; *Pipe Roll, 26 Henry II*, p. 75; *Pipe Roll, 27 Henry II*, p. 47; *28 Henry II*, p. 47.

7. Owen, 'The beginnings of the port of Boston', pp. 43-44; SBHAO, Cartulary of St Bartholomew's Hospital, SBHB.HC.2/1, f. 591v; SBHAO, St Bartholomew's Hospital Deeds, SBHB.HC.1, no. 438; *Cartulary of St Bartholomew's Hospital*, no. 1658; Thompson, *The history and antiquities of Boston*, pp. 226, 256-7.

8. Thompson, *The history and antiquities of Boston*, p. 345; Wright, *The book of Boston*, p. 28; Gurnham, *The story of Boston*, p. 15; Cope-Faulkner *et al.*, *Boston town historic environment baseline study*, p. 10.

9. SBHAO, Cartulary of St Bartholomew's Hospital, SBHB.HC.2/1, f. 593; SBHAO, St Bartholomew's Hospital Deeds, SBHB.HC.1, no. 875; *Cartulary of St Bartholomew's Hospital*, no. 1665.

10. *Early Yorkshire charters, volume IV*, p. 10; *Monasticon Anglicanum*, volume III, p. 547.

11. *CRR*, volume XVI, nos 1285, 1462, 1593; L. F. Salzman, 'A riot at Boston fair', *The History Teachers' Miscellany*, 6 (1928), p. 2; Owen, 'The beginnings of the port of Boston', pp. 42-3.

12. *Rotuli litterarum clausarumi*, volume I, pp. 137, 141, 363, 395, 418, 419, 498, 543, 606; *Rotuli litterarum clausarum*, volume II, pp. 45, 128, 129, 184, 191; *CPR 1216-25*, pp. 156-8, 293, 332; *Calendar of fine rolls of the reign of Henry III*, volume I, pp. 28-9, 35, 38, 58. For Bégard, see above, part 1, note 53.

13. *CPR 1216-25*, pp. 91, 156, 178, 401.

14. *CPR 1225-32*, pp. 40, 126; *Rotuli litterarum clausarum*, volume II, p. 119; Moore, *The fairs of medieval England*, pp. 166-7. For Multon, see above, part 2, note 93, and also *CPR 1225-32*, pp. 163, 207, 290, 364; for Haverhull, see *CPR 1225-32*, pp. 9, 25, 38, 40, 226, 241, 250, 425, 439, 458. For the names of the keepers in 1218, see *CPR 1216-25*, pp.156-8; *Calendar of fine rolls of the reign of Henry III, volume I*, pp. 28-9, 35. See also *CPR 1216-25*, p. 334.

15. Moore, *The fairs of medieval England*, pp. 173-80.

16. See, for instance, *Rotuli litterarum clausarum*, volume I, pp. 498; *Rotuli litterarum clausarum*, volume II, pp. 48, 191; *Calendar of fine rolls of the reign of Henry III, volume I*, pp. 28-9; *CPR 1216-25*, pp. 157, 334.

17. *CRR*, volume XVI, nos 1285; Salzman, 'A riot at Boston fair', p. 2.

18. Moore, *The fairs of medieval England*, pp. 160-5.

19. Moore, *The fairs of medieval England*, pp. 171-3.

20. LAO, 3 ANC 2/1, Huntingfield cartulary, f. 32v.

21. For fair income and courts in these fees, see below, notes 28-9.

22. *Widows, heirs, and heiresses in the late twelfth century: Rotuli de dominabus et pueris et puellis*, ed. J. Walmsley (Tempe, 2006), no. 12. The rent was not owed to Countess Constance (Rigby, 'Boston and Grimsby in the Middle Ages', p. 172).

23. For Glanville, see J. Hudson, 'Glanville, Ranulf de (1120s?–1190)', *Oxford Dictionary of National Biography* (Oxford University Press, 2004; online edition, January 2007). http://www.oxforddnb.com/view/article/10795, accessed 19 Dec 2013]. For a charter granting land in Boston to Reiner of Waxham, Ranulf's steward, see D. M. Owen, 'An early Boston charter', *Lincolnshire History and Archaeology*, 23 (1988), pp. 77-8; *The charters of Duchess Constance*, pp. 17-18; see also *Widows, heirs, and heiresses in the late twelfth century*, nos 8, 12.

24. *Pipe Roll, 19 Henry II*, p. 10; *Pipe Roll, 20 Henry II*, p. 49; Lloyd, *The English wool trade*, pp. 6-7; Warren, *Henry II* pp. 117-36; Okansen, *Flanders and the Anglo-Norman world*, pp. 39-41, 172, 174.

25. *Pipe Roll, 29 Henry II*, p. 57.

26. *Pipe Roll, 18 Henry II*, p. 5; *Pipe Roll, 19 Henry II*, p. 10; *Pipe Roll, 20 Henry II*, p. 49; *Pipe Roll, 21 Henry II*. p. 4; *Pipe Roll, 22 Henry II*, p. 121; *Pipe Roll, 23 Henry II*, p. 80; *Pipe Roll, 24 Henry II, p. 73; Pipe Roll, 25 Henry II*, p. 24; *Pipe Roll, 26 Henry II*, p. 75; *Pipe Roll, 27 Henry II*, p. 47; *Pipe Roll, 28 Henry II*, p. 47; *Pipe Roll, 29 Henry II*, p. 57; *Pipe Roll, 2 Richard I*, p. 5; *Pipe Roll, 3 Richard I*, p. 117; *Pipe Roll, 2 John*, p. 88; *Pipe Roll, 11 John*, p. 201; *Pipe Roll, 12 John*, p. 206; *Pipe Roll, 13 John*, p. 130; *Pipe Roll, 14 John*, p. 7.

27. Moore, *The fairs of medieval England*, pp. 14-16, 18, 193; Langdon and Masschaele, 'Commercial activity and population growth', p. 44.

28. TNA, Pipe Rolls, E.372/50, rot. 20d, m. 1; *Pipe Roll, 6 John*, p. 256

29. *Pipe Roll, 14 John*, p. 7.

30. Masschaele, 'The economy of England', p. 161; Moore, *The fairs of medieval England*, pp. 15-16.

31. *Pipe Roll, 14 John*, p. 7.

32. *The earliest Lincolnshire assize rolls*, no. 601; *Select pleas of the crown, volume I: A.D. 1220-1225*, ed. F. W. Maitland (Selden Society, 1 (1887)), p. 36; *Rolls of the justices in eyre being the rolls of pleas and assizes for Lincolnshire, 1218-19, and Worcestershire, 1221*, no. 1160; *CRR*, volume X, p. 231; *Rotuli litterarum clausarum*, volume I, p. 436.

33. *Rotuli litterarum patentium*, volume I, part I, p. 84; *Rotuli litterarum clausarum*, volume I, p. 419; W. R. Childs, *Anglo-Castilian trade in the later Middle Ages* (Manchester, 1978), p. 12.

34. Rigby, 'Boston and Grimsby in the Middle Ages', pp. 177-86.

35. *Pipe Roll, 22 Henry II*, pp. 121-2; *Calendar of fine rolls of the reign of Henry III, volume I*, p. 35.

36. SBHAO, Cartulary of St Bartholomew's Hospital, SBHB.HC.2/1, f. 593; SBHAO, St Bartholomew's Hospital Deeds, SBHB.HC.1, no. 875; *Cartulary of St Bartholomew's Hospital*, no. 1665; A. Sutton, 'Mercery through four centuries, c.1130s-c.1500', *Nottingham Medieval Studies*, 41 (1997), pp. 100-25, at pp. 100, 103; A. Sutton, 'The shop-floor of the London mercery trade, c.1200-c.1500: the marginalisation of the artisan, the itinerant merchant and the shopholder', *Nottingham Medieval Studies*, 45 (2001), pp. 12-50, at p. 12. Owen rightly equated references to the '*parmentaria*' of the fair with the 'mercerie' but described it as belonging to the 'Lincoln cloth-men' when it was actually that of the men of London (Owen, 'The beginnings of the port of Boston', p. 43).

37. *Rotuli litterarum clausarum*, volume I, pp. 499, 607, 612, 637; *Pipe Roll, 8 Henry III*, p. 50; Summerson, 'Calamity and commerce', p. 148. See also *Rotuli litterarum clausarum*, volume II, pp. 45, 128. For the siege of Bedford castle, see R. Allen Brown, *Allen Brown's English castles* (Woodbridge, 2004), pp. 140-3.

38. R. H. Hilton, *The English peasantry in the later Middle Ages* (Oxford, 1975), pp. 208-12; R. H. Hilton, *English and French towns in feudal society: a comparative study* (Cambridge, 1992), pp. 44-5; Baker and Holt, *Urban growth and the medieval church*, pp. 261, 371; Goddard, *Lordship and medieval urbanization*, pp. 93-4, 97-8, 111-12, 117.

39. *Transcripts of the charters relating to the Gilbertine houses*, pp. 45, 57; Thompson, *The history and antiquities of Boston*, p. 206.

40.  *CChR 1300-26*, p. 256; Owen, 'The beginnings of the port of Boston', p. 45; Thompson, *The history and antiquities of Boston*, pp. 41, 61, 64. For Louth Park's involvement in the wool trade, see *CCR 1272-79*. p. 321; *Rotuli hundredorum*, volume I, p. 317.

41.  BL, Cotton MS Claudius D.XI, Register of Malton priory, ff. 216, 216v; Owen, 'The beginnings of the port of Boston', p. 45; Golding, *Gilbert of Sempringham*, p. 440. Golding dates this grant to the mid-thirteenth century (*Ibid.*,) but it may date from the late twelfth century (see above, part 3, note 10).

42.  *Chartulary of Fountains*, volume I, pp. 114-21; *Memorials of the abbey of St Mary of Fountains*, ed. J. R. Walbran (Surtees Society, 42 (1862)), p. 256; *Memorials of the abbey of St Mary of Fountains*, volume II, part I, pp. 15, 19n, 95; *CPR 1272-81*, p. 141; *The Boston assembly minutes*, no. 390; Thompson, *The history and antiquities of Boston*, pp. 47, 63, 64, 212; Molyneux and Wright, *An atlas of Boston*, pp. 14-15; R. A. Donkin, *The Cistercians: studies in the geography of medieval England and Wales* (Toronto, 1978), pp. 166-7; G. Coppack, *Fountains Abbey* (London, 1993), pp. 85-7.  See also *Final concords of the county of Lincoln*, volume II, p. 152.

43.  *Durham cathedral priory rentals, volume I: bursars rentals*, eds R. A. Lomas and A. J. Piper (Surtees Society, 198 (1989 for 1986)), p. 221; *Extracts from the account rolls of the abbey of Durham*, volume I, ed. J. T. Fowler (Surtees Society, 99 (1898)), p. 177; *Ibid.*, volume II (Surtees Society, 100 (1898)), p. 500; Hill, *Medieval Lincoln*, pp. 318, 392-3; Thompson, *The history and antiquities of Boston*, pp. 45, 64, 212. For later property acquired by Durham in Boston, see *CIM*, volume I, no. 1582.

44.  *Extracts from the account rolls of the abbey of Durham*, volume I, p. 5; *Ibid.*, volume II, pp. 295, 491, 493, 495, 496, 498, 499, 503, 512, 529, 532, 534.

45.  *CChR 1327-41*, p. 416.

46.  BL, Cotton MS Vespasian E.XVIII, cartulary of Kirkstead priory, ff. 182v-185; BL, Harley Ch 48 G 41, Confirmation of grants to Kirkstead abbey; *Registrum honoris de Richmond*, appendix, p. 103; *Early Yorkshire charters, volume IV*, pp. 37-8, 42-3; Donkin, *The Cistercians* p. 166. For Kirkstead's involvement in the wool trade, see *Rotuli Hundredorum*, volume I, p. 317.

47  *Chartulary of Fountains*, volume I, pp. 114, 117; *Transcripts of the charters relating to the Gilbertine houses*, p. 99.

48.  *CChR 1327-41*, p. 416.

49.  *Transcripts of the charters relating to the Gilbertine houses*, pp. 109-10; Thompson, *The history and antiquities of Boston*, pp. 61, 64, 254. For Alvingham's later wool trade at Boston, see Golding, *Gilbert of Sempringham*, pp. 425-7; Redford, 'An edition of the cartulary of Alvingham priory', p. 64.

50.  BL, Additional MS 46701, Cartulary of Stixwold priory, ff. 37, 37v.; Owen,  'The beginnings of the port of Boston', p. 44; Thompson, *The history and antiquities of Boston*, pp. 61, 64, 254.

51.  Spalding Gentlemen's Society, Carta Regnum, f. 12; Spalding Gentlemen's Society, Wrest Park Cartulary, f. 138v; Page, *The estates of Crowland abbey*, p. 139 .

52.  BL, Cotton MS Faustina B.1, Cartulary of Barlings abbey, ff. 66, 66v.

53.  *Early Yorkshire charters, volume IV*, pp. 42-3 (but see also *Ibid.*, p. 76); Thompson, *The history and antiquities of Boston*, pp. 55, 56, 61, 64, 206.

54.  Donkin, *The Cistercians*, pp. 166, 169. For later references to Sallay, see *The charters of the Cistercian abbey of St Mary of Sallay in Craven*, volume II, ed. J. McNulty, (Yorkshire Archaeological Record Society Record Series, 90 (1934)), pp. 98-9.

55.  *Chronica monasterii de Melsa*, volume I, ed. E. A. Bond (London: Rolls Series, 1866), p. 323; Donkin, *The Cistercians*, p. 166. For Meaux's involvement wool trade at Boston in the late thirteenth century, see *Rotuli hundredorum*, volume I, p. 105; TNA, Ancient Corrsepondence, SC.1/10/1116. For lists of religious houses which held property in Boston at the Reformation, see Thompson, *The history and antiquities of Boston*, pp. 61-4; *Letters and papers, foreign and domestic, of the reign of Henry VIII*, , volume 20, part 1, no. 846/87; *List of the lands of dissolved religious houses. Index: A-G* (Public Record Office, List and Indexes, Supplementary Series, III, volume 5 (1964; first published 1949), p. 69.

56.  *Register and records of Holm Cultram*, eds, F. Grainger and W. G. Collingwood (Kendal, 1929), pp. 90-1, 128; *The Thurgarton cartulary*, ed. T. Foulds (Stamford, 1994), nos 1115-8.

57. G. Espinas, *La vie urbaine de Douai au Moyen Age*, volume III (Paris, 1913), pp. 232-4; *La practica della mercatura*, ed. A. Evans (Cambridge, Mass., 1936), pp. xiv, xxviii, 258-69.

## PART FIVE: BOSTON AS A BOROUGH

1 Rigby, 'An administrative contrast', pp. 51-66; Reynolds, *An introduction to the history of English medieval towns*, pp. 34, 97, 100, 116. See also Tait, *The medieval English borough*, pp. 211-12.

2. Britnell, *The commercialisation of English society*, pp. 134-5, 147-8.

3. For doubts about the significance of borough privileges, see A. R. Bridbury, *Economic growth: England in the later Middle Ages* (Hassocks, 1975), pp. 44-5; S. Reynolds, 'Medieval urban history and the history of political thought', *Urban History Yearbook 1982*, pp. 14-22, at pp. 16-17; S. Reynolds, *Kingdoms and communities in western Europe, 900-1300* (Oxford, 1984), p. 157; S. Reynolds, 'The writing of medieval urban history in England', *Theoretische geschiedenis*, 19 (1992), pp. 43-57, at pp. 47-8; D. Palliser, 'English medieval cities and towns: new directions', *Journal of Urban History*, 23 (1997), pp. 474-87, at p. 481; R. Holt and G. Rosser, 'Introduction: the English town in the Middle Ages', in R. Holt and G. Rosser, eds, *The medieval English town: a reader in English urban history, 1200-1540* (London, 1990), pp. 1-18, at p. 3; A. G. Rosser, 'The essence of medieval urban communities: the vill of Westminster, 1200-1540', *TRHS*, 5th series, 34 (1984), pp. 91-112, at pp. 92, 111; G. Rosser, *Medieval Westminster, 1200-1540* (Oxford, 1989), pp. 226-8, 245; C. Dyer, 'The hidden trade of the Middle Ages: evidence from the west midlands', in C. Dyer, *Everyday life in medieval England* (London, 1994), pp. 283-303, at 285, 291-2, 299-300.

4. *The manor and borough of Leeds, 1066-1400*, ed. J. Le Patourel (Thoresby Society, 45 (1957)), pp. xvii, xxix; Beresford, *New towns*, pp. 191-2, 206-25; Postan, *Medieval economy and society*, p. 213; Hilton, *English and French towns*, p. 7; Rigby, *Medieval Grimsby*, pp. 44-7; R. Britnell, *Britain and Ireland, 1050-1530: economy and society* (Oxford, 2004), p. 143; M. Bailey, *Medieval Suffolk: an economic and social history, 1200-1500* (Woodbridge, 2007), p. 120.

5. Davis, *Medieval market morality*, pp. 155-60, 181, 272, 389-90; Rigby, *Medieval Grimsby*, pp. 11-12.

6. Postan, *Medieval economy and society*, pp. 212-13; Goddard, *Lordship and medieval urbanization*, pp. 47, 68-9, 80, 90. For the interpenetration of base and superstructure, see S. H. Rigby, 'Historical materialism: social structure and social change in the Middle Ages', *The Journal of Medieval and Early Modern Studies*, 34 (2004), pp. 474-522, at pp. 508-9.

7. Rosser, *Medieval Westminster, 1200-1540*, p. 245; Dyer, *Making a living*, p. 222. See also Bailey, *Medieval Suffolk*, pp. 121-2.

8. Beresford and Finberg give the date of this extent as 1279 and say that it refers to 'burgages' (*Medieval English boroughs*, p. 136) but the Saturday after the Feast of St Philip and St James in the eighth year of Edward I's reign, when the inquisition was held, was 4 May 1280. The extent only refers to the town's burgages indirectly when it mentions the 'rents of assize' which were owed to the honour within the *'burgus'* of Boston (TNA, Inquisitions Post-Mortem, C.133/26/6; *Registrum honoris de Richmond*, appendix, pp. 37-9; *CIPM*, volume II, p. 211).

9. Grants of pavage were made to the the the 'bailiffs, burgesses and good men' of Boston in 1281 (*CPR 1272-81*, p. 462) and in 1285 (TNA, Patent Rolls, C.66/104, m. 20; *CPR 1281-92*, p. 165) and Boston was also referred to as a 'borough' in 1313 (*CCR 1307-13*, p. 519). For Boston as a *'municipium'* in 1389, see Leach, 'Boston Grammar School', p. 405.

10. *Inquisitions and assessments relating to feudal aids, volume III*, pp. 177-92.

11. R. Britnell, 'Burghal characteristics of market towns in medieval England', in R. Britnell, *Markets, trade and economic development in England and Europe, 1050-1550* (Farnham, 2009), VI: 147-51; Britnell, *The commercialisation of English society*, p. 147; Rigby, 'An administrative contrast', pp. 51-2.

12. Britnell, 'Burghal characteristics', p. 148.

13. Tait, *The medieval English borough*, pp. 354-5; Beresford and Finberg, *Medieval English boroughs*, p. 226; Britnell, 'Burghal characteristics', p. 147.

14. Holt and Rosser, 'Introduction', p. 4. See also Dyer, 'The hidden trade', p. 284; Reynolds, *An introduction to the history of English medieval towns*, pp. ix-x; Hilton, *English and French towns*, p. 6.

15. Rigby, *Medieval Grimsby*, pp. 75, 85; Hill, *Medieval Lincoln*, pp. 328-58; Hallam, *Settlement and society*, pp. 86, 173, 185, 186-7, 203.

16. *CRR*, volume I, pp. 177, 271; *CRR*, volume II, pp. 11, 57, 75, 164, 170, 177, 222, 270; *Select civil pleas, volume I: A.D. 1200-1203*, ed. W. P. Baildon (Selden Society, 3 (1890)), no. 158; C. T. Flower, *Introduction to the Curia Regis Rolls* (Selden Society, 62 (1944)), p. 296. See also *Pipe Roll, 3 John*, p. 20.

17. *CRR*, volume I, p. 271; *Abstracts of final concords, temp. Richard I, John and Henry III*, volume I, part I, ed. W. O. Massingberd (London, 1896), p. 84 (and see also pp. 164, 167, 170; *Abstracts of final concords, temp. Richard I, John and Henry III*, volume I, part II, ed., W. O. Massingberd (London, 1896), pp. 213, 228, 272); *Feet of fines for the county of Lincoln for the reign of King John, 1199-1216*, ed. M. S. Walker (Pipe Roll Society, n.s., 29 (1954 for 1953)), no. 264 (and see also *ibid*., no. 137). For free tenements in Boston, see also *CRR*, volume II, pp. 11, 75, 164, 170, 222; *Rolls of the justices of the eyre being the rolls of pleas and assizes for Lincolnshire, 1218-19, and Worcestershire, 1221*, nos 253, 874.

18. *Pipe Roll, 2 John*, p. 88; TNA, Pipe Rolls, E.372/50, rot. 17d., m.1; *Pipe Roll, 6 John*, p. 256.

19. *CIPM*, volume VI, no. 600; *CIPM*, volume VII, no. 597; *CIPM*, volume XIII, no. 199; *CPR 1391-96*, p. 217; TNA, Inquisitions Ad Quod Damnum, C.143/418/4. See also *CIPM*, volume XVI, no. 50.

20. A. Ballard, *The English borough in the twelfth century* (Cambridge, 1914), pp. 2-6; W. B. Simpson, *An introduction to the history of land law* (Oxford, 1967), p. 14; P. Vinogradoff, *The growth of the manor* (New York, 1968), p. 357; F. Pollock and F. W. Maitland, *The history of English law before the time of Edward I*, volume I (Cambridge, 1898), p. 295.

21. Tait, *The medieval English borough*, pp. 197, 134; 218; *Rotuli parliamentorum*, volume I, p. 213; *CIM*, volume II, no. 833.

22. *The Boston assembly minutes*, no. 561.

23. *British borough charters, 1042-1216*, pp. 180-94; J. Tait, *Medieval Manchester and the beginnings of Lancashire* (Manchester, 1904), pp. 92-4; Goddard, *Lordship and medieval urbanization*, pp. 75-6; Rigby, *Medieval Grimsby*, pp. 38, 41; Hill, *Medieval Lincoln*, p. 191.

24. J. Masschaele, 'Tolls and trade in medieval England', in L. Armstrong, I. Elbl and M. M. Elbl, eds, *Money, markets and trade in late medieval Europe: essays in honour of John H. A. Munro* (Leiden, 2014), pp. 146-83, at pp. 148, 151-2, 174-5; Masschaele, 'The English economy', pp. 156-7; Goddard, *Lordship and medieval urbanization*, p. 131; Davis, *Medieval market morality*, p. 369.

25. *Rotuli chartarum*, p. 138.

26. *Placita de quo warranto temporibus Edw. I, II and III* (London, 1818), p. 413.

27. C. Gross, *The gild merchant*, volume I (Oxford, 1890), pp. 37-44, 70-1, 92-3.

28. Thompson, *The history and antiquities of Boston*, p. 134; Cope-Faulkner *et al.*, *Boston town historic environment baseline study*, p. 11; Gross, *The gild merchant*, volume I, p. 10; Giles and Clark, 'St Mary's Guildhall, Boston, Lincolnshire', p. 233

29. *CCR 1256-59*, p. 64 (see also *Ibid*., pp. 110-11).

30. *CCR 1247-51*, p. 441; Birch, *The royal charters of the city of Lincoln*, pp. 62-7; *CPR 1377-81*, pp. 461-2; Hill, *Medieval Lincoln*, p. 319.

31. *CPR 1461-68*, p. 474. For earlier exemptions from toll enjoyed by the honour's tenants in Richmondshire (Yorkshire), see *CCR 1377-81*, pp. 188, 193-4, 301-2.

32. See, for instance, *Rotuli originalium in curia scaccarii abbrevatio*, volume I (London, 1805), p. 44.

33. Tait, *The medieval English borough*, pp. 355-8; Rigby, 'An administrative contrast', p. 53.

34. J. Campbell, 'Power and authority, 600-1300', in Palliser, *The Cambridge urban history*, volume I, pp. 51-78, at pp. 69-74; S. H. Rigby and E. Ewan, 'Government, power and authority, 1300-1540', in Palliser, *The Cambridge urban history*, volume I, pp. 291-312, at pp. 292-3.

35. Rigby, *English society*, pp. 163-9; M. Bailey, 'Self-government in the small towns of late medieval England', in B. Dodds and C. Liddy, eds, *Commercial activity, markets and entrepreneurs in the Middle Ages: essays in honour of Richard Britnell* (Woodbridge, 2011), pp. 107-28, at pp. 109-10, 126.

36. Tait, *Medieval Manchester*, p. 55. See also Rigby, 'An administrative contrast', pp. 51, 63.

37. *CCR 1237-42*, p. 351; *CCR 1256-59*, p. 62; *Rotuli hundredorum*, volume I, pp. 305, 348, 383, 385; *CPR 1281-92*, p. 57; *Registrum honoris de Richmond*, appendix, p. 136; *Rotuli originalium*, volume I, p. 44; *CPR 1436-41*, pp. 181, 345; *CPR 1430-37*, p. 267. For the burden of owing suit of court, see A. B. White, *Self-government at the king's command* (Minneapolis, 1933), pp. 7-8. For the assize of bread and ale, see Davis, *Medieval market morality*, pp. 232-48. For the frankpledge system, see *The English manor, c.1200-c.1500*, ed. M. Bailey (Manchester, 2002), pp. 178-89.

38. *CCR 1251-53*, p. 283. See also *CCR 1232-27*, p. 592; *CCR 1377-81*, p. 7; *CChR 1341*-1417, p. 236; *CPR 1321-24*, p. 36; *Registrum honoris de Richmond*, pp. 197-8; *CPR 1430-37*, p. 267

39. TNA, Charter Rolls, C.53/5, m. 14; *Rotuli chartarum*, p. 118; TNA, Pipe Rolls, E.372/50, rot 6, m. 1d. The printed edition of the pipe roll omits the supralinear '*et*' from '*et de socha*' which makes the sense of the grant difficult to follow (*Pipe Roll, 6 John*, p. 76). See also *Registrum honoris de Richmond*, appendix, pp. 271-2.

40. B. Brodt, 'East Anglian coasts and harbours', in Friedland and Richards, *Essays in Hanseatic history*, pp. 22-36, at p. 27.

41. For the Lynn charter, see *Rotuli chartarum*, p. 138. See also *The making of King's Lynn*, no. 412. For Boston as a soke, see *CChR 1226-57*, p. 259; *Registrum honoris de Richmond*, appendix, p. 120; *Rotuli hundredorum*, volume I, p. 348; *CPR 1321-24*, p. 31; *CIM*, volume I, p. 449. The charter was not granted to the 'sokemen' of Boston (Rigby, 'An administrative contrast', p. 58).

42. For grants of the right for townsmen to elect reeves elsewhere, see Goddard, *Lordship and medieval urbanization*, pp. 75, 82; *The charters of the Anglo-Norman earls of Chester, c.1071-1237*, ed. G. Barraclough (The Record Society of Lancashire and Cheshire, 126 (1988)), pp. 348, 434.

43. Reynolds, *An introduction to the history of English medieval towns*, p. 107; Campbell, 'Power and authority', pp. 69-70; TNA, Pipe Rolls, E.372/50, rot 6. m. 1d; *Pipe Roll, 6 John*, p. 76.

44. *The charters of Duchess Constance*, p. 135; *Rotuli litterarum patentium*, volume I, part I, p. 34; *The complete peerage*, volume VII, p. 535; Crouch, 'Breteuil, Robert de, fourth earl of Leicester (d. 1204)'.

45. Rigby, *Medieval Grimsby*, pp. 38-9. For a further indication that the men of Boston faced an increased level of interference in this period, see *Rotuli de oblatis et finibus in Turri Loninensi asservati tempore regis Johannis* (London, 1835), p. 261.

46. The charter specifies the 'count of Brittany', not the earl of Richmond (Rigby, 'An administrative contrast', p. 58).

47. Prior to Constance's death, Guy had used the title of 'duke of Brittany'. See *The charters of Duchess Constance*, pp. 137, 142-63. For Guy as count of Brittany in English sources, see TNA, Pipe Rolls, E.372/50, rot. 1d., m. 1; *Pipe Roll, 6 John*, p. 7.

48. *Historical Manuscripts Commission. Fourteenth report, appendix, part VIII*, pp. 237-9; Davis, *Medieval market morality*, p. 386.

49. E. Searle, *Lordship and community: Battle abbey and its banlieu, 1066-1538* (Toronto, 1974), p. 240); TNA, Charter Rolls, C.53/5, m. 14; *Rotuli chartarum*, p. 118.

50. *CCR 1268-72*, pp. 586-7.

51. *Records of the borough of Leicester, volume I*, p. xxiv; *British borough charters, 1216-1307*, eds A. Ballard and J. Tait (Cambridge, 1923), p. lxxxiv. The earliest Boston court roll for the honour of Richmond comes from as late as 1514 (TNA, Court Rolls, SC.2/184/27).

52. *The making of King's Lynn*, pp. 34-5. For the text of Boston's 1545 charter of incorporation, see Allen, *The history of the country of Lincoln*, volume I, pp. 233-8. Allen dates the charter to 1546 (*Ibid.*, pp. 226, 238), as does Thompson (*The history and antiquities of Boston*, p. 64) but it was actually dated 14 May 37 Henry VIII, i.e., 1545 (*LPFD*, volume 20, part 1, no. 846/38). It has been claimed that Boston had a mayor in 1500 (Jones, 'Lady Margaret Beaufort', p. 16) but the John Anderson who authenticated the delineation of the bounds between Holland and Kesteven which had been made in 1500 was actually mayor of the town in 1601 and 1609 (*Fenland Notes and Queries*, 2 (1892-94), pp. 143-4, 296; Thompson, *the history and antiquities of Boston*, p. 454).

53.  Maynard, 'The borough of Richmond', pp. 24-5; *Registrum honoris de Richmond*, appendix, pp. 100-101; *Early Yorkshire charters, volume IV*, p. 22; *British borough charters, 1042-1216*, p. 220.

54.  See, for instance, Tait, *The medieval English borough*, pp. 154-83; Campbell, 'Power and authority', pp. 60-70.

55.  *Widows, heirs and heiresses in the late twelfth century*, no. 12.

56.  For examples of manorial farms, see *Widows, heirs and heiresses in the late twelfth century*, nos 3, 5, 10, 11, 15. For the leasing of manors, see Rigby, *English society*, pp. 73-4.

57.  *Pipe Roll, 2 John*, p. 88; *Pipe Roll, 13 John*, p. 130; *Pipe Roll, 14 John*, p. 7. For the soke of Holland and its liberties, see *Early Yorkshire Charters*, volume IV, pp. 35-6; for farming out of specific sources of revenue, see Bailey, 'Self-government in the small towns of late medieval England', pp. 114-16.

58.  *Pipe Roll, 13 John*, p. 130; *Pipe Roll, 14 John*, p. 7.

59.  *Liber feodorum*, volume I, p. 195.

60.  TNA, Inquisitions Miscellaneous, C.145/19/22. This is given as £104 6s. 4½d. in *CIM*, no. 449, where the inquisition is undated. For the division of the honour in 1219, see above, part 2, note 28.

61.  TNA, Inquisitions Post-Mortem, C.133/26/6. The versions of these entries in *Registrum honoris de Richmond*, appendix, p. 39 and *CIPM*, volume II, p. 211 are slightly inaccurate.

62.  TNA, Ministers' Accounts, SC.6/1116/9, m. 2.

63.  *CPR 1343-45*, p. 298. For the Tattershall fee, see *CPR 1301-07*, p. 206; *Rotuli originalium*, volume I, p. 132; *Final concords of the county of Lincoln*, volume II, pp. 178-9; *Rotuli hundredorum*, volume I, pp. 348, 385. For the Croun fee, see below.

64.  *Placita de quo warranto*, p. 427; Summerson, 'Calamity and commerce', pp. 160-1.

65.  *CRR*, volume VII, p. 269; *CRR*, volume XIV, no. 2380; *Abstracts of final concords, temp. Richard I, John and Henry III*, volume I, part II, p. 345; *Final concords of the county of Lincoln*, volume II, pp. 305-6; Flower, *Introduction to the Curia Regis Rolls*, p. 216. For John de Gisors, see G. A. Williams, *Medieval London: from commune to capital* (London, 1963), pp. 68-70; Thompson, *the history and antiquities of Boston*, pp. 54, 55, 59, 63, 236-8; Wright, *The book of Boston*, pp. 25, 28, 78. In 1348, the citizens of Lincoln complained that the bailiffs of Gysors' Hall in Boston illegally charged them for tronage and pesage (*Rotuli parliamentorum*, volume II, p. 213). By 1357, the collection of tronage seems to have been moved away from Gysors' Hall (*CPR 1354-58*, pp. 545-6) and in 1372 was said be located at the manor house of the Richmond honour, at which time it was decided by inquisition that it should be returned to Gysors' Hall (TNA, Inquisitions Ad Quod Damnum, C.143/379/7).

66.  Rigby, 'Boston and Grimsby in the Middle Ages', pp. 110-19, 125-8; Rigby, 'An administrative contrast'. pp. 59-61.

67.  *CRR*, volume VI, pp. 199, 277, 353; *The earliest Lincolnshire assize rolls*, no. 1498; *Placitorum in domo capitulari Westmonastriensi asservatorum abbreviatio*, p. 79; *Pleas before the king or his justices, 1198-1212*, volume IV, nos 4597, 4656; Thompson, *The history and antiquities of Boston*, p. 620. For the Boston men's rights to common pasture in the fens, including West Fen, Eight Hundred Fen and Bolingbroke, see also Dugdale, *The history of imbanking*, pp 199, 239; *A terrier of Fleet*, pp. x-xii, xxiii, xxvii, 158, 179-80; Hallam, *Settlement and society*, pp. 162-4; Molyneux and Wright, *An atlas of Boston*, p. 29. For villagers defending their common rights and forms of rural collective organization, see H. Cam, *Law finders and law makers in medieval England* (London, 1962), pp. 71-84; C. West, 'Urban populations and associations', in Crick and Van Houts, *A social history of England*, pp. 198-207, at p. 207.

68.  TNA, Chancery Miscellanea, C.47/39/87; Giles and Clark, 'St Mary's Guildhall, Boston, Lincolnshire', p. 233.

69.  Rigby and Ewan, 'Government, power and authority, 1300-1540', p. 294.

70.  B. Brammer 'The guild of the Blessed Virgin Mary', in Ormrod, *The guilds in Boston*, pp. 45-54; Giles and Clark, 'St Mary's Guildhall, Boston, Lincolnshire'; Cross, 'Communal piety', p. 33; Rosser, *The art of solidarity*, pp. 84, 113n., 126-7, 129-30, 132, 136. However, the surviving sources may downplay the administrative role of such guilds (*Ibid.*, pp. 204-7). For claims about the existence of guilds in Boston before 1260, see Whitley, 'In the palmy days of Boston', p. 231; W. Cunningham, *The growth of English industry and commerce during the early and Middle Ages*, volume I (second edition; Cambridge, 1890), p. 181n.

71. Bonney, *Lordship and the urban community*, pp., 227-8; Rigby and Ewan, 'Government, power and authority', pp, 294-5.

72. Bailey, *Medieval Suffolk*, pp. 142-5; Davis, *Medieval market morality*, pp. 147-51, 291-3, 372, 380-1.

73. TNA, Inquisitions Post-Mortem, C.133/26/6; *Registrum honoris de Richmond*, appendix, p. 39; TNA, Ministers' Accounts, SC.6/1116/9.

74. TNA, Ministers' Accounts, SC.6/1116/10; SC.6/909/23; SC.6/Henry VII/1771; TNA, Duchy of Lancaster, Ministers' Accounts, DL.29/639/10376;

75. Dugdale, *The history of imbanking*, pp. 199, 26-7, 239; BL, Additional MS 35296, Spalding priory cartulary, f. 255.

76. *Rotuli hundredorum*, volume I, p. 349; *Placita de quo warranto*, p. 413.

77. *Rotuli hundredorum*, volume I, pp. 348-9.

78. R. C. Palmer, *The county courts of medieval England* (Princeton, 1982), pp. 255-6; Summerson, 'Calamity and commerce', p. 161; TNA, Court Rolls, SC.2/184/27.

79. *Rotuli hundredorum*, volume I, p. 348; KAO., De L'Isle Papers, Bailiff's Accounts, U1475 M93; U1475 M94; U1475 M96.

80. *The early records of medieval Coventry, with the Hundred Rolls of 1280*, eds P. R. Coss and T. John (London, 1986), pp. xix-xxviii; A. Gooder and E. Gooder, 'Coventry before 1355: unity or division? The importance of the Earl's half', *Midland History*, 6 (1981), pp. 1-38, at pp. 5-9.

81. J. Gould, 'The medieval burgesses of Tamworth: their liberties, courts and markets', *South Staffordshire Archaeological and Historical Society Transactions*, 13 (1971-72), pp. 17-42, at pp. 21-9.

82. Bonney, *Lordship and the urban community*, pp. 28-31, 41-2, 46-7, 199-205, 227; M. Carlin, *Medieval Southwark* (London, 1996), pp. 101, 108-16.

83. Hill, *Medieval Lincoln*, pp. 261-8.

84. Palliser, *Medieval York*, pp. 134, 153; Rees Jones, *York*, pp. 173-4, 177-8; Hill, *Medieval Lincoln*, pp. 261-8; S. H. Rigby, '"John of Gaunt's Palace" and the Sutton family of Lincoln', *Lincolnshire History and Archaeology*, 35 (2000), pp. 35-9, at pp. 37-8.

85. *Matthaei Parisiensis monachi Sancti Albani, Chronica majora, volume V*, p. 564. For later conflict, see *CPR 1343-45*, p. 298.

86. *Final concords of the county of Lincoln*, volume II, pp. 178-9.

87. Carlin, *Medieval Southwark*, p. 101; *The early records of medieval Coventry*, pp. xxv-xxix; Davis, *The early history of Coventry*, pp. 22-30, Gooder and Gooder, 'Coventry before 1355', pp. 5-12; Goddard, *Lordship and medieval urbanization*, pp. 98-9.

88. Gould, 'The medieval burgesses of Tamworth', pp. 25-6.

89. For the charter of incorporation, see note 52, above.

90. Bonney, *Lordship and the urban community*, pp. 31, 47-9, 199-203.

91. Summerson, 'Calamity and commerce', p. 161.

92. *CPR 1272-81*, p. 462; TNA, Patent Rolls, C.66/104, m. 20; *CPR 1281-92*, p. 165; *CPR 1301-07*, p. 322; *Records of the parliament holden at Westminster*, p. 94. For the earl's town and markets of Boston, see also *CPR 1317-21*, p. 361.

93. Goddard, *lordship and medieval urbanization*, p. 277; *CPR 1292-1301*, p. 583. For the medieval tendency to express inequalities of power and wealth as hierarchies of moral worth, see R. Hilton, 'Status and class in the medieval town', in Slater and Rosser, *The church in the medieval town*, pp. 9-19, at p. 13. For the 'good men' of Boston, see also *CPR 1385-89*, p. 227; *CPR 1396-99*, p. 180.

94. *CPR 1292-1301*, pp. 583-4; *CPR 1232-47*, p. 156.

95. TNA, Pipe Rolls, E. 372/50, rot. 20d., m. 1; *Pipe Roll, 6 John*, p. 256. For the later medieval sources for these fees, see Rigby, 'Boston and Grimsby in the Middle Ages', p.11.

96. *Placitorum in domo capitulari Westmonastriensi asservatorum abbreviatio*, pp. 155-6; Summerson, 'Calamity and commerce', p. 160.

97. Rigby, 'An administrative contrast', pp. 62-3; Rigby, 'Boston and Grimsby in the Middle Ages', pp. 129-32.

98. Rosser, 'The essence of medieval urban communities', p. 92; Rosser, *Medieval Westminster, 1200-1540*, p. 228; Holt and Rosser, 'Introduction', pp. 3-4; Davis, *Medieval market morality*, p. 21; ten Harkel, 'Urban identity and material culture', p. 158; G. Astill, 'Medieval towns and urbanization', in R. Gilchrist and A. Reynolds, eds, *Reflections: 50 years of medieval archaeology* (Leeds, 2009), pp. 255-70, at p. 256. For towns as 'non-feudal islands in the feudal seas', see Postan, *Medieval economy and society*, p. 213 and also M. W. Hemmeon, *Burgage tenure in medieval England* (Cambridge, Mass., 1914), p. 3.

99. Rigby, *Medieval Grimsby*, p. 47; G. Rosser, 'Review of Rigby, *Medieval Grimsby*', *Urban History*, 22 (1995), pp. 147-8, at p. 147.

100. Goddard, *Lordship and medieval urbanization*, pp. 3, 14, 47, 48, 68-9, 75, 90-1, 290-2; West, 'Urban populations and associations', pp. 204-5; A. Simms and H. B. Clarke, 'Introduction', to Simms and Clarke, *Lords and towns in medieval Europe*, pp. 1-9, at pp. 1-3.

101. N. Trenholme, *The English monastic boroughs* (University of Missouri Studies, no. 3 (1927)), *passim*; Rigby, *English society*, pp. 165-9; Goddard, *Lordship and medieval urbanization*, pp. 276-81; J. Röhrkasten, 'Conflict in a monastic borough: Coventry in the reign of Edward II', *Midland History*, 18 (1993), pp. 1-18.

102. A. Hannan, *et al.*, 'Tewkesbury and the earls of Gloucester: excavations at Holm Hill, 1974-5', *Transactions of the Bristol and Gloucestershire Archaeological Society*, 115 (1997), pp. 79-231, at pp. 81, 221; Bonney, *Lordship and the urban community*, pp. 212, 230-3; Rosser, *Medieval Westminster, 1200-1540*, pp. 237-8, 245-7; Rigby, *English society*, p. 169; Goddard, *Lordship and medieval urbanization*, p. 288.

103. *CPR 1345-8*, p. 381; *CPR 1348-50*, pp. 52-3. 292; TNA, King's Bench, Coram Rege Rolls, KB.27/350, m. 101; B. Sharp, 'The food riots of 1347 and the medieval moral economy', in A. Randall and A. Charlesworth, eds, *Moral economy and popular protest: crowds, conflict and authority* (Basingstoke, 2000), pp. 33-54; R. C. Palmer, *English law in the age of the Black Death, 1348-1381* (Chapel Hill, 1993), pp. 26, 55; Rigby, 'Boston and Grimsby in the Middle Ages', p. 136.

## PART SIX: CONCLUSION: BOSTON'S EARLY GROWTH

1. See for instance Miller and Hatcher, *Medieval England: rural society and economic change*, p 41

2. Miller, 'The English economy in the thirteenth century', pp. 23-4, 38: Carus-Wilson, 'The medieval trade of the ports of the Wash', pp. 183-5.

3. Britnell, *The commercialisation of English society*, p. 79; Miller and Hatcher, *Medieval England: rural society and economic change*, p. 64; Langdon and Masschaele, 'Commercial activity and population growth', pp. 41-2, 48, 55-6, 63-9, 73-4.

4. Sawyer, *The wealth of Anglo-Saxon England*, pp. 1, 16, 20, 26, 72, 111; Holt, 'Urban transformation in England', pp. 66-777; Hinton, 'The large towns', 230-33; J. Blair, 'The small towns, 600-1270', in Palliser, *The Cambridge urban history*, volume I, pp. 245-70, at p. 256; Eisenberg, *The rise of market society*, pp. 5, 23-35, 118; Miller and Hatcher, *Medieval England: rural society and economic change*, p. 64.

5. D. Griffiths, 'Towns and their hinterlands', in Crick and Van Houts, *A social history of England*, pp. 152-78, at pp. 152, 160-5.

6. Britnell, *The commercialisation of English society*, p. 79; Nightingale, *A medieval mercantile community*, pp. 59, 63; J. L. Bolton, *Money in the medieval English economy: 973-1489* (Manchester, 2012), p.305; Hinton, 'The large towns', p. 238; Blair, 'The small towns', p. 268; Masschaele, 'The English economy', pp. 153, 155-6, 159-64.

7. Holt, 'Urban transformation in England', pp. 66, 76-7.

8. Britnell, *Britain and Ireland, 1050-1530*, pp. 102, 119, 294.

9. On the chrono;ogy of new town foundations, see Beresford, *New Towns*, p. 328; Astill, 'Medieval towns and urbanization', p. 258.

10. A.R. Nielssen, 'Early commercial fisheries and the interplay among farm, fishing station and fishing village in north Norway', in Barrett and Orton, *Cod and herring*, pp. 42-9, at pp. 42-3.

11. Harden, *Medieval Boston*, p.2; Cope-Faulkner *et al.*, *Boston town historic environment baseline study*, pp. 8, 19, 20, 23.

12. LHER, MLI198729, Medieval pits and linear features, 3 Willoughhby Road, Boston; LHER, ML189035, Occupation deposits at South Square, Boston; LHER, MLII3327, Medieval remains from the junction of Wormgate and Fountains Lane, Boston; Thorpe, *Excavations at Wormgate, Boston, Lincolnshire*.

13. *CPR 1216–25*, p. 157; TNA, Patent Rolls, C.66/18, m. 3; *CCR. 1225–32*, p. 488; *The making of King's Lynn*, p. 96.

14. Summerson, 'Calamity and commerce', p. 149; CIM, volume II, no. 1221; TNA, Inquisitions Micellaneous, C.145/117.12.

15. See above, section 4.3. For 1280, see TNA, Inquisitions Post-Mortem, C.133/16/6; *Registrum honoris de Richmond*, appendix, pp. 39-40.

16. For a general survey of the town's later history, see Rigby, 'Medieval Boston', pp. 10-28; for the thirteenth century, see Summerson, 'Calamity and commerce'.

# Glossary

**alienation of land:** transferring legal ownership of land by sale, grant or bequest.

**appurtenances:** property, rights or privileges associated with a particular piece of property.

**assize:** a court session or an ordinance made at such a session.

**assize of bread and ale:** regulation controlling the price, quality and measures of these commodities when offered for sale.

**assize of cloth:** royal regulation of 1196 prescribing standard dimensions for cloth offered for sale.

**assize of wine:** regulation introduced by Henry II, *c*.1176, regulating the price and quality of wine offered for sale.

**attachment:** the seizure of something by order of a court of law.

**attainder:** to have been found guilty of treason and forfeited one's estate.

**bailiff:** a manorial official.

**bailiwick:** a jurisdiction, e.g. of a bailiff or sheriff.

**(town) bar:** a barrier marking the entrance to a town.

**bearing a rod:** carrying a rod of office.

**berewick:** a detached portion of a manor.

**borough:** a town with burgage tenure (or an equivalent form of tenure).

**bovate:** one eighth of a carucate. In Lincolnshire, bovates were often about twenty acres, although bovates ranging from ten to ninety-nine acres have also been identified in the county (see Platts, *Land and people in medieval Lincolnshire*, p. 22).

**burgage:** a plot of land held in burgage tenure, i.e. by free tenure, usually for a fixed money rent and being freely transferable.

**burgess:** the holder of a burgage tenure or, more generally, a privileged inhabitant of a borough.

**cartulary:** a register that includes copies of deeds relating to a particular person or institution.

**carucate:** the area of land that could be cultivated by an eight-oxen plough team, made up of eight bovates (q.v.).

**Chancery:** the office of state headed by the Chancellor which was the main royal writing-office.

**charter rolls:** the rolls containing enrolments (q.v.) of royal grants, or confirmations of grants, of lands or privileges.

**cell:** a religious house that was the dependant of another house.

**close rolls:** the rolls containing the enrolments (q.v.) of royal letters close conveying instructions and orders to royal officials.

**clowes:** sluice-gates.

**cog:** a flat-bottomed, keeled, high-volume ship used for carrying freight.

**commissioners** *de wallis et fossatis:* royal commissioners (later known as the commissioners of sewers) who oversaw the measures in place to ensure the drainage of low-lying land and its protection against flooding.

**cordwain:** leather, often made from goat-skins or horse-hides, often used for shoemaking. Originally from Cordova in Spain.

*curia:* a house with its adjoining land.

**disseisin:** wrongful dispossession of land.

**dower rights:** a woman's rights as a widow.

**enrolment:** entering something (e.g. a copy of royal charters, letters patent or letters close) onto a roll as an official record.

**essoin:** an excuse for absence from court.

**Exchequer:** the office of state headed by the Treasurer which was responsible for collecting and administering royal revenues.

**Esterling:** a Hanseatic merchant from east Germany or the Baltic.

**farm:** a fixed lump-sum paid by a lessee in return for the right to collect the revenues from a piece of property.

**fee-farm:** a permanent farm.

**fee:** a feudal estate.

**fine rolls:** the rolls recording payments to the Crown for the enjoyment of lands, offices and privileges and which note the appointment of sheriffs and other royal officers.

**fifteenth:** a duty on overseas trade levied by King John. See also 'tenth and a fifteenth'.

**(view of) frankpledge:** a court held once or twice a year, with a range of legal and policing responsibilities, including administration of the tithing (q.v.) system.

**(in) free alms:** land held perpetually by an ecclesiastical institution in return for specified religious duties.

**geld:** a tax on land paid to the Anglo-Saxon and Norman kings.

**gowt:** a channel of water or a sluice.

*grangia:* a grange or, more specifically, a warehouse.

**greywork:** winter squirrel skins.

**guild merchant:** an association of merchants, traders and artisans who enjoyed specific commercial privileges or monopolies.

**Hansard:** a merchant who enjoyed the privileges of the Hanseatic League.

**Hanseatic League:** a confederation of German cities whose members enjoyed commercial privileges in the countries in which they traded.

**in chief:** land held directly of the Crown.

**honorial court:** a court for feudal tenants of an honour.

**honour:** a lordship made up of a number of manors.

**hospice:** lodgings.

**hospital:** a charitable institution to maintain the poor, the sick or the aged.

**hundred:** in most of England, a hundred was a subdivision of a county but in most of Lincolnshire these subdivisions were known as 'wapentakes' (q.v.) and a 'hundred' was a much smaller unit of twelve carucates of land, which was assessed for geld and which had some legal responsibilities.

**Hustings court (London):** the chief court of the city of London.

**inquisition:** a judicial or official inquiry carried out by appointed commissioners.

**issues:** revenues (e.g. of a fair).

**justices in eyre:** itinerant royal justices.

**keepers of the fair:** officers with overall responsibility for running the fair.

**Knights Hospitaller:** a crusading monastic order with hospitals (q.v.) and possessions across Europe.

**lastage:** a levy on exports.

**lay subsidy:** taxation paid by the laity.

**liberate roll:** the roll containing enrolments (q.v.) of writs (q.v.) relating to royal expenditure.

**liberties:** rights and privileges enjoyed by a specific person or institution.

**mark:** two-thirds of a pound, i.e. 13s. 4d.

**mendicants:** friars.

**mercery:** mercery was comprised of a wide range of non-bulky goods including not only fustian, silk and linen but also girdles, ribbons, purses and other accessories, and even spices. The 'mercery' in Boston was the area where such goods were sold.

**messuage:** a plot of land.

***mort d'ancestor:*** a case brought by someone who claims to have been unjustly dispossessed of their rightful inheritance.

**murage:** a toll levied to raise revenue to build or maintain town walls.

**novel disseisin:** a case brought for the recovery of land by someone who claims to have been recently unjustly dispossessed.

**palfrey:** a small horse.

**patent roll:** the roll containing enrolments (q.v.) or royal letters patent dealing with a wide range of royal business and recording grants of liberties, offices and land.

**pavage:** a toll levied to raise revenue for the paving of a town.

**perquisites:** the proceeds of an office or court.

**pesage:** a duty imposed for the service of weighing commodities.

**pipe roll:** record of the audit of accounts of sheriffs and other royal officers made at the Exchequer (q.v.).

**pledge:** to act as a pledge is to offer surety in court on behalf of someone else.

**pontage:** a toll levied to raise revenue to build or repair a bridge.

**portmoot:** a borough court.

**quitclaim:** to renounce any right of possession to something.

**rents of assize:** fixed rents paid for free properties.

**revetment:** a retaining wall, e.g. on a quay.

**(in) scot and lot:** to bear the charges (and hence enjoy the privileges) of being a burgess (q.v.).

**seised:** to be in possession of something.

**serjeanty:** a feudal tenure based on the performance of a specific service to the king.

***servientes:*** serjeants.

*socage tenure:* the standard, non-military form of free tenure.

**soke:** a jurisdiction.

**sokemen:** a class of tenants who were common in Lincolnshire. They were of varying status and owed a range of different obligations but were often of an intermediate position between freemen and villeins.

**staithe:** a landing-stage or wharf.

**Statute of Mortmain:** statute of 1279 which, in theory, prohibited further acquisitions of land by the Church.

**steward:** an estate official, often one who presided over a manorial court.

**tallage:** a royal tax or a levy by a feudal lord.

**tenant-in-chief:** someone who holds land directly from the king.

**tenement:** a dwelling-place and its associated land.

**tenth and a fifteenth:** from 1334 the fixed tax assessments from specified taxation boroughs and the royal ancient demesne were known as 'tenths' whilst those of other places, including Boston, were known as 'fifteenths'.

**tithing:** a group of males, aged twelve or over, who were responsible for each other's behaviour as part of the frankpledge (q.v.) system.

**tronage:** a charge for using a 'tron', i.e. a weighing apparatus.

**tun (of wine):** a cask containing 252 gallons.

**vill:** a township.

*villa or villata:* a township.

**villeins:** unfree manorial tenants.

**wapentake:** in Lincolnshire and other eastern counties, a wapentake was the term used to refer to the subdivision of the shire which elsewhere was known as a 'hundred' (q.v.).

**writ:** a written command by the Crown.

# Bibliography of works cited in the text

PRIMARY SOURCES IN MANUSCRIPT

**Lincolnshire Archives Office, Lincoln**

3 ANC 2/1  Huntingfield cartulary.

BB1/1/1  Receipt by the Treasurer of Augmentations for property obtained by the borough of Boston.

MCD 234  Notes on the deeds of St Bartholomew's Hospital, London, relating to Boston.

Monson 7/27  Miscellaneous Book relating to the sluice at Boston.

Spalding Sewers, 503/55; 503/56.

**British Library, London**

Additional MS 35296  Cartulary of Spalding priory

Additional MS 38816  Miscellaneous volume including charters of St Mary's abbey, York.

Additional MS 40008  Cartulary of Bridlington priory.

Additional MS 46701  Cartulary of Stixwold priory.

Cotton MS Claudius D.XI  Register of Malton priory.

Cotton MS Faustina B.I  Cartulary of Barlings Abbey.

Cotton MS Vespasian E.XVIII  Cartulary of Kirkstead abbey.

Cotton MS Vespasian E.XX  Cartulary of Bardney abbey.

Harley Ch 48 G 41  Confirmation of grants to Kirkstead abbey.

Harley MS 742  Cartulary of Spalding priory.

**The National Archives, London**

C.47 Chancery Miscellanea

C.53 Charter Rolls

C.66  Patent Rolls.

C.133 Inquisitions Post-Mortem.

C.143 Inquisitions Ad Quod Damnum.

C.145 Inquisitions Miscellaneous.

DL.29 Duchy of Lancaster, Ministers' Accounts.

E.122 Particular Customs Accounts.

E.359 Enrolled Lay Subsidies.

E.372 Pipe Rolls.

KB.27 King's Bench, Coram Rege Rolls.

SC.1 Ancient Correspondence.

SC.2 Court Rolls.

SC.6 Ministers' Accounts.

**St Bartholomew's Hospital Archives Office, London**
SBHB.HC.1  St Bartholomew's Hospital Deeds.
SBHB.HC.2/1  Cartulary of St Bartholomew's Hospital.

**Kent Archives Office, Maidstone**
U 1475  De L'Isle Papers, Bailiffs' Accounts.

**John Rylands Library, Manchester**
Latin MS 221, Cartulary of St Mary's abbey.

**Reading University Library, Reading**
RUL MS 1148/14/12  Transcription of the Crowland cartulary.
RUL MS 1148/14/14 Calendar of the Huntingfield cartulary

**Spalding Gentlemen's Society, Spalding**
Carta Regnum
Wrest Park cartulary.

## PRINTED PRIMARY SOURCES

*Abstracts of the charters and other documents contained in the  chartulary of the Cistercian abbey of Fountains in the West Riding of the county of York*, ed. W. T. Lancaster (two volumes; Leeds, 1915).

*Abstracts of final concords, temp. Richard I, John and Henry III*, volume I, ed. W. O. Massingberd (two parts; London, 1896).

*The acta of Hugh of Wells, bishop of Lincoln, 1209-1235*, ed. D. M. Smith (L.R.S., 88 (2000)).

*Acta sanctorum Junii, tomus III* (Antwerp. 1701).

*Advance contracts for the sale of wool, c.1200-c.1327*, eds A. Bell, C. Brooks and P. Dryburgh (List and Index Society, 315 (2006)).

*Ancient charters, royal and private, prior to A.D.1200, part 1*, ed. J. H. Round (Pipe Roll Society, 1888).

*The Anglo-Saxon chronicle: a revised translation*, eds D. Whitelock, D. C. Douglas and S. I. Tucker.

*Annales or a general chronicle of England, begun by John Stow: continued and augmented with matters foraigne and domestique, ancient and moderne, unto the end of this present yeere, 1631, by Edmund Howes, gent.* (London, 1631).

*The Boston assembly minutes, 1545-1575*, ed. P. Clark and J. Clark (L.R.S., 77 (1986)).

*British borough charters, 1042-1216*, ed. A. Ballard (Cambridge, 1913).

*British borough charters, 1216-1307*, eds A. Ballard and J. Tait (Cambridge, 1923).

*Building accounts of King Henry III*, ed. H. M. Colvin (Oxford, 1971).

*Calendar of the charter rolls preserved in the Public Record Office* (six volumes; London, 1903-1927).

*Calendar of the close rolls preserved in the Public Record Office, 1227-1509* (sixty volumes; London, 1902-1963).

*Calendar of entries in the papal registers relating to Great Britain and Ireland, volume II: A.D. 1305-1342*, ed. W. H. Bliss (London, 1895)

*Calendar of fine rolls of the reign of Henry III preserved in The National Archives, volume I: 1 to 8 Henry III*, eds P. Dryburgh and B. Hartland (Woodbridge, 2007).

*Calendar of fine rolls of the reign of Henry III preserved in The National Archives, volume II: 9 to 18 Henry III*, eds P. Dryburgh and B. Hartland (Woodbridge, 2008).

*Calendar of inquisitions miscellaneous (Chancery) preserved in the Public Record Office* (eight volumes; London, 1916-2003).

*Calendar of inquisitions post mortem and other analogous documents preserved in the Public Record Office* (twenty-three volumes; London 1904-2004).

*Calendar of letter-books preserved among the archives of the corporation of the city of London. Letter Book I, circa A.D. 1400-1422*, ed. R. R. Sharpe (London, 1909).

*Calendar of the patent rolls preserved in the Public Record Office, 1216-1509* (fifty-three volumes; London 1901-1916).

*Cartulary of St Bartholomew's hospital, founded 1123*, ed. N. J. M. Kerling (London, 1973).

*The charters of the Anglo-Norman earls of Chester, c.1071-1237*, ed. G. Barraclough (The Record Society of Lancashire and Cheshire, 126 (1988)).

*The charters of the Cistercian abbey of St Mary of Sallay in Craven*, ed. J. McNulty (two volumes; Yorkshire Archaeological Record Society Record Series, 87 (1933) and 90 (1934)).

*The charters of Duchess Constance of Brittany and her family, 1171-1221*, eds J. Everard and M. Jones (Woodbridge, 1999).

*Christopher Saxton's 16th century maps: the counties of England and Wales*, ed. W. Ravenhill (Shrewsbury, 1992).

*Chronica Magistri Rogeri de Houedene*, volume IV, ed. W. Stubbs (London: Rolls Series, 1871).

*Chronica monasterii de Melsa*, volume I, ed. E. A. Bond (London: Rolls Series, 1866).

*The chronicle of Bury St Edmunds*, ed. A. Gransden (London, 1964).

'Chronicle of Florence of Worcester', in *The church historians of England*, volume II, part I, ed., J. Stevenson (London, 1853), pp. 171-372.

*The chronicle of St Mary's abbey, York, from Bodley MS. 39*, eds H. H. E. Craster and M. E Thornton (Surtees Society, 148 (1933)).

*The chronicle of Walter of Guisborough previously edited as the chronicle of Walter of Hemingford or Hemingburgh*, ed. H. Rothwell (Camden Society, third series, 89 (1957)).

*Chronicon Henrici Knighton vel Cnitthon, monachi Leycestrensis*, volume I, ed. J. R Lumby (London: Rolls Series, 1889).

*Chronicon Petroburgense*, ed T. Stapleton (Camden Society, 1849).

*Curia regis rolls* (twenty volumes; London 1922-2006).

'Dame Sirith', in *Early Middle English verse and prose*, eds J. A. W. Bennett and G. V. Smithers (Oxford, 1966), pp. 77-95.

*Documents illustrative of the social and economic history of the Danelaw from various collections*, ed. F. M. Stenton (London, 1920).

*Durham cathedral priory rentals, volume I: bursars rentals*, eds R. A. Lomas and A. J. Piper (Surtees Society, 198 (1989 for 1986)).

*The earliest Lincolnshire assize rolls, A.D. 1202-1209*, ed. D. M. Stenton (L.R.S., 22 (1926)).

*The early records of medieval Coventry, with the Hundred Rolls of 1280*, eds P. R. Coss and T. John (London, 1986).

*Early registers of writs*, eds E. De Haas and G. D. G. Hall (Selden Society, 87 (1990)).

*Early Yorkshire charters, volume I*, ed. W. Farrer (Edinburgh, 1914).

*Early Yorkshire charters, volume IV: the honour of Richmond, part I*, ed., C. T. Clay (Yorkshire Archaeological Society Record Series, extra series, 1 (1935)).

*Early Yorkshire charters, volume V: the honour of Richmond, part II*, ed. C. T. Clay (Yorkshire Archaeological Society, Record Series, extra series 2 (1936)).

'An edition of the cartulary of Alvingham priory (Oxford, Bodleian Library Laud Misc. 642)', ed. J. E. Redford (Unpublished University of York Ph.D. thesis, 2010).

*English episcopal acta, 1: Lincoln 1067-1185*, ed. D. M. Smith (Oxford, 1980).

*English episcopal acta, 31: Ely, 1109-1197*, ed. N. Karn (Oxford, 2005)

*The English manor, c. 1200-c. 1500*, ed. M. Bailey (Manchester, 2002).

*Extracts from the account rolls of the abbey of Durham*, ed. J. T. Fowler (two volumes; Surtees Society, 99 and 100 (1898)).

*Feet of fines for the county of Lincoln for the reign of King John, 1199-1216*, ed. M. S. Walker (Pipe Roll Society, n.s., 29 (1954 for 1953)).

*Feet of fines of the reign of Henry II and of the first seven years of the reign of Richard I, A.D. 1182 to A.D. 1196* (Pipe Roll Society, 17 (1894).

*Feet of fines of the tenth year of the reign of King Richard I, A.D. 1198 to A.D. 1199* (Pipe Roll Society, 24 (1900)).

*Final concords of the county of Lincoln, A.D. 1242-1272, with additions A.D. 1176-1250, volume II*, ed. C. W. Foster (L.R.S., 17 (1920)).

*The great roll of the pipe, 31 Henry I-7 Henry III* (Publications of the Pipe Roll Society, 1884-2012).

*Henry, archdeacon of Huntingdon, Historia Anglorum: The history of the English people*, ed. D. Greenway (Oxford, 1996).

Herman of Laon, 'De Miraculis S. Mariae Laudunensis', in *Patrologia Latina*, 156 (Paris, 1853), cols 962-1018.

*Historia Anglicanae scriptores, X* (London, 1652).

*Historiae Anglicanae scriptores varii et codicibus manuscriptis nunc primum editi* (London, 1723).

*Historical Manuscripts Commission, fourteenth report, appendix, part VIII* (London, 1895).

*Historical Manuscripts Commission: report on manuscripts in various collections, volume I* (London, 1901).

'Ingulfi Croylandensis Historia', in *Rerum Anglicarum scriptorum veterum*, Volume I, ed. W. Fulman (Oxford, 1684).

*Ingulph's chronicle of the abbey of Croyland with the continuations of Peter of Blois and anonymous writers*, ed. H. T. Riley (London, 1854).

*Inquisitions and assessments relating to feudal aids; with other analogous documents preserved in the Public Record Office, 1284-1431, volume III: Kent-Norfolk* (London, 1904).

*The itinerary of John Leland in or about the years 1535-1543, parts I-III*, ed. L. Toulmin Smith (London, 1907).

*The itinerary of John Leland in or about the years 1535-1543, parts IX, X, XI*, ed. L. Toulmin Smith (London, 1910).

*Joannis Lelandi antiquarii, De rebus Britannicis collectanea*, ed. T. Hearne (six volumes; Oxford, 1715).

*John of Gaunt's register*, volume II, ed. S. Armitage-Smith (Camden Society, third series, 21 (1911)).

John of Tynemouth, *Explicit (Nova legenda Anglie)* (London: printed by Wynkyn de Worde, 1515/16).

*The Knights Hospitaller in England: being the report of Prior Philip de Thame to the Grand Master, Elyan de Villa Nova for A.D. 1338*, eds L. B. Larking and J. M. Kemble (Camden Society, 65 (1857)).

*La practica della mercatura*, ed. A. Evans (Cambridge, Mass., 1936).

*Letters and papers, foreign and domestic, of the reign of Henry VIII*, volume 20, part 1, eds J. Gairdner and R. Brodie (London, 1905).

*Liber Albus: the White Book of the city of London*, ed. H. T. Riley (London, 1861).

*Liber feodorum: the book of fees commonly called Testa de Nevill reformed from the earliest MSS* (three volumes; London: 1920, 1923, 1931).

*The Lincolnshire Domesday and the Lindsey survey*, eds C. W. Foster and T. Longley (L.R.S., 19 (1921)).

*Lincoln wills registered in the diocesan probate at Lincoln, volume I: A.D. 1271 to 1526*, ed. C. W. Foster (L.R.S., 5 (1914)).

*Lincoln wills registered in the diocesan probate at Lincoln, volume II: A.D. 1505 to May 1530*, ed. C. W. Foster (L.R.S., 10 (1918 for 1914))

*Lincoln wills registered in the diocesan probate at Lincoln, volume III: A.D. 1530 to 1532*, ed. C. W. Foster (L.R.S., 24 (1930)).

*The manor and borough of Leeds, 1066-1400*, ed. J. Le Patourel (Thoresby Society, 45 (1957)).

*Materials for the history of Thomas Becket, archbishop of Canterbury*, volume III, ed. J. C. Robertson (London: Rolls Series, 1877).

*Matthaei Parisiensis, monachi Sancti Albani, Chronica majora, volume I: the Creation to A.D. 1066*, ed. H. R. Luard (London: Rolls Series, 1872).

*Matthaei Parisiensi, monachi Sancti Albani, Chronica majora, volume V: A.D. 1238 to A.D. 1259*, ed. H. R. Luard (London: Rolls Series, 1880).

*Memorials of the abbey of St Mary of Fountains*, ed. J. R. Walbran (Surtees Society, 42 (1862)).

*Memorials of the abbey of St Mary of Fountains*, volume II, part I, ed. J. R. Walbran (Surtees Society, 67 (1876)).

*Memorials of London and London life in the XIIIth, XIVth and XVth centuries*, ed. H. T. Riley (London, 1868).

*Munimenta Gildhallae Londoniensis: Liber Albus, Liber Custumarum et Liber Horn*, volume I, ed. H. T. Riley (London, 1859).

*The overseas trade of Boston in the reign of Richard II*, ed. S. H. Rigby (L.R.S., 93 (2005)).

*The Peterborough chronicle*, ed. H. A. Rositzke (New York, 1951).

*The Peterborough chronicle (The Bodleian manuscript Laud Misc.636)*, ed. D. Whitelock (Copenhagen, 1964).

'Petri Blesensis Continuatio', in *Rerum Anglicarum scriptorum veterum*, volume I, ed. W. Fulman (Oxford, 1684).

*Placita de quo warranto temporibus Edw. I, II and III* (London, 1818).

*Placitorum in domo capitulari Westmonastriensi asservatorum abbreviatio, temporibus regum Ric. I, Johann., Henr. III, Edw. I, Edw. II* (London, 1811).

*Pleas before the king or his justices, 1198-1212*, volume IV, ed. D. M. Stenton (Selden Society, 84 (1967)).

*The poll taxes of 1377, 1379 and 1381, part 2: Lincolnshire-Westmoreland* ed. C. Fenwick (Oxford, 2001).

*Records of the borough of Leicester, volume I, 1103-1327*, ed. M. Bateson (London, 1899).

*The records of the commissioners of sewers in the parts of Holland, 1547-1603*, ed. A. Mary Kirkus (L.R.S., 54 (1959)).

*Records of early English drama: Lincolnshire*, volume II, ed. J. Stokes (Toronto, 2009).

*Records of the parliament holden at Westminster on the twenty-eighth day of February in the thirty-third year of the reign of King Edward I (A.D. 1305)*, ed. F. W. Maitland (London: Rolls Series, 1893).

*Regesta regum Anglo-Normannorum, 1066-1154*, volume I, eds H. W. C. Davis and R. J. Whitwell (Oxford, 1913).

*Regesta regum Anglo-Normannorum, 1066-1154*, volume III, eds H. A. Cronne and R. H. C. Davis (Oxford, 1956).

*Register and records of Holm Cultram*, eds F. Grainger and W. G. Collingwood (Kendal, 1929).

*The register of Henry Burghersh, 1320-1342, volume I*, ed. N. Bennett (L.R.S., 87 (1999)).

*The Registrum Antiquissimum of the cathedral church of Lincoln, part VII*, ed. K. Major (L.R.S., 46, 1950)).

*Registrum honoris de Richmond*, ed. R. Gale (London, 1722).

*The rolls and register of Bishop Oliver Sutton, 1280-1299, volume IV.* ed. R. M. T. Hill (L.R.S., 52 (1958)).

*Rolls of the justices in eyre, being the rolls of pleas and assizes for Lincolnshire, 1218-19, and Worcestershire, 1221*, ed. D. M. Stenton (Selden Society, 53 (1934)).

*Rotuli chartarum in Turri Londinensi asservati* (London, 1837).

*Rotuli de oblatis et finibus in Turri Loninensi asservati tempore regis Johannis* (London, 1835).

*Rotuli Hugonis de Welles, episcopi Lincolniensis, A.D. MCCIX-MCCXXXV,* volume I, ed. W. P. W. Phillimore (L.R.S., 3 (1912)).

*Rotuli Hugonis de Welles, episcopi Lincolniensis, A.D. MCCIX-MCCXXXV,* volume III, ed. F. N. Davies (L.R.S., 9 (1914)).

*Rotuli hundredorum*, volume I (London, 1812).

*Rotuli litterarum clausarum in Turri Londinensi asservati*, volume I, ed. T. D. Hardy (London, 1833).

*Rotuli litterarum patentium in Turri Londinensi asservati*, volume I, part I, ed. T. D. Hardy (London, 1835).

*Rotuli originalium in curia scaccarii abbrevatio*, volume I (London, 1805).

*Rotuli parliamentorum* (six volumes; London, 1783).

*The royal charters of the city of Lincoln, Henry II to William III*, ed. W. de Gray Birch (Cambridge, 1911).

*The saga of King Sverri of Norway*, trans. J. Sephton (London, 1899).

*Saxton's survey of England and Wales with a facsimile of Saxton's wall map of 1583*, ed. R. A. Skelton (Amsterdam, 1974).

*Select civil pleas, volume I: A.D. 1200-1203*, ed. W. P. Baildon (Selden Society, 3 (1890)).

*Select pleas of the crown, volume I: A.D. 1220-1225*, ed. F. W. Maitland (Selden Society, 1 (1887)).

*Sibton abbey cartularies and charters*, ed. P. Brown (four parts, Suffolk Records Society, Suffolk Charters, 7-10 (1985-88).

*Sir Christopher Hatton's book of seals,* eds L. C. Loyd and D. M. Stenton (Oxford, 1950).

*A summarie of the chronicles of England, diligently collected, abridged and continued unto this present yere of Christ, 1598 by John Stow* (London, 1598).

*Symeonis Monachi opera omnia*, volume II, ed. T. Arnold (London: Rolls Series, 1885).

*A terrier of Fleet, Lincolnshire, from a manuscript in the British Museum*, ed. N. Neilson (London, 1920).

*The Thurgarton cartulary*, ed. T. Foulds (Stamford, 1994).

*Transcripts of the charters relating to the Gilbertine houses of Sixle, Ormsby, Catley, Bullington and Alvingham*, ed. F. M. Stenton (L.R.S., 18 (1920)).

*Widows, heirs, and heiresses in the late twelfth century: Rotuli de dominabus et pueris et puellis*, ed. J. Walmsley (Tempe, 2006).

*William of Malmesbury, Historia regum Anglorum. The history of the English kings, volume I*, eds R. A. B. Mynors, R. M. Thomson and M. Winterbottom (Oxford, 1998).

## SECONDARY WORKS

Alexander, J. S., 'Building stone from east Midland quarries: sources, transportation and usage', *Medieval Archaeology*, 39 (1995), pp. 107-35.

Allen, T. H., *The history of the county of Lincoln, from the earliest period to the present time*, volume I (London, 1834).

Allison, K. J., 'Medieval Hull', in K. J. Allison and P. M. Tillott, eds, *The Victoria history of the county of York: East Riding, volume I: the city of Kingston-upon-Hull* (Oxford, 1969), pp. 11-89.

Astill, G., 'Medieval towns and urbanization', in R. Gilchrist and A. Reynolds, eds, *Reflections: 50 years of medieval archaeology* (Leeds, 2009), pp. 255-70.

Ayers, B., 'Cities, cogs and commerce: archaeological approaches to the material culture of the North Sea world', in D. Bates and R. Liddiard, eds, *East Anglia and its North Sea world in the Middle Ages* (Woodbridge, 2013), pp. 63-81.

Badham. S. and Cockerham, P., eds, *'The beste and fayrest of al Lincolnshire': the church of St Botolph's, Boston, Lincolnshire, and its medieval monuments* (British Archaeological Reports, British Series, 554 (2012)).

Bagley, G. S., *Boston: its story and people* (Boston, 1986).

Bailey, I., *Pishey Thompson: man of two worlds* (Boston, 1991).

Bailey, M., 'The commercialisation of the English economy, 1086-1500', *Journal of Medieval History*, 24 (1998), pp. 297-311.

Bailey, M., 'Trade and towns in medieval England: new insights from familiar sources', *The Local Historian*, 29 (1999), pp. 194-211.

Bailey, M., *Medieval Suffolk: an economic and social history, 1200-1500* (Woodbridge, 2007).

Bailey, M., 'Self-government in the small towns of late medieval England', in B. Dodds and C. Liddy, eds, *Commercial activity, markets and entrepreneurs in the Middle Ages: essays in honour of Richard Britnell* (Woodbridge, 2011), pp. 107-28.

Baillie, M., *New light on the Black Death: the cosmic connection* (Stroud, 2006).

Baillie, M., 'The case for significant numbers of extraterrestrial impacts through the late Holocene', *Journal of Quaternary Science*, 22 (2007), pp. 101-9.

Baker, F. T., 'The Iron Age salt industry in Lincolnshire', *Lincolnshire Architectural and Archaeological Society Reports and Papers*, n.s., 8 (1959-60), pp. 26-34.

Baker, N., and Holt, R., *Urban growth and the medieval church: Gloucester and Worcester* (Aldershot, 2005).

Ballard, A., *The English borough in the twelfth century* (Cambridge, 1914).

Banks, T.C., *The dormant and extinct baronage of England*, volumes I and II (London, 1807, 1808).

Barley, M. W., 'Lincolnshire rivers in the Middle Ages', *Architectural and Archaeological Society of Lincolnshire, Reports and Papers*, volume I, part I (1936), pp. 1-21.

Barley, M. W., 'Town defences in England and Wales after 1066', in M. W. Barley, ed., *The plans and topography of medieval towns in England and Wales* (Council for British Archaeology Research Report no., 14 (1976)), pp. 57-71.

Barrow, J., 'Urban planning', in J. Crick and E. Van Houts, eds, *A social history of England, 900-1200* (Cambridge, 2011), pp. 188-97.

Beckett, J. V., *The east Midlands from A.D. 1000* (London, 1988).

Beeston, A. F. L., 'Idrisi's account of the British Isles', *Bulletin of the School of African and Oriental Studies*, 13 (1950), pp. 265-81.

Bell, A. R., Brooks, C., and Dryburgh, P. R., *The English wool market, c.1230-1327* (Cambridge, 2007).

Benedictow, O., *The Black Death, 1346-1353: a complete history* (Woodbridge, 2004).

Bennett, N., 'Religious houses', in S. Bennett and N. Bennett, eds, *An historical atlas of Lincolnshire* (Hull, 1993), pp. 48-9.

Beresford, M., *New towns of the Middle Ages: town plantation in England, Wales and Gascony* (London, 1967).

Beresford, M., '*English medieval boroughs: a handlist*: revisions, 1973-1981', *Urban History Yearbook 1982*, pp. 59-64.

Beresford, M. W., and Finberg, H. P. R., *English medieval boroughs: a hand-list* (Totowa, 1973).

Beresford, M. W., and St Joseph, J. K. S., *Medieval England: an aerial survey* (second edition; Cambridge, 1979).

*The big dig: Boston marketplace, Boston, Lincolnshire. Community excavation* (Network Archaeology for Lincolnshire County Council, report no. 591 (May, 2012)).

Blair, J., 'The small towns, 600-1270', in D. M. Palliser, ed., *The Cambridge urban history of Britain*, volume I (Cambridge, 2000), pp. 245-70.

Blair, J., 'Botwulf (*fl.* 654–*c.*670)', *Oxford Dictionary of National Biography*, online edition [http://www.oxforddnb.com/view/article/2963, accessed 25 March 2015].

Blanchard, I. S. W., 'Derbyshire lead production, 1195-1505', *Derbyshire Archaeological Journal*, 91 (1971), pp. 119-40.

Blanchard, I., *Mining, metallurgy and minting in the Middle Ages*, (three volumes; Stuttgart, 2001-5).

Bolton, J. L., *Money in the medieval English economy: 973-1489* (Manchester, 2012).

Bond, F., *Dedications and patron saints of English churches: ecclesiastical symbolism; saints and their emblems* (London, 1914).

Bond, J., 'Canal construction in the early Middle Ages: an introductory review', in J. Blair, ed., *Waterways and canal-building in medieval England* (Oxford, 2007), pp. 153-206.

Bonney, M., *Lordship and the urban community: Durham and its overlords, 1250-1540* (Cambridge, 1990).

'Boston, Lincolnshire', in *Encyclopedia Britannica, Volume IV* (eleventh edition; Cambridge, 1910), pp. 289-90.

'Boston, Lincolnshire', https://en.wikipedia.org/wiki/Boston,_Lincolnshire. Accessed 6 June 2016.

Brammer, B., 'The guild of the Blessed Virgin Mary', in W. M. Ormrod, ed., *The guilds in Boston* (Boston, 1993), pp. 45-54.

Bridbury, A. R., *England and the salt trade in the Middle Ages* (London, 1955).

Bridbury, A. R., *Economic growth: England in the later Middle Ages* (Hassocks, 1975).

Bridbury, A. R., *Medieval English clothmaking: an economic survey* (London, 1982).

Britnell, R. H., *The commercialisation of English society, 1000–1500* (second edition; Manchester, 1996).

Britnell, R. H., 'The economy of English towns, 600-1300', in D. M. Palliser, ed., *The Cambridge urban history of Britain*, volume I (Cambridge, 2000), pp. 105-126.

Britnell, R., *Britain and Ireland, 1050-1530: economy and society* (Oxford, 2004).

Britnell, R., 'Burghal characteristics of market towns in medieval England', in R. Britnell, *Markets, trade and economic development in England and Europe, 1050-1550* (Farnham, 2009), VI: 147-51.

Britnell, R., 'Commerce and markets', in J. Crick and E. Van Houts, eds, *A social history of England, 900-1200* (Cambridge, 2011), pp. 179-87.

Broadberry, S., Campbell, B. M. S., Klein, A., Overton, M., and van Leeuwen, B., *British economic growth, 1270-1870* (Cambridge, 2015).

Brodt, B., 'East Anglian coasts and harbours', in K. Friedland and P. Richards, eds, *Essays in Hanseatic trade: the King's Lynn symposium, 1998* (Dereham, 2005), pp. 22-36.

Brown, R. A., 'Early charters of Sibton Abbey, Suffolk', in P. M. Barnes and C. F. Slade, eds, *A medieval miscellany for D. M. Stenton* (London, 1962), pp. 65-76.

Brown, R. Allen, *Allen Brown's English castles* (Woodbridge, 2004).

Brown, R. Allen, and Colvin, H. M., 'The Angevin kings, 1154-1216', in R. Allen Brown, H. M. Colvin and J. Taylor, eds, *The history of the king's works*, volume I (London, 1963), pp. 51-91.

Burkhardt, M., 'One hundred years of thriving commerce at a major English sea port: the Hanseatic trade at Boston between 1370 and 1470', in H. Brand and L. Müller, eds, *The Dynamics of European culture in the North Sea and Baltic region* (Hilversum, 2007), pp. 65-85.

Burkhardt, M., 'The German Hanse and Bergen: new perspectives on an old subject', *Scandinavian Economic History Review*, 58 (2010), pp. 60-79.

Burton, J., *St Mary's abbey and the city of York* (York, 1989).

Burton, J., 'The monastic revival in Yorkshire', in D. Rollason, M. Harvey and M. Prestwich, eds, *Anglo-Norman Durham, 1093-1193* (Woodbridge, 1994), pp. 41-51.

Burton, J., *The monastic order in Yorkshire, 1069-1215* (Cambridge, 1999).

Butler, L., 'The evolution of towns: planted towns after 1066', in M. W. Barley, ed., *The plans and topography of medieval towns in England and Wales* (Council for British Archaeology Research Report no., 14 (1976)), pp. 32-48.

Cam, H., *Law finders and law makers in medieval England* (London, 1962).

Campbell, B. M. S., and Bartley, K., *England on the eve of the Black Death: an atlas of lay lordship, land and wealth* (Manchester, 2006).

Campbell, J., 'Power and authority, 600-1300', in D. M. Palliser, ed., *The Cambridge urban history of Britain*, volume I (Cambridge, 2000), pp. 51-78.

Canfield, N., 'The guilds of St Botolph's', in W. M. Ormrod, ed., *The guilds in Boston* (Boston, 1993), pp. 25-34.

Carlin, M., *Medieval Southwark* (London, 1996).

Carus-Wilson, E. M., 'The medieval trade of the ports of the Wash', *Medieval Archaeology*, VI-VII (1962-3), pp. 182-201.

Carus-Wilson, E. M., and Coleman, O., *England's export trade, 1275-1547* (Oxford, 1963).

Chandler, J., 'Introduction', in *John Leland's Itinerary: travels in Tudor England*, ed. J. Chandler (Stroud, 1993).

Childs, W. R., *Anglo-Castilian trade in the later Middle Ages* (Manchester, 1978).

Chisholm, M., 'Water management in the Fens before the introduction of pumps', *Landscape History*, 33 (2012), pp. 45-68.

Clarke, H., 'The archaeology, history and architecture of the medieval ports of the east coast, with special reference to King's Lynn, Norfolk', in S. McGrail, ed., *The archaeology of medieval ships and harbours in northern Europe* (British Archaeological Reports, International Series, 66 (1979)), pp. 155-65.

*The complete peerage, volume VI: N to R*, by G. E.C[okayne] (first edition; London, 1895).

*The complete peerage*, by G. E.C[okayne], enlarged by V. Gibbs *et al.*, (new edition; thirteen volumes; London, 1910-1959).

Cook, A. M., *Boston (Botolph's Town)* (second edition; Boston, 1948).

Cope-Faulkner, P., Hambly, J., and Young, J., *Boston town historic environment baseline study* (Heckington, 2007).

Cox, E. L., *The eagles of Savoy: the house of Savoy in thirteenth-century Europe* (Princeton, 1974).

Cross, C., 'Communal piety in sixteenth century Boston', *Lincolnshire History and Archaeology*, 25 (1990), pp. 33-8.

Crouch, D., 'Urban government and oligarchy in medieval Scarborough', in D. Crouch and T. Pearson, eds, *Medieval Scarborough: studies in trade and civic life* (Yorkshire Archaeological Society Occasional Paper, 1 (2002)), pp. 41-7.

Crouch, D., 'Breteuil, Robert de, fourth earl of Leicester (*d.* 1204)', *Oxford Dictionary of National Biography*, online edition [http://www.oxforddnb.com/view/article/47202, accessed 5 Aug 2015].

Cullum, P. H., 'Leper houses and borough status in the thirteenth century', in P. R. Coss and S. D. Lloyd, eds, *Thirteenth century England, volume III: proceedings of the Newcastle upon Tyne conference, 1989* (Woodbridge, 1991), pp. 37-46.

Cunningham, W., *The growth of English industry and commerce during the early and Middle Ages*, volume I (second edition; Cambridge, 1890).

Dalton, P., *Conquest, anarchy and lordship: Yorkshire, 1066-1154* (Cambridge, 1994).

Darby, H. C., *The Domesday geography of eastern England* (Cambridge, 1952).

Darby, H. C., *The medieval fenland*, (Newton Abbot, 1974; first published 1940).

Darby, H. C., *Domesday England* (Cambridge, 1977).

Darby, H C., *The changing fenland* (Cambridge, 1983).

Davis, G. R. C., *Medieval cartularies of Great Britain* (revised edition; London, 2010).

Davis, J., *Medieval market morality: life, law and ethics in the medieval marketplace, 1200-1500* (Cambridge, 2012).

Davis, R. H. C., *The early history of Coventry* (Dugdale Society Occasional Papers, 24 (1976)).

Ditchfield, P. H., 'Proceedings of the congress', *Journal of the British Archaeological Association*, n.s., 27 (1921), pp. 8-60.

Dollinger, P., *The German Hansa* (London, 1970).

Donkin, R. A., *The Cistercians: studies in the geography of medieval England and Wales* (Toronto, 1978).

Dover, P., *The early medieval history of Boston, A.D. 1086-1400* (second edition; Boston, 1972).

Dugdale, W., *The history of imbanking and draining* (second edition; London, 1772).

Dugdale, W., *Monasticon Anglicanum* (six volumes; London, 1817-1830).

Dury, A., *A collection of the plans of the principal cities of Great Britain and Ireland* (London, 1764).

Dyer, A., 'Ranking lists of English medieval towns', in D. M. Palliser, ed., *The Cambridge urban history of Britain*, volume I (Cambridge, 2000), pp. 747-70.

Dyer, C., 'The hidden trade of the Middle Ages: evidence from the west midlands', in C. Dyer, *Everyday life in medieval England* (London, 1994), pp. 283-303.

Dyer, C., *Making a living in the Middle Ages: the people of Britain, 850-1520* (New Haven, 2002).

Eales, R., 'Ranulf (III), sixth earl of Chester and first earl of Lincoln (1170–1232)', *Oxford Dictionary of National Biography*, online edition http://www.oxforddnb.com/view/article/2716, accessed 27 July 2015].

Eisenberg, C., *The rise of market society in England, 1066-1800* (New York, 2013).

Espinas, G., *La vie urbaine de Douai au Moyen Age*, volume III (Paris, 1913).

Evans, M. R., '"A far from aristocratic affair": poor and non-combatant crusaders from the Midlands, c.1160-1300', *Midland History*, 21 (1996), pp. 23-36.

Everard, J. A., *Brittany and the Angevins: province and empire, 1158-1203* (Oxford, 2000).

Faith, R., 'The structure of the market for wool in early medieval Lincolnshire', *EcHR*, 65 (2012), pp. 674-700.

Farrer, W. 'An outline itinerary of King Henry the First', *EHR,* 34 (1919), pp. 303-82, 505-79.

Finn, R. Welldon, *Domesday Book: a guide* (Chichester, 1973).

Fleet, P., 'Markets in medieval Lincolnshire', *East Midland Historian,* 3 (1993), pp. 7-14.

Fowler, R. C., 'Abbey of Waltham Holy Cross', in W. Page and J. H. Round, eds, *The Victoria history of the county of Essex,* volume II (London, 1907), pp. 166-70.

Friel, I., *Maritime history of Britain and Ireland, c. 400-2001* (London, 2003).

Fudge, J. D., *Cargoes, embargoes and emissaries: the commercial and political interaction of England and the German Hanse, 1450-1510* (Toronto, 1995).

Gardner, C. J., 'The behaviour and ecology of adult common bream *Abramis brama* (L.) in a heavily modified lowland river' (Unpublished University of Lincoln Ph.D. thesis, 2013).

Gilchrist, R., 'Christian bodies and souls: the archaeology of life and death in late medieval hospitals', in S. Bassett, ed., *Death in towns: urban responses to the dying and the dead, 100-1600* (Leicester, 1992), pp. 101-18.

Giles, K., '"A table of alabaster with the story of the Doom": the religious objects and spaces of the Guild of Our Blessed Virgin, Boston (Lincs.)', in T. Hamling and C. Richardson, eds, *Everyday objects: medieval and early modern material culture and its meanings* (Farnham, 2010), pp. 267-85.

Giles, K., and Clark, J., 'St Mary's Guildhall, Boston, Lincolnshire: the archaeology of a medieval "public" building', *Medieval Archaeology,* 55 (2011), pp. 226-56.

Gillett, E., and MacMahon, K. A., *The early history of Hull* (Oxford, 1980).

Glasscock, R. E., 'The distribution of wealth in East Anglia in the early fourteenth century', *Transactions of the Institute of British Geographers,* 32 (1963), pp. 113-23.

Glasscock, R. E., 'The lay subsidy of 1334 for Lincolnshire', *Lincolnshire Architectural and Archaeological Society Reports and Papers,* 10/2 (1964), pp. 115-33.

Goddard, R., *Lordship and medieval urbanization: Coventry, 1043-1355* (Woodbridge, 2004).

Gooder, A., and Gooder, E., 'Coventry before 1355: unity or division? The importance of the Earl's half', *Midland History,* 6 (1981), pp. 1-38.

Golding, B., *Gilbert of Sempringham and the Gilbertine order, c.1130-c.1300* (Oxford, 1995).

Gould, J., 'The medieval burgesses of Tamworth: their liberties, courts and markets', *South Staffordshire Archaeological and Historical Society Transactions,* 13 (1971-72), pp. 17-42.

Gras, N. S. B., *The early English customs system* (Cambridge, Mass., 1918).

Green, C., 'Islamic gold dinars in eleventh- and twelfth-century England', http://www.caitlingreen.org/2016/04/islamic-gold-dinars-anglo-norman.html.

Griffiths, D., 'Towns and their hinterlands', in J. Crick and E. Van Houts, eds, *A social history of England, 900-1200* (Cambridge, 2011), pp. 152-78.

Gross, C., *The gild merchant,* volume I (Oxford, 1890).

Gurnham, R., *The story of Boston* (Stroud, 2014).

Hallam, H. E., *The new lands of Elloe* (Department of English Local History, University College of Leicester, Occasional Papers 6 (1954)).

Hallam, H. E., 'Some thirteenth century censuses', *EcHR,* second series, 10 (1957-8), pp. 340-61.

Hallam, H. E., 'Salt making in the Lincolnshire fenland during the Middle Ages', *Lincolnshire Architectural and Archaeological Society Reports and Papers,* n.s., 8 (1959-60), pp. 85-112.

Hallam, H. E., 'Population density in the medieval fenland', *EcHR*, second series, 14 (1961–2), pp. 71-81.

Hallam, H. E., *Settlement and society: a study of the early agrarian history of south Lincolnshire* (Cambridge, 1965).

Hallam, H. E., 'Drainage techniques', in H. E Hallam, ed., *The agrarian history of England and Wales, volume II: 1042-1350* (Cambridge, 1988), pp. 497-507.

Hallam, H. E., 'New settlement: eastern England', in H. E Hallam, ed., *The agrarian history of England and Wales, volume II: 1042-1350* (Cambridge, 1988), pp. 139-74.

Hallam, S. J., 'The Romano-British salt industry in south Lincolnshire', *Lincolnshire Architectural and Archaeological Society Reports and Papers*, n.s., 8 (1959-60), pp. 35-75.

Hannan, A., *et al.*, 'Tewkesbury and the earls of Gloucester: excavations at Holm Hill, 1974-5', *Transactions of the Bristol and Gloucestershire Archaeological Society*, 115 (1997), pp. 79-231.

Harden, G., *Medieval Boston and its archaeological implications* (Sleaford, 1978).

Harden. G., 'Four dagger sheaths from the Barditch, Boston', *Lincolnshire History and Archaeology*, 18 (1983), pp. 108-110.

Haslett, S. K., 'Historic tsunami in Britain since AD 1000: a review', *Natural Hazards and Earth System Sciences*, 8 (2008), pp. 587-601.

Haward, W. I., 'The trade of Boston in the fifteenth century', *Associated Architectural Societies Reports and Papers*, 41 (1932-33), pp. 169-78.

Harkel, L. ten, 'Urban identity and material culture: a case study of Viking-age Lincoln, *c.* A.D. 850-1000', in H. Hamerow, ed., *Anglo-Saxon Studies in Archaeology and History*, 18 (2013), pp. 157-73.

Harrison, D., *The bridges of medieval England: transport and society, 400-1800* (Oxford, 2007).

Harvey, P. D. A., 'The English trade in wool and cloth, 1150-1250: some problems and suggestions', in M. Spallanzani, ed., *Produzione, commercio e consumo dei panni di lana (nei secoli XII-XVIII)* (Florence, 1976), pp. 369-75.

Hayes, P. P., and Lane, T. W., *The Fenland project, number 5: the south-west fens* (East Anglian Archaeology Report, 55 (1992).

Healey, H., 'A medieval salt-making site in Bicker Haven, Lincolnshire', in A. Bell, D. Gurney and H. Healey, *Lincolnshire salterns: excavations at Helpringham, Holbeach and Bicker Haven* (East Anglian Archaeology Report, 89 (1999)), pp. 82-101.

Hemmeon, M. W., *Burgage tenure in medieval England* (Cambridge, Mass., 1914).

Hill, J. W. F., *Medieval Lincoln* (Stamford, 1990; first published 1948).

Hilton, R. H., *The English peasantry in the later Middle Ages* (Oxford, 1975).

Hilton, R. H., *English and French towns in feudal society: a comparative study* (Cambridge, 1992).

Hilton, Y., 'La Bretagne et la rivalité Capétiens-Plantagenets. Un exemple: la duchesse Constance (1186-1202)', *Annales de Bretagne*, 92 (1985), pp. 111-44.

Hinde, A., *England's population: a history since the Domesday survey* (London, 2003).

Hindle, B. P., *Medieval town plans* (Prince Risborough, 1990).

Hinton, D. A., 'The large towns, 600-1300', in D. M. Palliser, ed., *The Cambridge urban history of Britain*, volume I (Cambridge, 2000), pp. 217-43.

Holt, R., 'Urban transformation in England, 900-1100', *Anglo-Norman* Studies, 32 (2010), pp. 57-78.

Holt, R., and Rosser, G., 'Introduction: the English town in the Middle Ages', in R. Holt and G. Rosser, eds, *The medieval English town: a reader in English urban history, 1200-1540* (London, 1990), pp. 1-18.

Hoskins, W. G., *The making of the English landscape* (London, 1955).

Hudson, J., 'Glanville, Ranulf de (1120s?–1190)', *Oxford Dictionary of National Biography* (Oxford University Press, 2004; online edition, January 2007). http://www.oxforddnb.com/view/article/10795, accessed 19 Dec 2013].

Huffman, J. P., *Family, commerce and religion in London and Cologne: Anglo-German emigrants c.1000-c.1300* (Cambridge, 1998).

Hutchinson, G., *Medieval ships and shipping* (London, 1994).

Hutchinson, J., and Palliser, D. M., *York* (Edinburgh, 1980).

Jebb, G., *A guide to the church of S. Botolph with notes on the history and antiquities of Boston and Skirbeck* (Boston, 1896).

Jenks, S., *England, Die Hanse und Preußen: Handel und Diplomatie, 1377-1474* (thee volumes; Koln, 1992).

Johns, S. M., *Noblewomen, aristocracy and power in the twelfth-century Anglo-Norman realm* (Manchester, 2003).

Jones, E. T., 'River navigation in medieval England', *Journal of Historical Geography*, 26 (2000), pp. 60-75.

Jones, M., 'Lady Margaret Beaufort, the royal council and an early fenland drainage scheme', *Lincolnshire History and Archaeology*, 21 (1986), pp. 11-18.

Jones, M., 'Arthur, duke of Brittany (1187–1203)', *Oxford Dictionary of National Biography*, online edition [http://www.oxforddnb.com/view/article/704, accessed 27 July 2015].

Jones, M., 'Conan (IV), duke of Brittany (c.1135–1171)', *Oxford Dictionary of National Biography*, online edition [http://www.oxforddnb.com/view/article/59576, accessed 13 Oct 2015].

Jones, M., 'Constance, duchess of Brittany (c.1161–1201)', *Oxford Dictionary of National Biography*, online edition [http://www.oxforddnb.com/view/article/46701, accessed 24 July 2015].

Jones, M., 'Eleanor, *suo jure* duchess of Brittany (1182x4–1241)', *Oxford Dictionary of National Biography*, online edition [http://www.oxforddnb.com/view/article/46702, accessed 5 Aug 2015].

Jones, S. Rees, *York: the making of a city, 1068-1350* (Oxford, 2013).

Jukes-Browne, A. J., *The geology of the south-west part of Lincolnshire, with parts of Leicestershire and Nottinghamshire* (London, 1885).

Jurkowski, M., Ramsay, N., and Renton, S., *English monastic estates, 1066-1540: a list of manors, chapels and churches* (three parts; List and Index Society, special series, 40-42 (2007)).

Keats-Rohan, K. S. B., 'Alan Rufus (d. 1093)', *Oxford Dictionary of National Biography* online edition [http://www.oxforddnb.com/view/article/52358, accessed 24 February 2013].

Keats-Rohan, K. S. B., 'William I and the Breton contingent in the non-Norman Conquest, 1066-1087', *Anglo-Norman Studies*, 13 (1991), pp. 157-72.

Keats-Rohan, K. S. B., 'The Bretons and the Normans of England, 1066-1154: the family, the fief and the feudal monarchy', *Nottingham Medieval Studies*, 36 (1992), pp. 42-78.

K. S. B. Keats-Rohan, 'Le rôles des Bretons dans la colonisation normande de l'Angleterre (vers 1042-1135'), *Mémoires de la Société d'histoire et d'archaéologie de Bretagne*, 74 (1996), pp. 181-215.

Keats-Rohan, K. S. B., *Domesday people: a prosopography of persons occurring in English documents, 1066-1166. I: Domesday Book* (Woodbridge, 1999).

Kingsford, C. L., 'Moulton, Sir Thomas of (*d.* 1240)', rev. Ralph V. Turner, *Oxford Dictionary of National Biography*, online edition [http://www.oxforddnb.com/view/article/19521, accessed 9 Oct 2015].

Knowles, D., and Hadcock, R. N., *Medieval religious houses, England and Wales* (second edition; Harlow, 1971).

Kowaleski, M., 'Port towns: England and Wales, 1300-1540', in D. M. Palliser, ed., *The Cambridge urban history of Britain*, volume I (Cambridge, 2000), pp. 467-94.

Lambert, M. R., and Walker, R., *Boston, Tattershall and Croyland* (Oxford, 1930).

Lander, J. H., and Vellacott, C. H., 'Lead mining', in W. Page, ed., *The Victoria history of the county of Derby*, volume II (London, 1907), pp. 323-49.

Lane, T. W. *et al.*, *The Fenland project, number 8: Lincolnshire survey, the northern fen edge* (East Anglian Archaeology Report, 66 (1993)).

Langdon, J., 'The efficiency of inland water transport in medieval England', in J. Blair, ed., *Waterways and canal-building in medieval England* (Oxford, 2007), pp. 110-30.

Langdon, J., and Masschaele, J., 'Commercial activity and population growth in medieval England', *Past and Present*, 190 (2006), pp. 35-82.

Leach, A. F., 'Boston Grammar School', *Associated Architectural Societies Reports and Papers*, 26/2 (1902), pp. 398-405.

Letters, S., *et al.*, eds, *Gazetteer of markets and fairs in England and Wales to 1516* (two parts; List and Index Society, Special Series, 32-33, (2003)).

Lewis, M. J. T., 'The trade and shipping of Boston', in M. J. T. Lewis and N. R Wright, *Boston as a port (Proceedings of the seventh East Midlands industrial archaeology conference: Lincolnshire Industrial Archaeology special issue*, 8/4 (1973)), pp. 1-22.

LHER, MLI12644, Barditch and Bargate, Boston.

LHER, MLI12688, The Carmelite friary at Boston.

LHER, MLI12691, St John's the Baptist's Hospital, Boston.

LHER, MLI12695, The Augustinian friary at Boston.

LHER MLI13313, Medieval masonry, 35 Paddock Grove, Boston.

LHER, MLI13327, Medieval remains from the junction of Wormgate and Fountains Lane, Boston.

LHER, MLI13351, A Middle Saxon settlement at Church Road, Boston.

LHER, MLI13360, Medieval remains, 3 New Street, Boston.

LHER, MLI83896. Medieval wall and associated deposits, 71 High Street, Boston.

LHER, MLI89035, Occupation deposits at South Square, Boston.

LHER, MLI98729, Medieval pits and linear features, 3 Willoughby Road, Boston.

*Lincolnshire Archives Committee, Archivists' Report*, no. 7 (1955-56).

Lipson, E., *The economic history of England, volume I: the Middle Ages* (eleventh edition; London, 1956).

*List of the lands of dissolved religious houses. Index: A-G* (Public Record Office, List and Indexes, Supplementary Series, III, volume 5 (1964; first published 1949).

Little, A. G. 'Austin friars of Boston', in W. Page, ed., *The Victoria history of the county of Lincoln*, volume II (London, 1988; first published 1906), pp. 213-14.

Little, A. G., 'Black friars of Boston', in W. Page, ed., *The Victoria history of the county of Lincoln*, volume II (London, 1988; first published 1906), pp. 214-15.

Little, A. G., 'Grey friars of Boston', in W. Page, ed., *The Victoria history of the county of Lincoln*, volume II (London, 1988; first published 1906), pp. 215-16.

Little, A. G. 'White friars of Boston', in W. Page, ed., *The Victoria history of the county of Lincoln*, volume II (London, 1988; first published 1906), pp. 216-17.

Lloyd, T. H., *The English wool trade in the Middle Ages* (Cambridge, 1977).

Lloyd, T. H., *England and the German Hanse, 1157-1611: a study of their trade and commercial diplomacy* (Cambridge, 1991).

Lopez, R. S., *The commercial revolution of the Middle Ages, 950-1350* (Cambridge, 1976).

Marrat, W., *The history of Lincolnshire, topographical, historical and descriptive* (two volumes; Boston, 1814),

Maritt, S., 'Drogo the sheriff: a neglected lost romance tradition and Anglo-Norwegian relations in the twelfth century', *History*, 80 (2007), pp. 157-84.

Masschaele, J., 'The English economy in the era of Magna Carta', in J. S. Loengard, ed., *Magna Carta and the England of King John* (Woodbridge, 2010), pp. 151-67.

Masschaele, J., 'Tolls and trade in medieval England', in L. Armstrong, I. Elbl and M. M. Elbl, eds, *Money, markets and trade in late medieval Europe: essays in honour of John H. A. Munro* (Leiden, 2014), pp. 146-83.

Mattinson, A., 'Topography and society in Boston, 1086-1400' (Unpublished University of Nottingham M.Phil. thesis, 1996).

Maynard, M., 'The borough of Richmond', in W. Page, ed., *The Victoria county history of the county of York: North Riding*, volume I (London, 1914), pp. 17-35.

Maynard, M., 'Honour and castle of Richmond', in W. Page, ed., *The Victoria county history of the county of York: North Riding*, volume I (London, 1914), pp. 1-16.

McDonald, J., and Snooks, G. D., *Domesday economy: a new approach to Anglo-Norman history* (Oxford, 1986).

Meier, D., *Seafarers, merchants and pirates in the Middle Ages* (Woodbridge, 2006).

Millea, N., *The Gough Map: the earliest road map of Great Britain* (Oxford, 2007).

Miller, E., and Hatcher, J., *Medieval England: rural society and economic change, 1086-1348* (London, 1978).

Miller, J., and Hatcher, J., *Medieval England: towns, commerce and crafts, 1086-1348* (London, 1995).

Miller, K., *Mappae Arabicae*, volume II (Stuttgart, 1927).

Miller, S. H., and Skertchly, S. B. J., *The fenland, past and present* (London, 1878).

Milne, G., and Hobley, B., *Waterfront archaeology in Britain and northern Europe* (Council for British Archaeology Research Report, 41 (1981)).

Minnis, J., Carmichael, K., Fletcher, C., Anderson, M., *Boston, Lincolnshire: historic North Sea port and market town* (Swindon, 2015).

Molyneux, F. H., and Wright, N. R., *An atlas of Boston* (Boston, 1974).

Monckton, L., '"The beste and fayrest of al Lincolnshire": the parish church of St Botolph, Boston', in S. Badham and P. Cockerham, eds, *'The beste and fayrest of al Lincolnshire': the church of St Botolph's, Boston, Lincolnshire, and its medieval monuments* (British Archaeological Reports, British Series, 554 (2012)), pp. 29-48.

Morgan, P., 'Medieval settlement and society', in A. D. M. Phillips and C. B. Phillips, *A new historical atlas of Cheshire* (Chester, 2002), pp. 32-3.

Moore, E. W., *The fairs of medieval England: an introductory study* (Toronto, 1985).

Moorhouse, S., 'Finds in the refectory at the Dominican friary, Boston', *Lincolnshire History and Archaeology*, 7 (1972), pp. 21-53.

Morris, A. E. J., *History of urban form before the industrial revolution* (third edition; Harlow, 1994).

Nedkvitne, A., *The German Hansa and Bergen, 1100-1600* (Cologne, 2014).

Nedkvitne, A., 'The development of the Norwegian long-distance stockfish trade', in J. H. Barrett and D. C. Orton, eds. *Cod and herring: the archaeology and history of medieval sea fishing* (Oxford, 2016), pp. 50-9.

Nicholas, D., 'Of poverty and primacy: demand, liquidity and the Flemish economic miracle, 1050-1200', *American Historical Review*, 96 (1991), pp. 17-41.

Nicholas, D., *Medieval Flanders* (London, 1992).

Nicholas, D., *The growth of the medieval city: from late antiquity to the early fourteenth century* (London, 1997).

Nielssen, A. R., 'Early commercial fisheries and the interplay among farm, fishing station and fishing village in north Norway', in J. H. Barrett and D. C. Orton, eds. *Cod and herring: the archaeology and history of medieval sea fishing* (Oxford, 2016), pp. 42-9.

Nightingale, P., *A medieval mercantile community: the Grocers' Company and the politics and trade of London, 1000-1485* (New Haven, 1995).

Norton, C., 'The buildings of St Mary's abbey, York, and their destruction', *Antiquaries Journal*, 74 (1994), pp. 256-88.

O'Brien, C., Bown, L., Dixon, S., Nicholson, R., et al., *The origins of the Newcastle quayside: excavations at Queen Street and Dog Bank* (Newcastle, 1988).

Oggins, R. S., *The kings and their hawks: falconry in medieval England* (New Haven, 2004).

Okansen, E., *Flanders and the Anglo-Norman world, 1066-1216* (Cambridge, 2012).

Okansen, E., 'Economic relations between East Anglia and Flanders in the Anglo-Norman period', in D. Bates and R. Liddiard, eds, *East Anglia and its North Sea world in the Middle Ages* (Woodbridge, 2013), pp. 174-203.

O'Malley, G., *The Knights Hospitaller of the English langue, 1460-1565* (Oxford, 2010).

Ormrod, W. M., ed., *The guilds in Boston* (Boston, 1993).

O'Sullivan, D., *In the company of preachers: the archaeology of medieval friaries in England and Wales* (Leicester Archaeology Monograph, no. 23 (2013)).

Owen, A. E. B., 'Beyond the sea bank: sheep on the Huttoft outmarsh in the early thirteenth century', *Lincolnshire History and Archaeology*, 28 (1993), pp. 39-41.

Owen, D. M.. *Church and society in medieval Lincolnshire* (Lincoln, 1971).

Owen, D. M., 'Bishop's Lynn: the first century of a new town?', in R. A. Brown, ed., *Proceedings of the Battle Conference on Anglo-Norman studies*, volume II (Woodbridge, 1979), pp. 141-53.

Owen, D. M., 'The beginnings of the port of Boston', in N. Field and A. White, eds, *A prospect of Lincolnshire being collected articles on the history and traditions of Lincolnshire in honour of Ethel H. Rudkin* (Lincoln, 1984), pp. 42-5.

Owen, D. M., 'An early Boston charter', *Lincolnshire History and Archaeology*, 23 (1988), pp. 77-8.

Owen, L. V. D., 'Lincolnshire and the wool trade in the Middle Ages', *Reports and Papers of the Architectural Societies of the County of Lincoln, County of York, Archdeaconries of Northampton and Oakham and County of Leicester*, 39 (1928-9), pp. 259-63.

Page, F. M., *The estates of Crowland abbey: a study in manorial organization* (Cambridge, 1934).

Painter, S., *The scourge of the clergy: Peter of Dreux, duke of Brittany* (Baltimore, 1937).

Palliser, D., *Domesday York* (York: Borthwick Paper, 78 (1990)).

Palliser, D., 'English medieval cities and towns: new directions', *Journal of Urban History*, 23 (1997), pp. 474-87.

Palliser, D. M., 'Town defences in medieval England and Wales', in D. M. Palliser, *Towns and local communities in medieval and early modern England* (Aldershot, 2006), V: 105-21.

Palliser, D. M., *Medieval York, 600-1540* (Oxford, 2014).

Palmer, R. C., *The county courts of medieval England* (Princeton, 1982).

Palmer, R. C., *English law in the age of the Black Death, 1348-1381* (Chapel Hill, 1993).

Parker, V., *The making of King's Lynn* (London, 1971).

Patten, J., *English towns 1500-1700* (Folkestone, 1978).

Pevsner, N., Harris, J., and Antram, N., *The buildings of England: Lincolnshire* (second edition; London, 1989).

Pezzolo, L., 'The *via italiana* to capitalism', in L. Neal and J. G. Williamson, eds, *The Cambridge history of capitalism, volume I: the rise of capitalism from ancient origins to 1848* (Cambridge, 2014), pp. 267-313.

Platt, C., *The English medieval town* (London, 1976).

Platt, C., 'The evolution of towns: natural growth', in M. W. Barley, ed., *The plans and topography of medieval towns in England and Wales* (Council for British Archaeology Research Report no., 14 (1976)), pp.48-56.

Platts, G., *Land and people in medieval Lincolnshire* (Lincoln, 1985).

Poole, A. L., *From Domesday Book to Magna Carta, 1087-1216* (second edition; Oxford 1955).

Pollock F., and Maitland, F. W., *The history of English law before the time of Edward I*, volume I (Cambridge, 1898).

Postan, M. M., *Medieval economy and society: an economic history of Britain in the Middle Ages* (London, 1972).

Poynton, E. M., 'The fee of Creon', *The Genealogist*, n.s., 18 (1901), pp. 162-66, 219-25.

Raban, S., *The estates of Thorney and Crowland: a study in medieval monastic tenure* (Cambridge, 1973).

Rawcliffe, C., 'The earthly and spiritual topography of suburban hospitals', in K. Giles and C. Dyer, eds, *Town and country in the Middle Ages: contrasts, contacts and connections, 1100–1500* (Leeds, 2005), pp. 251-74.

Reynolds, S., *An introduction to the history of English medieval towns* (Oxford, 1977).

Reynolds, S., 'Medieval urban history and the history of political thought', *Urban History Yearbook 1982*, pp. 14-22.

Reynolds, S., *Kingdoms and communities in western Europe, 900-1300* (Oxford, 1984).

Reynolds, S., 'The writing of medieval urban history in England', *Theoretische geschiedenis*, 19 (1992), pp. 43-57.

Richards, P., 'The hinterland and overseas trade of King's Lynn, 1205-537: an introduction', in K. Friedland and P. Richards, eds, *Essays in Hanseatic trade: the King's Lynn symposium, 1998* (Dereham, 2005), pp. 10-21.

Richardson, H. G., *The English Jewry under the Angevin kings* (London, 1960).

Rigby, S. H., 'Boston and Grimsby in the Middle Ages' (Unpublished University of London Ph.D. thesis, 1983).

Rigby, S. H., 'Boston and Grimsby in the Middle Ages: an administrative contrast', *Journal of Medieval History*, 10 (1984), pp. 51-66.

Rigby, S. H., 'The customs administration at Boston in the reign of Richard II', *Bulletin of the Institute of Historical Research*, 58 (1985), pp. 12-24.

Rigby, S. H., '"Sore decay" and "fair dwellings": Boston and urban decline in the later Middle Ages', *Midland History*, 10 (1985), pp. 47-61.

Rigby, S. H., 'Urban society in the early fourteenth century: the evidence of the lay subsidies', *Bulletin of the John Rylands Library*, 72 (1990), pp. 169-184.

Rigby, S. H., *Medieval Grimsby: growth and decline* (Hull, 1993).

Rigby, S. H., *English society in the later Middle Ages: class, status and gender* (Basingstoke, 1995).

Rigby, S. H., '"John of Gaunt's Palace" and the Sutton family of Lincoln', *Lincolnshire History and Archaeology*, 35 (2000), pp. 35-9.

Rigby, S. H., 'Historical materialism: social structure and social change in the Middle Ages', *The Journal of Medieval and Early Modern Studies*, 34 (2004), pp. 474-522.

Rigby, S. H., 'Social structure and economic change in late medieval England', in R. Horrox and M. Ormrod, eds, *A social history of England, 1200-1500* (Cambridge, 2006), pp. 1-30.

Rigby, S. H., 'Urban population in late medieval England: the evidence of the lay subsidies', *Economic History Review*, 63 (2010), pp. 393-417.

Rigby, S. H., 'Medieval Boston: economy, society and administration', in S. Badham and P. Cockerham, eds, *'The beste and fayrest of al Lincolnshire': the church of St Botolph's, Boston, Lincolnshire, and its medieval monuments* (British Archaeological Reports, British Series, 554 (2012)), pp. 6-28.

Rigby, S. H., and Ewan, E., 'Government, power and authority, 1300-1540', in D. M. Palliser, ed., *The Cambridge urban history of Britain*, volume I (Cambridge, 2000), pp. 291-312.

Roffe, D., 'The *Historia Croylandensis*: a plea for reassessment', *EHR*, 110 (1995), pp. 95- 108.

Roffe, D., *Decoding Domesday* (Woodbridge, 2007).

Rogers, A., *A history of Lincolnshire* (Chichester, 1985).

Röhrkasten, J., 'Conflict in a monastic borough: Coventry in the reign of Edward II', *Midland History*, 18 (1993), pp. 1-18.

Röhrkasten, J., 'The origin and development of the London mendicant houses', in T. R. Slater and G. Rosser, eds, *The church in the medieval town* (Aldershot, 1998), pp. 76-99.

Rose, S., *The wine trade in medieval Europe, 1000-1500* (London, 2011).

Rosser, A. G., 'The essence of medieval urban communities: the vill of Westminster, 1200-1540', *TRHS*, 5th series, 34 (1984), pp. 91-112.

Rosser, G., *Medieval Westminster, 1200-1540* (Oxford, 1989).

Rosser, G., 'Review of Rigby, *Medieval Grimsby*', *Urban History*, 22 (1995), pp. 147-8.

Rosser, G., *The art of solidarity in the Middle Ages: guilds in England, 1250-1550* (Oxford, 2015).

Roth, C., *A history of the Jews in England* (second edition; London, 1949).

Round, J. H., *Feudal England: historical studies in the XIth and XIIth centuries* (London, 1895).

Rudkin, E. H., and Owen, D. M., 'The medieval salt industry in the Lindsey marshland', *Lincolnshire Architectural and Archaeological Society Reports and Papers*, n.s., 8 (1959-60), pp. 76-84.

Russell, J. C., *British medieval population* (Albuquerque, 1948).

Rylatt, J., *Report on a programme of archaeological fieldwork undertaken at Boston Grammar School, Boston, Lincolnshire* (2002), p. 4 (*Library of Unpublished Fieldwork Reports* [data-set]. York: Archaeology Data Service [distributor] (doi:10.5284/1014344)).

Salzman, L. F., 'A riot at Boston fair', *The History Teachers' Miscellany*, 6 (1928), p. 2.

Sanders, I. J., *English baronies: a study of their origin and descent, 1086-1327* (Oxford, 1960).

Sawyer, P. H., 'Medieval English settlement: new interpretations', in P. H. Sawyer, ed., *English medieval settlement* (London, 1979), pp. 1-8.

Sawyer, P., *Anglo-Saxon Lincolnshire* (Lincoln, 1998).

Sawyer, P., *The wealth of Anglo-Saxon England* (Oxford, 2013).

Searle, E., *Lordship and community: Battle abbey and its banlieu, 1066-1538* (Toronto, 1974).

Sharp, B., 'The food riots of 1347 and the medieval moral economy', in A. Randall and A. Charlesworth, eds, *Moral economy and popular protest: crowds, conflict and authority* (Basingstoke, 2000), pp. 33-54.

Shinn, H., *Boston through time* (Stroud, 2014).

Simms, A., and Clarke, H. B., 'Introduction', in A. Simms and H. B. Clarke, eds, *Lords and towns in medieval Europe: the European Historic Towns Atlas project* (Farnham, 2015), pp. 1-9.

Simon, A. L., *The history of the wine trade in England*, volume I (London, 1964).

Simpson, W. B., *An introduction to the history of land law* (Oxford, 1967).

Sister Elspeth, 'The abbey of Kirkstead', in W. Page, ed., *The Victoria history of the county of Lincoln*, volume II (London, 1988; first published 1906), pp. 135-8.

Sister Elspeth, 'The hospital of St John the Baptist without Boston', in W. Page, ed., *The Victoria history of the county of Lincoln*, volume II (London, 1988; first published 1906), p. 233.

Sister Elspeth, 'The monastery of Ikanho', in W. Page, ed., *The Victoria history of the county of Lincoln*, volume II (London, 1988; first published 1906), pp. 96-7.

Sister Elspeth, 'The priory of Freiston', in W. Page, ed., *The Victoria history of the county of Lincoln*, volume II (London, 1988; first published 1906), pp. 128-9.

Skertchly, J. B. J., *The geology of the fenland* (London, 1877).

Slater, T. R., 'Lordship, economy and society in English medieval marketplaces', in A. Simms and H. B. Clarke, eds, *Lords and towns in medieval Europe: the European Historic Towns Atlas project* (Farnham, 2015), pp. 213-31.

Smith, T. P., 'Hussey Tower, Boston: a late medieval tower-house', *Lincolnshire History and Archaeology*, 14 91979), pp. 31-7.

Spufford, P., *Power and profit: the merchant in medieval Europe* (London, 2002).

*St Botolph's church, Boston Stump, parish of Boston* (n.p., n.d.).

Stenton, F. M., *The first century of English feudalism, 1066-1166* (Oxford, 1932).

Stevenson, F. S., 'St Botolph (Botwulf) and Iken', *Proceedings of the Suffolk Institute of Archaeology and Natural History*, 18 (1922-4), pp. 29-51.

Stukeley, W., *An account of Richard of Cirencester, monk of Westminster, and of his work* (London, 1757).

Stukeley, W., *Itinerarium curiosum: or, an account of the antiquities and remarkable curiosities in nature or art observed in travels through Great Britain* (second edition; two volumes; London, 1776).

Summerson, H., 'Calamity and commerce: the burning of Boston fair in 1288', in C. M. Barron and A. F. Sutton, eds, *The medieval merchant: proceedings of the 2912 Harlaxton symposium* (Donington, 2014), pp. 146-65.

Sutton, A., 'Mercery through four centuries, c.1130s-c.1500', *Nottingham Medieval Studies*, 41 (1997), pp. 100-25.

Sutton, A., 'The shop-floor of the London mercery trade, c.1200-c.1500: the marginalisation of the artisan, the itinerant merchant and the shopholder', *Nottingham Medieval Studies*, 45 (2001), pp. 12-50.

Swanson, H., *Medieval British towns* (Basingstoke, 1999).

Swanson, R. N., *Indulgences in late medieval England: passports to paradise?* (Cambridge, 2007).

Sweetinburgh, S., *The role of the hospital in medieval England: gift-giving and the spiritual economy* (Dublin, 2004).

Tait, J., *Medieval Manchester and the beginnings of Lancashire* (Manchester, 1904).

Tait, J., *The medieval English borough: studies on its origins and constitutional history* (Manchester, 1936).

Tanner, T., *Notitia monastica* (London, 1744).

Thomas, A., 'Rivers of gold? The coastal zone between the Humber and the Wash in the mid-Saxon period', in H. Hamerow, ed., *Anglo-Saxon Studies in Archaeology and History*, 18 (2013), pp. 97-118.

Thompson, A. Hamilton, 'Registers of John Gynewell, bishop of Lincoln for the years 1347-1350', *Archaeological Journal*, 68 (1911), pp. 301-60.

Thompson, P., *Collections for a topographical and historical account of Boston and the hundred of Skirbeck in the County of Lincoln* (London, 1820).

Thompson, P., 'On the early commerce of Boston', *Associated Architectural Societies Reports and Papers*, 2 (1852-53), pp. 362-81.

Thompson, P., *The history and antiquities of Boston, and the villages of Skirbeck, Fishtoft, Freiston, Butterwick, Benington, Leverton, Leake and Wrangle; comprising the hundred of Skirbeck in the County of Lincoln* (Sleaford, 1997; first published 1856).

Thorpe, R., *Excavations at Wormgate, Boston, Lincolnshire* (1989) (*Library of Unpublished Fieldwork Reports* [data-set]. York: Archaeology Data Service [distributor] (doi:10.5284/1012869)).

Topham, J., 'Subsidy roll of 51 Edward III', *Archaeologia,* 7 (1785), pp. 337-47.

Trenholme, N., *The English monastic boroughs* (University of Missouri Studies, no. 3 (1927)).

Turner, H. L., *Town defences in England and Wales: an architectural and documentary study, A.D. 900-1500* (London, 1971).

Turner, R. V., *Men raised from the dust: administrative service and upward mobility in Angevin England* (Philadelphia, 1988).

Turner, R. V., 'Huntingfield, William of (d. in or before 1225)', *Oxford Dictionary of National Biography*, online edition [http://www.oxforddnb.com/view/article/14238, accessed 26 Aug 2014].

Unger, R. W., *The ship in the medieval economy, 600-1600* (London, 1980).

Unger, R. W., 'Changes in ship design and construction: England in the European mould', in R Gorski, ed., *Roles of the sea in medieval England* (Woodbridge, 2012), pp. 25-39.

Veale, E. M., *The English fur trade in the later Middle Ages* (Oxford, 1966).

Vince, A., 'Lincoln in the Viking Age', in J. Graham-Campbell, R. Hall, J. Jesch and D. N. Parsons, eds, *Vikings and the Danelaw: select papers from the proceedings of the thirteenth Viking congress, Nottingham and York, 21-30 August 1997* (Oxford, 1997), pp. 157-79.

Vincent, N., 'Savoy, Peter of, count of Savoy and de facto earl of Richmond (1203?–1268)', *Oxford Dictionary of National Biography*, online edition [http://www.oxforddnb.com/view/article/22016, accessed 5 Aug 2015].

Vinogradoff, P., *The growth of the manor* (New York, 1968).

Warren, W. L., *Henry II* (Berkeley, 1973).

Watson, S., 'City as charter: charity and the lordship of English towns, 1170-1250', in C. Goodson, E. Lester and C. Symes, eds, *Cities, texts and social networks: experiences and perceptions of medieval urban space* (Farnham, 2010), pp. 235-62.

West, C., 'Urban populations and associations', in J. Crick and E. Van Houts, eds, *A social history of England, 900-1200* (Cambridge, 2011), pp. 198-207.

West, S. E., Scarfe, N., and Cramp, R., 'Iken, St Botolph and the coming of East Anglian Christianity', *Proceedings of the Suffolk Institute of Archaeology and History,* 35 (1984), pp. 279-301.

W. H. B. B., 'The Kirkstead chartulary', *The Genealogist*, n.s. 18 (1902).

Wheeler, W. H., *A history of the fens of south Lincolnshire* (second edition; Boston, 1896).

White, A. B., *Self-government at the king's command* (Minneapolis, 1933).

Whitley, W. T., 'Botulph's Ycean-ho', *Journal of the British Archaeological Association*, n.s., 36 (1930), pp. 233-8.

Whitley, W. T., 'In the palmy days of Boston: the Hospitallers of St John and the men of St Botolph at Skirbeck', *Journal of the British Archaeological Association*, n.s., 37 (1932), pp. 225-42.

Whittingham, A. B., 'St Mary's abbey, York: an interpretation of its plan', *Archaeological Journal*, 120 (1971), pp. 118-46.

Whitwell, J. B., *Roman Lincolnshire* (Lincoln, 1970).

Williams, A., 'Ralph the Staller, earl of East Anglia (*d.* 1068x70)', *Oxford Dictionary of National Biography*, Oxford University Press, 2004 [http://www.oxforddnb.com/view/article/52354, accessed 7 June 2016].

Williams, G. A., *Medieval London: from commune to capital* (London, 1963).

Williamson, T., *England's landscape: East Anglia* (London, 2006).

Wilson, C., and Burton, J., *St Mary's abbey, York* (York, 1988).

Wilson, D. M., and Hurst, J. G., 'Medieval Britain in 1957', *Medieval Archaeology*, 2 (1958), pp. 183-213.

Wilson, D. M., and Hurst, J. G., 'Medieval Britain in 1960', *Medieval Archaeology*, 5 (1961), pp. 309-39.

Wubs-Mrozewicz, J., '"Alle goede coeplyden...": strategies in the Scandinavian trade politics of Amsterdam and Lübeck, *c.*1440-1560', in H. Brand and L. Müller, eds, *The Dynamics of European culture in the North Sea and Baltic region* (Hilversum, 2007), pp. 86-101.

Wright, N. R., *The book of Boston* (Buckingham, 1986).

Wright, N., *Boston: a pictorial history* (Chichester, 1994).

Wright, N., *Boston: a history and celebration* (Salisbury, 2005).

Wright, N., 'Grand deviations: the course of the River Witham in Boston', *Lincolnshire History and Archaeology*, 44 (2009), pp. 48-53.

Young, A., *General view of the agriculture of Lincolnshire* (second edition; London, 1813).

# Index